GREEN HELL

Adventures in the Mysterious Jungles of Eastern Bolivia

By JULIAN DUGUID

With a Foreword by
HIS EXCELLENCY MARQUES
DE MERRY DEL VAL, G.C.V.O.
Ambassador of His Majesty The King of Spain to the Court of St. James

*Illustrated from Photographs
Taken by Members of the Expedition*

THE CENTURY CO.

NEW YORK   LONDON

OPENING WORDS

TO THE AUTHOR

To WRITE well is one thing, to write vividly another. How many descriptive narratives do we read powerfully designed and beautifully rounded off as in hard cold marble. They are useful but through their pages our interest flags. You in "Green Hell" have reached the unsurpassable. At once we are rushed into the midst of your surroundings, your experiences, your feelings physical and moral, your very thoughts. They do not rise like water-colors in distant beauty and perfection before us. They do not even pass in realistic views under our eyes as on the ribbon of a film. We simply live your life with you. We are blinded by the sun's glare, scorched by its rays, entranced by the glow of its setting, cowed by the eerie, living, creeping silence of the forest, which in its fearful eloquence is no silence. We agonize under festering stings, the cracking drought of throat and lips, the misery of tropical rain. We exult in the cool relief of a vivifying pool. The soft treading Indians march with us threateningly on either side of the jungle-path. We actually hear their bullfrog war-cry, we are eye-witnesses of their sudden emergence and disappearance. We trek with you over waste and mountain, through thorny, clammy, intertwined woods, and gigantic swollen rivers. What is more admirable still we think the daring thoughts and feel the strong emotions of your hearts. And as we leave you at the End, we turn about once more and doff our hats to the ground in mute homage and wonder, the highest praise!

How you achieve this magical feat it is not for me to question. A foreigner may not presume to scrutinize English style. I am content to thank you and devoutly hope for more.

TO THE READER

THIS book has taken from the "Queen of Cats" an arresting quality. If you put your hand on it you cannot shake it off until at the finish you are cut off. It is as if the author had learnt the trick from the engaging creepers of the jungle. A book for men of all ages, the adventures it describes thrill and attract the more because true. You will enjoy every line. For me it possesses an added charm in its recognition of the heroism of two peculiarly Spanish products of Spain, the "adelantados" of the early colonial days and the Jesuit Missionaries, of the Chaco. Both were breeds of supermen. No other "race" has given the world such explorations nor the ideal "reductions" of the Guarani Indians. Because we know that among our arid mountains and our wind-swept plains the wood still grows from which those men were hewn, because we know that their blood flows from Rio Grande to the Horn, we in Spain have faith and hope in the future of the "race." I am sorry to stumble in Mr. Duguid's entrancing pages on an account of Atahualpa's death notoriously concocted by Spain's untiring detractors. The reason was very different from that therein given. Modern research explains. Read its testimony. But also read this book. You will feel all the better for it and in your heart you will erect four more niches to virility of body and soul.

MERRY DEL VAL

To My
Companions In Adventure

MAMERTO URRIOLAGOITIA

J. C. BEE-MASON

ALEJANDRO SIEMEL (TIGER-MAN)

with
admiration and respect

FOREWORD

Two roads of almost equal peril lie open to the chronicler of travel. He may describe with tedious detail each moment of his trip and quote long passages from his diary in support of his contentions. Or, artistically, he may select this incident and that, seeking to weld his experiences into a harmonious whole. In either case he is doomed, for, if he adopt the former he will send his audience to sleep; if the latter, he will do himself an injustice by causing the expedition to appear short and shallow as a picnic.

For good or ill I have chosen to select. Whenever anything happened which threw a light, either on the characters of my incomparable companions or on the curiosities of the country through which we passed, I have set it down as vividly as I could, but the imaginative reader will remember that between each scene that is worthy of record there were long stretches of weary days in which nothing occurred at all. Behind each bright memory is a background of dark forest, of common daily tasks that call for no publicity, of interminable weeks spent in a stuffy atmosphere of decay, of self-control practised so quietly that it had become a habit almost before we were aware of its necessity.

Seven readers out of every ten skip those references to scenery which occupy more than a paragraph. I have tried to save them the labor.

ILLUSTRATIONS

HUAINA POTOSÍ, NEAR LA PAZ	*Frontispiece*
	FACING PAGE
INTERIOR OF CHURCH AT SANTO CORAZÓN LEFT BY THE JESUITS	20
A BAG OF WILD DUCK	37
BEFORE A JAGUAR HUNT	41
DUGUID AND HIS FIRST BIG VICTIM	48
VILLAGE IN THE TROPICS IN BOLIVIA	52
HUT MADE BY THE INDIANS TO ATTRACT THE ATTENTION OF THE TRAVELERS, IN ORDER TO ATTACK THEM AFTERWARD	69
RUSTIC SUGAR-CANE CRUSHER USED BY THE CHIQUITOS INDIANS	73
SQUARE IN SANTA CRUZ	80
AN INDIAN MARKET, NEAR COCHABAMBA	88
PANORAMIC VIEW OF LA PAZ WITH ILLIMANI IN THE BACKGROUND	97
CROSSING THE RIO GRANDE IN FULL SWING	108
NATIVES ADMIRING A MOTOR-CAR FOR THE FIRST TIME	117
HUT IN THE BOLIVIAN FORESTS	132
HOW WE CROSSED RIVERS IN THE BOLIVIAN TROPICS	136
FLOCK OF LLAMAS CARRYING TIN ORE IN THE MINING DISTRICT NEAR ATOCHA	145
OPENING UP A MOTOR ROAD IN THE BOLIVIAN FORESTS	149
CROSSING A RIVER	164
CROSSING A RAPID	168
"TIGER-MAN" AT FOOT OF THE ANDES	177
RESERVOIR IN PATIÑO TIN MINES	181

ILLUSTRATIONS

	FACING PAGE
NATIVES IN TARIJA, WEARING THEIR CARNIVAL GARMENTS	196
WATERFALL NEAR TARIJA	200
PANORAMIC VIEW OF THE ANDES	209
WATERFALL NEAR TARIJA	229
CAVE IN THE BOLIVIAN ANDES	244
VILLAGE OF LAGUNILLAS IN THE HEART OF THE OIL DISTRICT	260
RUINS OF AN OLD CEMETERY, NEAR POTOSÍ	277
THE PATIO OF THE MINT HOUSE IN POTOSÍ	281
CLOSER VIEW OF POTOSÍ MOUNTAIN SHOWING HOW THE EARTH HAS BEEN REMOVED IN ORDER TO EXTRACT MINERALS	288
POTOSÍ MOUNTAIN FROM WHENCE GREAT TREASURES HAVE BEEN EXTRACTED	308
WHERE TALL STORIES ARE UNNECESSARY	325

PART ONE

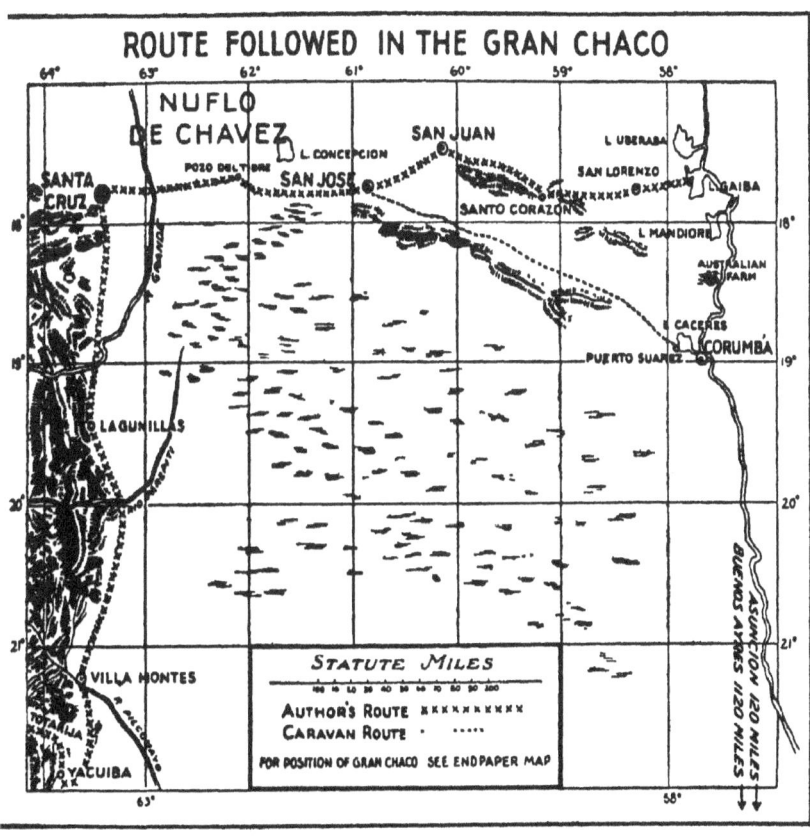

CHAPTER I

WHEN a man yields to the urge of Ishmael, the voice of Sarah is raised at tea parties; for there is more heart-burning over the one sheep that escapes than over the ninety and nine that catch the 8:15 to town every morning. Consequently, since Sarah's favor counts for a good deal in the race for a living, Ishmael is forced to prevaricate. He becomes a prospecting engineer, a sailor, a rubber planter, or even an exploratory journalist, anything in fact which will remove the strangle-hold of a collar from his neck; and he takes care to explain that the whole glorious business of walking into the horizon is honestly rather a bore. Those who neglect this precaution are known as beach-combers.

Thus Mamerto Urriolagoitia, Consul-General for Bolivia in London, let it be known in diplomatic circles that he was about to range the forests of his country at the request of his Government. J. C. Bee-Mason, cinematographer of repute, told everybody that he was going to make a film of an expedition on strictly commercial lines. And I, hardly able to control my excitement, said gravely I had been commissioned to write this chronicle.

In a way we were speaking the truth. Urriolagoitia

whose name is such a snare to his English friends that he contracts it to Urrio, really had been sent to explore the interior of a savage strip of jungle. Bee-Mason really did mean to film the result; and it really was my first chance to show what I could do with a pen. Nevertheless we lied. Ishmael was stirring in each of us, making us dream of camp-fires in a place where the richest man on earth could not find us if he wished. The terrible and wonderful scourge of wanderlust whipped us all, so that we tore off the calendar leaves in a frenzy during the weeks before our departure.

A light gray mist hung low above the river as we stood on the deck of a South Atlantic liner at Tilbury. Odd noises breaking through the fog joined the salt flavor of the air in a promise of adventure. Cranes clanked and rumbled, with now and again the nasal whine of taut wire racing over a pulley when a load of luggage shot into the hold. Tugs swore fussily on their hooters, hawsers splashed overside, from the distant railway station came the dim scream of a whistle. While over and under these noises, interwoven like the pattern of a carpet, was the ship's band. Suddenly a dance tune died away, and the National Anthem echoed through the passages. The anchor chain rattled to a standstill and we were gliding down the river while rows of warehouses vanished in the mist.

We felt like sixteenth century buccaneers masquerading in lounge suits.

Mamerto Urriolagoitia, our leader, was a diplomat

and scholar, and his profession had stamped him with a deep-cut seal. For twelve long years he had battled with his nature, curbing his southern fire and the bright speed of his wit until, at the age of thirty-two, his manner with strangers was a perfect blend of gravity and charm. In the process his swarthy Spanish features had acquired a dignity beyond his years, an effect that was heightened by a marked baldness. He still felt the strain, for at those times when diplomacy demanded a quiet tongue, his dark eyes would flash as one repartee after another passed unspoken. It was only when he was alone with his friends that one realized the depth of humor and sincerity that underlay the mask.

Bee-Mason was also bald, but there the likeness ended. He was lean and wiry, tough as a balk of last year's timber, and, unhampered by diplomatic considerations, he spoke his mind with breezy candor. A pair of light, restless eyes, set in the face of an ascetic priest, glinted through steel-rimmed glasses. He was close on forty when he first yielded to the voice of Ishmael, and his later history spoke for itself. War photographer in France, Belgium and Russia; cinematographer to Shackleton on the last trip south; member of the Commander Worsley and Oxford Expeditions to the North, his brain ran on the glory of the ice. He would speak for hours of the thunder of the breaking pack, of vessels crushed to matchwood in the hands of winter, of the wonderful, steel-blue coloring, and the dancing air that banished weariness from the bones of men, and finally, of three days of blinding hurricane when they hauled on freezing ropes in their pajamas.

In spirit, our tiny expedition went straight back to the Conquistadores. We had no more idea of tropical exploration than Pizarro had when he led his Spaniards through the jungles of Peru. Urrio had been born in Bolivia, but his country stretches from the gigantic backbone of the Andes to the swamps of the Rio Paraguay, and like most of his compatriots he had never descended into the plains. Bee-Mason was exceptionally well-traveled, but a day in Rio de Janeiro was his sole knowledge of South America; and I had never left Europe. It was a mad trip to have undertaken, a solemn request for death, but we did not recognize our folly till we were faced with the unknown, and then the lure of the sky-line seized us almost against our wills.

So three cheerful Ishmaels threw off the dust of cities.

Nevertheless, for all our ignorance of the dangers and discomforts that lay ahead, we knew definitely where we wanted to go and why. Urrio's Government had promised him nine months of freedom if he would follow the route of an old explorer and report on the agricultural possibilities of the land. At first it seemed absurd that any statesman should have to send an expedition to inquire about his country, but it became rapidly more credible as we struggled with the geography of Bolivia.

Bolivia is the Switzerland of South America, a Republic without access to the sea. In shape it resembles the hall of a great hotel, a huge green carpet at the foot of a staircase that rises to a flat landing a good deal nearer the stars. Nine tenths of the population live either at the top or half way down, and the vast forest plain that merges into Brazil in the center of the continent is unknown. The very people are different. Up in the mountains there are fine buildings and stone cities, where the descendants of Spanish colonists live cheek by jowl with Quechua and Aymará Indians, the races over whom the Incas ruled. Down in the jungle, savage man-killing tribes still range the thickets and dwell in huts made of boughs. In Chiquitos, where the Jesuits held sway until the King of Spain expelled them, the Indians are tamer, and exist in mud and wattle houses, but to this day they confuse Christianity with their own barbarous customs. Chiquitos was our goal.

Nuflo de Chavez, the explorer whose course we were to take, was many sorts of hero. In 1557 he set out from Asuncion with three hundred soldiers, two priests, and five women. These last were no mere vivandières, but Castilian ladies of the highest birth and most sacred complexions. Why he took them no one knows. But he did, and they went through with him to the end. For seven hundred miles this tough, indomitable band of wanderers sailed up the waters of the Rio Paraguay and landed on the shores of Lake Gaiba. From there they cut their way through five hundred miles of utterly pathless forest, and after the desertion of half the soldiers, founded Santa Cruz de la Sierra. Their courage and endurance were terrific. Day after day they marched and stumbled and bled, never certain of the next water-hole, always on guard against an ambush. Weeks passed into months, and still the open land eluded them, until, worn out, their stuffy quilt garments cut to shreds, they paused under a ridge of rock, and called it "Sacred Cross of the Mountains."

Since then the Spanish Empire has faded, and Bolivia has emerged from the old Vice-Royalty of Peru, but the romance and glamor of a virile age still cling to this continent of jungles. As we passed smoothly through phosphorescent seas, a new spirit invested us, and the slanting beacon of the Southern Cross became the symbol of a flaming sword pointing the road to adventure. Flying fish leaped from the glassy water as if to warn us of perils that lurked unseen; porpoises rolled with easy grace; deep in the ship the engines rumbled, and all the while the careless glory of the sunlight called to us from cloudless skies.

From the hour that the Sugar Loaf in Rio harbor reared up out of the horizon, a new restlessness took hold of Urrio. It was the white cliffs of Dover once again, the sign that the exile had returned to the land of his birth. All the way down the coast of Brazil he walked with a lighter step and spoke repeatedly of the time when we should cast off the garments of politeness and roam the forests to our heart's desire.

On a dead calm August evening, when the muddy waters of the River Plate shone like beaten silver we came to Buenos Aires,

CHAPTER II

Rio de la Plata is the most misnamed sheet of water in the world. It is not a river at all, but an estuary, a vast, shallow, muddy, fresh-water sea, sixty miles in width, which pours the turgid streams of Paraná and Uruguay into the Atlantic. Nor has it anything to do with silver. There is none in the hills of the interior through which these rivers pass; there is none in the Province of Buenos Aires. Only an imaginative man could have so described it, an explorer for instance who happened to strike it towards evening on a calm day when the opaque surface of the water gleamed like metal. Still, adventurers must be men of fancy or they would stay behind a counter; and the epithet is undoubtedly attractive.

In the seventeenth century Buenos Aires was the iron bar that blocked the back entrance to the treasure house of Peru. From the grim stockade above the shore, a battery of long-range guns was trained on the one deep channel in the estuary as a perpetual challenge to the world at large. For His Most Catholic Majesty, the King of Spain, was a jealous monarch, and had issued the strictest orders to the Governor of the Fort that neither English nor French nor Dutch should trade with the New World.

Unfortunately, His Majesty made no allowance for the type of man that he was forced to employ. It was only the hard-bitten swashbuckler, the cut-throat, and the get-rich-quick bravo who ventured as far as South America; and the spiritual descendants of the Conquistadores cared nothing for the slower fruits of agriculture. Consequently, when they landed in Buenos Aires with their eyes glistening for the ingots of Peru, their dreams crashed in a heap of star dust, for the road across the Andes was forbidden them. Instead of an Eldorado blazing with emeralds and gold they found a dull, stuffy fort reeking with fever on a barren strip of desert at the end of nowhere.

The Governors of Buenos Aires were loyal soldiers, hidalgos of the highest birth and honor, but they were not supermen. Rulers over an insubordinate, greedy, time-serving band of desperadoes, their burden was rendered doubly galling by the nature of their duties. Since no foreign ship might anchor off the shore, it stood to reason that Spanish merchantmen took advantage of the monopoly, and the common necessities of life became ruinously expensive. To this there could only be one answer—smuggling, and, although the early Governors did their utmost to suppress it, those who came later recognized the inevitable and connived. Six thousand miles of sea can be a wonderful salve to conscience, and by degrees the roadstead of the River Plate turned into an open market where English, French and Dutchmen chaffered for cargoes of hides.

Towards the end of the eighteenth century the world rolled in its sleep. Rousseau wrote suggestively about the change, and the colonial grievance-mongers of South America gobbled his pamphlets whole. They watched with burning interest the struggle for independence in the North, and sighed enviously when a king's head tumbled from a scaffold in Paris. They stared with all their eyes when Napoleon invaded Spain in 1809, only to strike with sudden fury on the accession of Joseph Bonaparte.

For fifteen bloody years a haze of gun-smoke hung over the New World. Simón Bolivar, a tall, thin Venezuelan with a face of flame ranged the continent from the Orinoco to the Pilcomayo, fighting his seven hundred battles in the snows of the Andes and the fever-swamps of the Amazon, until, long after Argentina had won her liberty, his troops dropped dauntless, but exhausted, out of bondage.

When the smoke cleared, a new era had begun. Instead of the Vice-Royalties of Lima and Buenos Aires, eight separate countries with eight separate souls sprang into life. Buenos Aires split into Argentina, Paraguay and the eastern half of Bolivia; Lima into Chile, Peru, Western Bolivia, Ecuador, Colombia and Venezuela. Nevertheless there was no unity among the states as there was in the North, and the politics of South America are still governed by an uneasy balance of power.

Freed from the fetters of Spain, Buenos Aires became the center of a nation. It was no longer a useful blockhouse to ward off raids against Peru. It had its own destiny and its people learned to be a race. It ceased to think in terms of metals, and putting its faith in the land, ensured that Argentine cattle and horse-flesh should become a by-word for excellence. It welcomed foreign capital, placed its public works in the hands of Englishmen, and lay back on its ownership of the soil while the gringo labored. In this simple manner many fortunes were made, and railroads crept across the pampas.

The Argentino to-day is an enthusiastic creature, passionately proud of his country, and devoted to sport. The European conception of a nation of greasy dagoes wasting its manhood on the fruits of the white slave trade is rather sillier than most generalizations. In actual fact there are more football and boxing clubs, more yachting and rowing and wrestling than in any country in the Old World, except England and Germany. These swarthy sons of the old colonists have got sport on the brain. They live for sport, and the athlete is as much worshiped as he is at a British public school. One third of every newspaper published in Buenos Aires is devoted to athletic events, and the annual Association Football match between Argentina and Uruguay may be heard half way across the Plata. Nor is the standard unworthy. The Uruguayans carried the world before them at the Olympic games.

If there be one flaw in this spirit it is the excessive keenness with which it is carried out. When Firpo faced Dempsey in New York, the streets of Buenos Aires were swollen with a fiery, cheering mob, which for hours before the fight was broadcast, rent the skies with shouts of "Viva, Firpo." When Dempsey knocked the wild bull of the Pampas through the ropes, a thoroughly chastened multitude drooped off home, and ordered its sons to attend school next morning in black ties.

So race-proud has the Argentino become, that he has invented a dialect of his own by which he may be recognized from Lima to Madrid. Always imaginative he has surpassed himself in the pronunciation of double "l" and "uy," which are rendered alike by a soft "j"; and the power and range of his slang would shame a New Yorker into speaking English. His ideal is Paris, Paris clothes, Paris perfumes, Paris gaiety, and especially a visit to Paris, which is the ultimate heaven where all good Argentinos foregather when they die.

As regards the conventions, Buenos Aires is deep in the reign of the late Queen Victoria. Latin blood is ideal fodder for chaperons, and these graceful, well-groomed, charming middle-aged ladies may be seen at every function in which their beautiful daughters take part. Britain has taught the Argentino a lot, but it is doubtful whether he will ever take it as a compliment to be trusted alone with a woman. Such is the country from which Urrio, Bee-Mason and I jumped off for Bolivia.

I have often regretted that Buenos Aires did not stoop to win our affection. It would have been so easy for her to smile during the ten days we lodged with her, so gracious to have sent us away with nothing but sun in our hearts. With her wealth of historical reminiscence, her magnificent buildings, and reputation for gaiety, she could have made us her slaves for life. Still, she chose differently, and can blame none but herself for the clammy memories which are all that remain with us. Urrio was perpetually busy with men of high degree, so Bee-Mason and I took each other in hand and explored the greatest city south of New York. In raincoats and misery we splashed up the Avenida de Mayo, that vast boulevard, and gazed in wonder at the stupendous façades of the newspaper offices. We leered at the Palacio de Congreso, the Parliament House, which seemed to our disordered fancies to resemble a gigantic cinema designed by Sir Christopher Wren. We lingered in Recoleta, the most expensive cemetery in the world, and agreed that it fell in with our mood. In short, we fumed our way through ten wet, weary days, while we awaited the river steamer that was to take us a step further along Nuflo de Chavez's route.

Three incidents stand out against a streaming background. One afternoon Bee-Mason and I, wearied with sight-seeing, stumbled down a staircase out of the street, and found ourselves in one of the most remarkable rooms we had ever seen. It was entirely underground, a beershop more than a hundred feet long and, from floor to ceiling, was entirely lined with blue and white tiles. We sat down at a table, and I fingered the glaze before signing for the proprietor, who advanced beaming through a miasma of tobacco smoke. He admitted they were late eighteenth century Delft, and told me that his grandfather had brought them over from Holland. There must have been close on twenty thousand, an amazing room.

Soon afterwards I presented an introduction to an Irish-Argentine, one of that race of hardy ranchers whose fathers had migrated from Ireland in the eighties. To-day they own miles of productive pampas, play polo like demons, and chatter lightheartedly in a bastard mixture of English and Spanish. They are immensely wealthy, fear nothing in this world, and are as good company as one could meet in a year's travel. This one treated me kindly, but his jaw dropped when he heard the reason for our journey.

"Cross Bolivia on a mule!" he said. "You are mad. It is a deadly country full of snakes and swamps and fever. What you want is a canoe."

He went on to say that Bolivia and Paraguay were in the middle of a squabble about a piece of land called the "Chaco," that we might blunder into a war at any moment, and that a number of savage Indians, disturbed by the movement of troops, had established themselves in our path, and were killing the owners of caravans almost weekly.

"I should not care to go myself," he ended.

I departed with my brain in a whirl. It is one thing to yield to the lust for adventure, and quite another to hear a tough young man who knows the country rejoice at his absence from the game; so I returned to Bee-Mason and drew the picture with colored words.

He sprang up, his face aflame with emotion, and just as I was congratulating myself on having passed the old explorer's guard, he burst into speech.

"If only those Indians would kill you or Urrio," he cried, "my film would be worth something."

There are difficulties in working with a monomaniac.

Next morning we collected Urrio and took him to a toy shop. We might be amateurs in the art of exploration, but at any rate we knew our literature. Every man who goes off the beaten track arms himself with bright knick-knacks, and we hastened to follow their lead. Under the tolerant gaze of a young woman we ransacked the store and came away with enough Christmas cheer to distract the attention of a whole nation of savages.

At long last our ten days ran out, and in teeming rain we turned our backs on Buenos Aires. For several hours we sat at the window of a train and watched league upon league of sodden pampa flash by, and then we drew into Rosario where we were to join the river steamer. Unfortunately we had trusted to a dreamy friend of Urrio's, so that when we swept down to the quay we found a squat, tug-shaped boat with a black and white funnel, a sleepy Italian waiter, but no luggage. Nobody had heard of us, our tickets had not been booked, and a casual fellow who looked like a red monkey with a pilot's hat badge, told us without emotion that they were due to sail in an hour's time. It was then midday.

Black fury settled about the hearts of Bee-Mason and myself, for it is a curious fact that Englishmen who rather enjoy a sinking liner behave like fretful children over a lost connection. Urrio blew cigarette smoke through his nose and tried to calm us.

"You do not know the country," he said. "We have hours to spare."

After an hour and a half during which the taximeter turned over a new leaf and began again, we ran our luggage to ground in a distant shed. By this time Bee-Mason and I were quite frantic, but Urrio was imperturbable, and to make matters worse, insisted upon lunch directly the trunks had been despatched to the ship.

Seething with rebellion we followed him to an eating-house and listened in silent wrath while he urged us to enjoy our poached eggs on steak because boiled rice would be our portion in the wilds. On receipt of the bill he informed us mildly that Rosario was more expensive than the Ritz. Against such tactics we were powerless. Towards half past two we strolled into the offices of the shipping company where Urrio took possession of a small brown junior clerk. He did not slap the money down on the counter and ask haughtily for three tickets, nor did he stare through the youngster as if he were part of the furniture. He greeted him like a very dear friend from whom he had been separated for years. Gradually the two dark heads drew together, jokes and laughter rattled about the room, and within ten minutes the mysterious ailments of their respective families were receiving sympathetic attention. Bee-Mason and I held an indignation meeting on the pavement.

The manager's eyes were heavy with sleep when he returned from his siesta about an hour later, but he took to Urrio at once. His junior faded automatically into the background and a new edition of chit-chat began.

"Of course the ship will wait for you," he said cheerfully. "The captain will be over in a minute. I heard him snoring as I passed his house."

Gradually, as dawn breaks over a clouded hill, the reason for all this courtesy entered my northern mind. The South American is a born idler, a carefree creature of the sun who lives for the small artistic gaieties of life. The bright quality of the air is vivid in his blood, making him lust for color and music and romance. He regards work as a necessary evil without which he would go hungry, but he never absorbs himself in his job to the extent of selling his personality to his employer. He never forgets that he is José Maria Garcia, with a heavy accent on the José Maria, to distinguish him from all the rest of the noble army of Garcias. Consequently he must be approached as a human being. Reared in a land where tomorrow is the busiest day of the week he distrusts bustle, and, lest by an oversight he should be forced to hurry, he has erected a strick zareba of red-tape through which he gazes with a stony, departmental attention to business. Only as a friend will he consent to leave that zareba and help a brother wayfarer to catch his boat. This is the reason why foreigners belittle him as something slow and stupid.

The captain turned out to be a sturdy Brazilian with a taste for Englishmen. In response to a nod from the weary Urrio I leaped into the breach and took him in hand. It was an easy task, the only necessities being a friendly smile and a quick appreciation of the alternative ways of pronouncing English. In under twenty minutes we were striding arm in arm towards the quay, and talking hard about the trip across Bolivia.

At ten o'clock in brilliant moonshine we weighed anchor and churned over the smooth water towards the north. We leaned against the bulwarks for a long time after the lights of Rosario had vanished, and the scented peace of the night laid hold on us, making speech a blasphemy. Only when the moon sank and a chill crept into the air did we retire to our separate bunks.

The Paraná River is possibly the most treacherous in the world. Like the House of the Fool its foundations are of sand, shifting and restless, a bank one day, a deep pool the next, a silent obedient slave to the whims of the muddy water. A thousand islands mark its course, barren yellow spits that change shape over night and harbor nothing but screaming wild fowl and a few snakes. A steamer of five and a half feet draught can journey from Cuyabá to Buenos Aires, a distance of two thousand five hundred miles, and call on five countries in its passage; for Brazil, Bolivia, Paraguay, Uruguay and Argentina, all come down to the waterway which is international and free from tariffs. In the dry season the river is anything from four miles to a hundred yards across; but when the skies open, the low cattle-land on either bank becomes one vast sea, two hundred miles in width, and the main channel is drowned in a waste of waters. Small wonder that a pilot's apprentice must spend nine years in study for his ticket. It is impossible to know the exact position of every shoal, so by constant practice he acquires an instinct for sand that is akin to genius. Even then he must specialize at the outset of his career, for it is not permitted that one man shall know the whole River. Buenos Aires to Asuncion, Asuncion to Corumbá, he must make his choice—and heaven help him if he ground his ship, for the culprit must stay with his handiwork. There was one poor devil who paid with ten months of vigil. The rains were late that year.

One day Bee-Mason and I, aware of the prejudice against disturbing the pilot, tip-toed to the door of the wheel-house and peeped in. There was our red-haired friend, standing impassively magnificent in the uniform of the Brazilian Navy, his great mustache dipped towards the pages of an erotic novel. The wheel was lashed to the stem of the tall brass compass with a piece of string. Silently we departed.

As the days passed a subtle alchemy took place within us, and we ceased to be ourselves. Diplomat, cinematographer, writer, merged and softened into a merry band of adventurers. From the narrow deck we watched the sun lean out of heaven to touch the

INTERIOR OF CHURCH AT SANTO CORAZÓN LEFT BY THE JESUITS

surface of the water, and narrowed our eyes at the bright flash of the retort. On the branches of fallen trees sat thousands of cormorants with hard, cruel beaks. Once in a while a bird would dive, scarcely rippling the reflection, and emerge with a squirming, silver fish. *Urubu,* the black and white vulture of South America swept noiselessly and without effort, high above the forest that lined the banks. It was on one of these occasions that Bee-Mason said:

"Thank God for wanderlust," quite quietly.

A bright color burned in his cheeks, and he swept his arm in an upward semicircle that embraced the river, the trees, and the sky. For the first time Urrio and I realized the consuming fire that underlay the sober, priest-like shell.

CHAPTER III

IF an ordinary, intelligent layman were asked to name the greatest dangers of a tropical forest, he would refer to savages, wild beasts and snakes. If a well-read Eskimo wrote an essay on the marriage customs of the English he would quote the symbolic initials of Mr. Masefield, "One Divorce Trial after Another." Both would have abundant literary backing, and both would be astoundingly mistaken. One of the profoundest joys in store for the amateur of travel is the gradual shedding of preconceived ideas, and the slow accumulation of outlandish knowledge. Urrio, Bee-Mason and I left London with an incredibly childish conception of what we were in for. We dreamed of charging jaguars and coiled rattlesnakes, and we thought of naked men brandishing spears under our noses. We made solemn resolutions never to leave the camp-fire without knee-high boots, and we practised the art of throwing a gun in case a bad character should menace our innocent approach. It never occurred to us that in all that wealth of trees it might be hard to find water, or that game might be shy of sampling the cook-pot. It never entered our heads that swarms of tiny insects might keep us awake for days, or that prolonged lack of sleep is every bit as deadly as a bullet. And, crowning folly, none of us brought a compass.

Three days north from Rosario we encountered the gigantic and terrible personality that we came to call Green Hell. It is a truly colossal block of forest, so vast that the mind refuses to grasp the full immensity of its range. Shaped like a human body it stands foursquare on the top of Argentina. Its trunk is Brazil and Paraguay and Eastern Bolivia, its far-flung shoulders dip into two oceans at Ecuador and Pernambuco, and its scraggy neck twists at Panama into the Republics of Central America. At its widest it stretches without break the distance between Labrador and Liverpool, or Southampton and Suez. It has the Amazon, the Orinoco and the Paraguay for its main arteries, and some six hundred different breeds of Indians flit like fleas through the green covering of its skin.

Naturally it is not of equal density. In the southern portion it is often wooded parkland shot with belts of thicker trees. Cattle roam the plains near the Rio Paraguay, but the forest is never far distant, and ranchers have to take care lest their charges run wild. In the north it is horrible, a dense, fever-stricken thicket, shimmering in the heat with a perpetual glassy haze dancing through the topmost branches. It is evil, swampy, miasmic, like a warm, festering wound. An Englishman may obtain some slight insight into the discomfort of penetration if he lock himself into a hot-house, water the flowers, close all windows, and allow a blazing sun to shine through the glass while he rides on a stationary bicycle. Even then he will not be bothered by insects.

At first sight, especially if seen from a boat, Green Hell is just a wood, silent, empty, a little aloof as it paddles its roots in the river. Except for an occasional palm-tree, it might be a slice of England such as Symonds Yat on the Wye, or some parts of the Devon and Somerset border. Shady, cool and green, motionless in the sunlight, it gives an impression of beauty and security that has lured many a novice to his death. During the next seven months I began to know that forest, and to understand the fiendish, callous power that underlay the calm exterior. Under the shadow of its leaves I was tired, elated, thirsty, hungry and afraid. It hedged us in, dared us to venture through its bowers, coyly hid its water-holes from our sight, and loosed a covey of vampire bats when our animals could ill afford the blood. I make no claims against the snakes and jaguars that we met, for we sought them deliberately for our own ends. And the Indians that surrounded us were poor, driven creatures who knew no better.

By degrees I realized that the ancients were right about the sex of their symbolic deities. Ceres, Nature, Green Hell—either name will pass—is a woman. A man, Mars for instance, or Jupiter, would sport awhile with a victim before it died. Green Hell is logical, with all the cold clear-headedness of a woman who is responsible for the welfare of her kingdom. A traveler is at perfect liberty to wander in her domain, she places no insuperable obstacles in his path; but he must have experience and nerve, for if once he lose his head or make a wrong decision his doom is signed. She will not lift a finger to his aid. For all she cares his bones may whiten in oblivion. Still, she is not malevolent, and will grant fair play to all who subscribe to her rules.

Her dress is magnificent, a rich, eternal garment of every shade of green dappled with gold sun-spots. In a measure it portrays the inflexibility of her character, for she never relapses into the browns and reds of autumn, nor into the joyous innocence of the young spring. A deep sage at the hem, it rises in steady waves of color, until, towards the top, the sun has bleached the life-blood in the leaves. Her clothes are indestructible, for her wood is for the most part hardwood, and may not be burned while it lives. But for this fact South America would have been colonized long ago. Thousands of gardeners sweep her paths, and their children are reared to her service. She flatters them with her smile, shelters them with her gown, lulls them to sleep in the great silence of her bosom; but she starves without mercy any creature that does not minister to the increase of her body. She grants a landing ground to *Urubu* on condition that he buries the dead in the warmth of his gizzard. Purple beetle has a safe home beneath a leaf so long as he play the sexton to minor carrion. Painted jaguar may range her undergrowth till his beauty fades and the younger generation forces him into a corner to die.

Bang!

It was only Urrio shooting at a cormorant, but the rumbling echo was merged in the mocking laughter of Green Hell. A loud noise is the only method of arousing her interest, then she laughs, a chuckling, hollow, mocking sound, with the wickedness of the Ages behind it, but no mirth.

"That forest looks lived in," said Urrio, reloading.

There, in five words, is her secret and her danger.

She looks lived in.

Suddenly the red monkey pilot deserted the wheel and clattered down the companionway.

"*Jacaré*," he screamed and waved his arms up stream. It was a new blasphemy to us, but we made a note of it.

"*Jacaré*," he repeated, and then, "*cocodrilo.*"

This was more intelligible, and we ran to the rail. On a brown mud bank not twenty yards away from the ship's side was a knobbly, gray-green reptile with a pale throat. Its eyes were glassy and half-closed, its jaws wrinkled and half open and its expression was as wicked as a monkish gargoyle. There it lay, utterly still in the sunlight, a sinister, evil shape that looked as though a bad fairy had created it, only to repent and turn it into stone. Even as we gazed, the swirling wake of the steamer picked it off the ground and left it struggling in rough water.

This was our first encounter with a creature whose length varies from six inches to twenty feet, whose belly is white horn set in the form of plates, and whose "woof" of displeasure has led many a tenderfoot to look nervously round for a jaguar. Some years ago, when reptile skins first became fashionable, an enthusiastic trader tried to make a fortune out of *Jacaré*. He set up a factory and offered one shilling and sixpence for each hide. Thousands of Indians loaded their blunderbusses, and the air became foul with the stripped bodies of alligators. Then, and not till then did the speculator realize that the South American cayman is not tannable. Horn is horn, even when grown in strips, and by no process can it be turned into leather.

We steamed into the wide lagoon at the foot of Asuncion, where the town shines white above the river, on an evening that lives with me yet. It was absolutely still. The air smelt cool, and the mudflats showed wild and barren, shadowed in purple, apparently as free from life as when Nuflo de Chavez arrived. Fireflies were not awake, no fish mottled the face of the water, even the bullfrogs had not begun their nightly choir practice. It was as though Nature had peeped in a mirror, and had snatched her breath at the beauty of the reflection. For the sun and the moon were blazing at each other, not palely apart as the moon is sometimes, a distant echo of the flame of her lord's passing, but each a fiery personality low in the sky, glowing, vivid, alive. The lagoon was no longer dirty water, but solid metal, oddly luminous. The eastern side was silver, slightly tinged with mauve. The west was blinding gold hammered into a vast sheet, after the fashion of the Incas in the Temple of the Sun at Cuzco. The glory lasted for ten minutes, and then the sun slid over the horizon hoisting his consort into the sky with the weight of his descent. Whereupon the lights shone out from the town, a lantern crept to the peak of a river steamer, and the bullfrogs sang.

We were now at the capital of Paraguay, a city that is drenched in history. In 1527 Sebastian Cabot, fresh from his discoveries in North America entered the mouth of the Plata, and sailed up the aisles of Green Hell to Asuncion. From there, too, the Spaniard, Juan de Ayolas, pushed up to the head waters of the Rio Paraguay, and was lost in the hopeless, trailless wastes of the great Xarayes marsh. Cabeza de Vaca and Irala followed him, only to return appalled at the forests that cut off the river from the silver mines of Peru. Nuflo de Chavez and his gallant company alone drove their way through, and they opened up the Province of Chiquitos, which for a century and a half was a field of honor for the Jesuit missionaries.

When the time came for the Spanish adventurers to settle down in Asuncion they built a stockade and started to tame the Guaraní Indians. This proved comparatively easy, and as there were many priests and few women of their own race mixed marriages became fashionable. Thus the present breed of Paraguayan was born.

That night, as I stood by the prow under the full glare of the stars and listened to the boatman shouting across the water, I seemed in another age. Bearded men in gay clothes with rapiers at their hips swaggered in fantasy before my eyes. Dark-eyed, ascetic priests, black-robed, tonsured, strode with absorbed gaze through their jovial flock. Painted Castilian ladies, haughty and dangerous, secure in the numbers that sought their hand, reclined on couches in the shady *patios* and held their courts. And the ships with emblazoned sails and sunken waists, tall and proud on the glassy river. And the arquebusses and jeweled hilts; and the fine linen of the warriors, patched and torn and patched again; and the grand air of frivolity and stubborn purpose that drove men from padded homes into glory and dust and despair and death that lurked beside each path in the New World. All these and a thousand more passed before me.

Then a fish jumped, and the vision faded.

It is just at this spot that the Rio Pilcomayo brings a sporting career to a close by flowing into Rio Paraná. It is a navigable river at each end, both up in Bolivia and at Asuncion, but for three hundred miles in the center it is a vast, foul-smelling, oozy stretch of bog, with as much movement as an unsqueezed sponge. Incidentally it is the southern border of a huge, inhospitable tract of forest which is hotly claimed by Bolivia and Paraguay, and which nearly embroiled the expedition in what would have been a nasty, guerilla war. This strip, called the Chaco, is almost waterless, it being no uncommon fate for a man to ride forty miles between the waterholes. Indeed, adventurers have been known to tear the leaves from a spiky plant and lap the brackish acid liquid that lies concealed at the base of the spines.

Naturally these two eminently practical countries are

not disputing the ownership out of a desire for the right to go thirsty in this terrible land. The matter has a commercial side, for it is the home of a red hardwood, rather like the oak, named *quebracho* which contains thirty per cent of tannin. During the past half century Bolivia has concentrated her powers entirely on the extraction of metals from the Andean mines, and Paraguay has taken the opportunity with both hands. Year by year, as the line of the forest has receded under the ax, the *quebracho* companies have marched farther from the river until now a full hundred miles of territory has been irrevocably picketed.

A few years ago Bolivia awoke to her danger, and lodged a protest before Paraguay could carry her logging machines to the foothills of the Cordilleras. In July, 1928, a commission sat in Buenos Aires to fix a boundary, but negotiations broke down. Two days before we arrived the Bolivian Air Force dropped derisive pamphlets on Asuncion. Two days after we left, an absent-minded Bolivian colonel wandered into the neighborhood of *Bahia Negra*, the port of contention, at dead of night, and was arrested as a spy. Thus the rumblings of international thunder were already volleying across Green Hell, but it was not until we reached Santa Cruz at Christmas that blood was shed.

Meanwhile we chugged on up the river towards the most lawless and romantic province in the whole of South America.

CHAPTER IV

A FEW days out from Asuncion, to the east, lies the province of Matto Grosso. It is a land of wooded plains and cattle swamps, sun, seraglios, and erring women, and the Law is a 44 Smith & Wesson slung loose at the hip. In theory it is a country of stark terror, where judges go in fear of their lives, and acquitted scoundrels often die as they leave the Court. Assassins ply their trade at ten shillings a body, and pray earnestly to the Saints for a clear eye and a steady hand. Even the President of the United States of Brazil dare not send police after a criminal who has gained the tree-girt sanctuary of Matto Grosso.

The province is full of the most friendly and warm-hearted blackguards in the world. It is almost a second Mexico, though purer and more manly, freed to a great extent from the greasy trickery of the former nation. For Matto Grosso has a soul that is neither black nor white nor gray, but gaily colored and appreciative of bravery. Most of its sons are Brazilians, dark-skinned and passionate, descendants of the Portuguese settlers of the sixteenth century. They are the hardest materials for an Englishman to handle in the whole of South America, being as proud and prickly as Scottish crofters, and morbidly suspicious of strangers. No power on earth can drive them, and a hasty blow is answered with a knife; but a straight dealer who treats them as human beings may lead them where he will and a Brazilian who has once given his hand in friendship can be trusted to the end.

Sprinkled among the native population are a large number of Negroes whose ancestors came chained from Africa in foul-smelling slave ships. To-day they are mostly cattlemen, tough and springy and smiling, in love with the gaudy clothes in which they gallop the plains. Moreover, any one who has not seen one of these blue-trousered, yellow-scarved, silver-spurred *gauchos* dropping a lasso over the horns of a jumping steer and then leaning back in the saddle as the strain falls on the cinch and the dust is kicked into a cloud—that person has not lived.

The rest of the province is made up of traveling Syrian hucksters, Japanese coffee planters and Americans. The Syrians are small-eyed, shrewd, peaceable men, who range the country with a couple of mules and a cargo of knick-knacks, and give no trouble to anybody. The Japanese keep to themselves, live on rice and beer, and retire after twenty years with comfortable fortunes. For the Americans there can be no retirement because in seven cases out of ten they failed to observe the laws of Texas and Arizona, and beat the sheriff to the border by a short neck. They are sun-dried and small and pathetic, ranchers for the most part with tight mouths and sharp faces. Incredibly swift with a gun they are bleakly contemptuous of their neighbors, and only burst out on Saturday nights when the bitter taste of exile and the raw Brazilian gin cause them to shoot up the lights in memory of happier times.

With such a hotch-potch of destinies jumbled together in a savage land, it is surprising that there should be any code of rules at all. That there should be a particularly rigid one, is nothing short of amazing. The remainder of South America deny the existence of this code, swearing that it is just a vivid blaze of murder; but it is there for all that.

The whole root basis of the matter lies in the treatment of women. Matto Grosso is quite frankly medieval and Moslem in its denial of feminine rights, and if the ranchers had ever heard of the *ceinture de chasteté* they would certainly use it. Now a woman is quite unable to invent a code of morals for herself. She takes her character at her husband's valuation and draws it to a logical close. If he trust her she will pay him the compliment of feeling guilty for a lapse from virtue. If he shut her up like a milch cow she will risk her life to commit adultery. Brazilian men are well aware of this, and although an inhospitable curmudgeon is despised from Cuyabá to Camp Grande, no rancher in his senses would introduce a stranger to his wife and daughters. These are kept in the kitchen, and a sudden bullet is the portion of a guest who shows too much interest in cooking. Indeed, there is a very strict etiquette for the conduct of strangers. A man may have ridden all day and be dead tired, but he must never dismount and hammer on the door. He must sit his horse outside the palings and shout "*o de casa*" at the top of his lungs. Then he will be admitted and given free meals for himself and his mount. If the owner is away he must depart unquenched or the serving women will hope for the worst, and the mistress of the house will stand an excellent chance of burial on her lord's return. Small wonder that the sexes stray from light conversation when they find themselves together and alone.

This fidelity at the pistol's mouth has the same effect on the female mind as bandaging has on Chinese feet. It restricts and thwarts and numbs, and in the end renders them furtive and suspicious, useless for any but the simplest problems. The women of Matto Grosso cook and sew and bear children, but their lives are singularly narrow. They have no small talk, and their views, if they exist at all, are suppressed. At the same time their one-track minds are constantly on the alert for the means to outwit their men. There was a case in Corumbá when we passed through which perfectly illustrates the life. A man had lived with a woman for eighteen years. They were not married, just *amigados*, but they had always worked well together. He had ranched and she had tended the house, and they had prospered. That is to say, rich farmers had come to stay, and the woman had listened to the laughter from the kitchen without being asked to join. Lately their eldest daughter had been married, and the man had suggested to his mistress that, as a wedding gift, they should legitimize the child. Concealing her pleasure, the woman had agreed, and now, after eighteen years of unbroken servility, she had turned into a shrew. She was too old to be beaten, and the man had lost his fire through long obedience. So he just wandered about with a broken heart, and kept away from his home as much as possible. An almost perfect tragedy, for both were right according to their ethics.

Next to adultery, theft is the most discouraged vice in Matto Grosso. A thief is regarded as lacking in self-respect, and as such is relieved of the burden of living; for pride in oneself is the first virtue in the wilds. Nobody bothers to deliver him to the police. A bullet supplies the means, and the vultures the end.

Of course, when the use of firearms is so universal, and each man is his own law, there must be a certain measure of abuse. Buenos Aires would say it is all abuse, but this is not so. It is true that a man may hire an assassin, may even commit the murder himself, but in few countries is public opinion so strong as it is there. If a scoundrel has stolen a wife, or burgled a house, he must die, and the law of Matto Grosso barks approval, but heaven help the Ahab who ousts a Naboth from his rightful vineyard. From that hour he will live a life of fear, glancing uneasily at the shadows that fall from trees. Sooner or later, as well he knows, a bullet will strike between the shoulders, for even the poorest Naboth has a brother.

Taken as a whole the justice of Matto Grosso is temperate. It is based on a fierce pride of possession, and if the police are often ignored, it is because delay would grant the criminal a sanctuary. It is at least a manly creed, in which cowardice and theft and inhospitality are reckoned unpardonable, and in which a man who sued his wife for infidelity would be laughed into the grave. There would be less slime and filth in Anglo-Saxon Divorce Courts if the penalty for adultery were the same.

From time to time as we steamed up river, we passed small, wooden buildings on small red cliffs. They were always shaped the same, just a palm pole at each corner, a thatched roof, and a long, sloping chute that hung over the water. One day, when we drew level, we discovered their use. A slaughtered bullock lay on the top, and the blood from its entrails flowed down the boards into the stream. A dozen cowboys in leather aprons and gaudy scarves waved cheerfully in our direction, and stabbed at the air with flashing knives. A large herd of oxen gazed passively at the scene and blinked without regret at the blankets of meat that were drying in the sun. We had stumbled on a manufactory of *charqui*, the jerked beef and staple food of South America. From the cloud of flies that hovered above the slabs we concluded that the drying process was a cheap one.

Suddenly, Urrio pointed to the foot of the chute. There, in the muddy water, was a leaping, struggling mass of silver fish. It lurked like a cloud beneath the surface and stretched for many yards in a great circle. A piece of offal slithered out of the carcass and dropped

A BAG OF WILD DUCK

into their midst. In an instant it was gone, rent in pieces by the waiting shoal. One of the cowboys, seeing our amazement, cut off chunks of meat and threw them into the river. They, too, vanished in a swirl of fins.

"*Piranha,*" said the red pilot, spitting thoughtfully.

We pressed him for details, and he told us that *piranha* is the most dangerous creature in South America, the man-eating fish of the Rio Paraguay. More terrible than a tiger it herds together in numberless swarms, and preys on every sort of flesh. Cattle drovers always reckon to lose a bullock at each ford, because these blunt-jawed demons single out the weakest and tear its vitals into strings as it plunges in agony through the water. Nobody in his senses swims in these parts, though a healthy man may sometimes pass unscathed. Anything in the shape of a boil or an open wound is fatal, for the smell of blood travels with the current and draws *piranha* to the fountain head in a moment. Urrio watched the carnage in silence, and then said grimly:

"No need to forbid mixed bathing here."

At Puerto Esperanza, the railhead of the Trans-Brazilian railway, Green Hell has wilted. Vast, arid plains drop away to the horizon, brittle speargrass that lacerates like a saber covers the drab landscape, and drowsy bullocks meander from clump to clump at great risk to their tongues. From time to time a tiny breed of deer, yellow as a hare, with a white scut, dodges and leaps across the open, and a flaming sun scorches the ground for ten hours a day. In the rains this flat prairie country is a huge sea, and river steamers drop their anchors off the booking office two stations down the line.

We hitched up to the bank, near a pile of sleepers and started to unload salt for the meat factories. Growing tired of an endless chain of sweating Negroes, and the monotonous rumble of cranes, we took possession of a motor dinghy, and installed Bee-Mason's cinema in the bows. Then we commandeered the pilot's brother-in-law as a mechanic, and pushed off down stream in search of alligators.

Within ten minutes all trace of man had faded from the scene. Great beds of water-rushes came down into the river, and an astounding collection of brilliant river-birds chattered out at our approach. Little purple and orange fellows with trailing legs and the flight of a partridge leaped up with a squeak and then plunged into the sedge. *Carancho* with his fine, free, eagle's head, yellow-eyed, dressed in buff plus fours and a speckled Fair Isle jumper, strolled demurely on a sand-spit. Baker-birds peeped cheekily out of their small mud ovens and posed for their picture, while urubu swept through the skies and preyed for carrion.

By and by we turned off the main stream and entered a creek where evergreen shrubs reached down to the water. In a far corner was a sand bar, its yellow back hunched above the surface, and eight large alligators lay sleeping in the sun. The heavy, drenched languor of a tropical midday hung breathlessly in wavering mists, and

GREEN HELL

the silence was absolute when Urrio switched off the motor. In a strained, aching quietude the boat glided across the lagoon. Suddenly the pilot's brother-in-law leaned far out over the starboard gunwale and gave tongue.

"Ssh," said Bee-Mason, turning the handle of his camera at an angle of forty-five degrees.

"Whirr," went the machine.

The mechanic leaned obediently inwards and kicked an empty gasoline tin. The noise was incredible, a war drum beaten in the very ears of the foe. Instantly seven of the alligators lifted their heads from their paws, and the eighth, with the air of an old hand, slipped into the water.

"Ooooh!"

The long-drawn wail of sorrow sent five of the remaining reptiles off the bank.

"Ssh, you black devil," said Bee-Mason, swinging to the motion of the boat.

Once again the launch was righted, once again the challenge of a hollow tin rang across the water, and, with a flourish of displeasure, the last two tails vanished. Bee-Mason spoke angrily to Urrio:

"Can't you keep him in order? He's spoilt a wonderful picture."

Urrio, the diplomat, threw an orange to the repentant crew, and told him he would be crucified if he moved so much as a toe. Then we settled down to wait. Half an hour passed before the first alligator decided that the green depths of the water were an ill place to spend such a brilliant afternoon, and came to the surface. Soon the whole eight were swimming lazily in circles, hardly rippling the glassy smoothness of the lagoon. Only the arched protuberances above the eyes were visible, and these gleamed wickedly as they watched the boat. For a while Bee-Mason persisted with his camera. But at last he stepped down in disgust.

"They won't return to the bank," he grumbled. "Stir 'em up with a shot."

Urrio steadied his rifle on the gunwale and fired. Fifty yards away an evil eye went blank, a long snout dipped, and a gray-green body was floating on the face of the pool. Every other eye disappeared. Suddenly Urrio had an idea.

"Let's prove the *piranha* theory for ourselves," he suggested.

"Going for a swim?" I asked.

Bee-Mason fingered his beloved camera.

"It would be a unique picture," he said.

Urrio's idea was more original.

"Let's cut off the alligator's tail and see how long it takes for the *piranhas* to clean him out."

This was felt to be genius, so we passed a rope under the fore paws and returned to the main river. Amongst our armory of weapons (which incidentally had convinced the Customs officials in Buenos Aires that we were revolutionaries) was a *machete,* a heavy, curved, South American cross between a bill hook and a scimitar. Rest-

BEFORE A JAGUAR HUNT

ing the tail on the thwart we dealt it a smart blow, and then lowered the body at the end of a long rope. Almost at once we were conscious of strife. The dark water kindled, a troubled cloud grew to immense proportions, and a silver terror shone beneath the surface. Occasionally there was a bright flash of scales and a flourish of fins as a fish was forced into the daylight by the weight of its companions. An air of concealed energy, horrible and intense, kept our eyes fixed on the jerking rope, and I reflected that, if ever a liquid may be said to heave, the Rio Paraguay did that afternoon. Gradually, even as we watched, the knobbly back sank, until it hung vertical beneath the boat. At last, we could bear it no longer. We hauled with all our strength, and as the body slithered over the side, a gout of water shot into the engine. Queer, flapping noises came from the interior, and a deep-bellied fish fluttered on the floor boards. Bee-Mason stooped to touch the strange, grotesque head that was opaque, like talc, but with a snap and a wriggle the *piranha* jumped, missing his fingers by a fraction. More cautious this time, he placed a piece of string between the jaws, and stared at the speed with which it was sawn through.

Meanwhile the alligator had shrunk rather in the manner of a pricked football. It was no longer rounded and fat, the sides had fallen in, and when we rammed an oar up the stump of the tail it sounded muffled. Indeed, it was little more than a water skin, bloated and raw and leaking. Urrio eyed the submarine cloud as it still patrolled the river.

"Bathing's off," he said.

Corumbá, the chief commercial town of Matto Grosso, came next. It is without dispute the most unpleasant place I ever saw. A low range of limestone hills rears up out of the cattle plains, and the sun devours the yellow streets. The whiteness of the houses is blinding, the heat comes up in a haze, and a vast, heavy stillness broods over the terraced town. By day the porous stone sucks in the hot savagery of the tropics, and breathes it out like an evil odor by night. It is a strange, barbaric formation, for this terrible atmosphere is quite local. Two miles distant in all directions the evenings are cool.

On the day of our arrival we dined in a great room overlooking the river. For some reason the talk turned on spiders, and Bee-Mason shuddered with what, at the time, we took to be an exaggeration of feeling.

"I hate them," he said bitterly. "Even a house-spider in England makes me feel queer."

Urrio and I looked at him in surprise, but there was no amusement in his face. His eyes were serious, his expression troubled, and we realized suddenly that he felt the same primeval repulsion towards spiders as Lord Roberts felt towards cats. Impulsively he thrust a leathery arm across the table.

"I have kept bees for years," he said, "and hundreds sting me every season, but put an ordinary, harmless house-spider on my hand, and I'll faint."

"Probably there aren't as many tarantulas as travelers make out," soothed Urrio.

"I shan't answer for myself if we meet them," said Bee-Mason.

After dinner we went for a stroll through the streets. It was terribly hot, with the oppressive, expectant stillness that precedes a thunder-storm. Great banks of black clouds climbed gloomily up the sky and erased the stars in their ascent. Little puffs of warm air were blown across the river. Pieces of paper eddied in the dust and suddenly died. Men moved slowly, and sweated as they moved, while the dark forest behind the town seemed to pant for a release.

We walked past the listless tinkle of a piano played in an upstairs room, past the incessant rattle of dice in the wine shops, on past the garish lights of the local cinema to the road which led away from the smarting brilliance of the street lamps into the shadows of the jungle. We took this road, partly because the darkness seemed cooler, partly because we were too listless ourselves to care what we did. Anything was better than the tired cackle in the hotel bar, or the heavy warmth of our own bedrooms.

At intervals of a hundred paces a single arc lamp hung over the middle of the road. With each puff of wind it swayed, and the shadows of the trees danced a weary measure in the sandy ruts. Far away in the distance towards Bolivia, the white track stretched, lonely, silent, inviting. We followed it, and our feet sounded not at all on the soft carpet that had never known Macadam.

Suddenly, when we had walked about a mile, a dark

shape scuttled into the glare of a lamp. It came from the trees where, pale and aloof, gleamed the white face of a small house.

"There's a kitten," said Urrio, breaking a long silence. "Let's talk to it."

"Puss, puss!" cried Bee-Mason, slapping his leg and whistling.

The little beast stopped and squatted down in the center of the road, as though it were lonely and would like company. It sat in a compact ball, black and motionless, and we were struck by the fact that it did not seem to be crouching quite in the manner of a kitten. It seemed to be just a thought too round, and there was something in its immobility that was vaguely disquieting. A kitten, even when silent, is a friendly creature, this dark patch was not, but crouched taut and strained in an attitude of hostility.

I do not say that we felt all this as we advanced up the road, but we did notice the strangeness of demeanor, and it made us careful. It was just as well, because as we reached a spot some ten yards away Bee-Mason touched my arm.

"My God," he said quietly. "That's no kitten. What is it?"

He stood where he was, while Urrio and I advanced cautiously. There was no doubt about the feeling now; a distinct and potent menace emanated from the small black ball. A definitely evil atmosphere hung over us. Suddenly, the creature sank back on its haunches and raised two long, hairy feelers, which waved slowly and mesmerically before its face, and we realized that we were in the presence of Bee-Mason's most deadly enemy, a tarantula. Now that we were closer we could see the full horror and enormity of the brute. Eight legs of various lengths covered with long, coarse hair, supported an obscene fat sack, round and bulging, while a pair of unpleasant eyes glared from a kind of watch tower above the body. It was sitting back on four of the legs, the other four were waving in the air.

I had read of the phenomenal speed and leaping power of these creatures in one of W. H. Hudson's books, and I took great care to keep myself and Urrio out of range. So, five paces apart, we stood and looked at one another for the space of a minute. Then the forelegs dropped, and the beast moved rapidly away into the shadows with a curious, furtive, gliding motion that was unbelievably sinister.

When it had gone Urrio and I turned round and perceived that Bee-Mason was already some way back towards the town. Simultaneously the promised thunder broke.

CHAPTER V

FROM the first I distrusted that launch, even when it lay at ease in the lagoon below Corumbá. It was rusty and dented and queer, and a green scum of water weed fouled its steel flanks. There was an evil air about it, a perpetual grin of malice, that was neither faint nor elusive, but very obvious, like the set of a mule's ears. The gross praises of its owner, a sharp-faced Brazilian, caused it to smirk complacently, but it was the only vessel that could be induced to take us northwards, and we reluctantly chartered it. For several hours it coughed and rattled like a skeleton with croup up the exact center of the Rio Paraguay. The noise was outrageous, the smell appalling, and with every beat of its diseased engines the clampings strained against the plates. Wheezing triumphantly it bore us for precisely forty miles, and then, having made certain that no help could reach us, gave a spluttering cough and died. Very gently it backed into a reed bed.

If there is one thing that can turn a man into a blasphemous nonentity it is a machine with a sense of humor. There was no reason on earth why the launch should have stopped, except that the sun had set and the rushes made a soft berth for the night. It was pure cussedness of heart, supported by an ingrained wickedness which knew that we were novices and, therefore, liable to be worried by mosquitoes. An unmistakable spirit of mockery hung about the craft; it was grimly, sardonically alive, and we could feel the devilish joy that leaped through the shadows. Of course the mechanic did everything in his power. With the secret air of a witch doctor he produced an ancient blow-lamp from a cupboard below the water-line, and shot a jet of flame into the vitals of the motor. What he expected to achieve I have no idea, but the engine sat up on its supports and laughed at him. One by one we took our turn at the starting handle and swung until we were tired.

At last we gave it up and settled down to a night that was just as eerie and uncomfortable as those spent in churches by the squires of the Middle Ages. Moreover we were not upheld by the thought of knighthood in the morning. I shall never forget that watch, not because it was particularly eventful, but because it was our first under the stars. Men whose lives are passed in the open would have called it commonplace, would have thrown a blanket over their faces and slept till dawn. For us this was impossible. An amazing, vivid magic spoke to us each by name, bidding us regard the naked beauty of the silence, and we sat very quietly staring at the sky.

It is wonderful experience, that first glimpse of immensity, when the heavens are a deep, ink-blue, and the stars flutter their eyelids in the silence. It makes a man realize his place in the world, a presumptuous louse, crawling through the garments of Green Hell, dependent for his life on the accident of a scratch. If every man in authority were forced to spend a fortnight in a forest, and alone, there would be less arrogance and misery in this life.

By and by the moon rose in a blaze of deep, rich yellow, and a rather paler reflection shimmered on the face of the river. The blueness vanished from the sky, millions of fireflies jigged through a mad dance, and the woods on the other side of the river became as black as a silhouette. Suddenly we were conscious of a dark shape that floated down the middle of the bright line of the stream. It seemed to be about ten yards square, and traveling fast on the smooth current.

"*Camelotte*," said the mechanic, speaking instinctively in a whisper. He told us that these islands of sedge broke off from the bank, and drift until they are caught by the next sharp bend. Whenever possible they are avoided by boatmen, because of the large, furious brand of mosquito that nests in them. Meanwhile we were having enough trouble of our own on that score. Hitherto we had been either moving quickly in a river steamer, or had used nets across the windows, but now the whole insect population of Matto Grosso leaped on us with a yell. Their high, tinny squeaks distracted us, and we beat about us with our arms, so that they had little chance to settle on our bare flesh. For a while the mechanic watched us, and then, smiling a little in the moonlight,

DUGUID AND HIS FIRST BIG VICTIM

showed us how to deal with the pests. Quite calmly he allowed them to alight before squashing them with his thumb, though, as a matter of fact, the mosquitoes of the Upper Paraguay are harmless, for malaria is unknown, and three weeks of suffering is enough to inure the newcomer to their charms.

None of us slept a wink that night. We watched the moon drop down the sky, and we pulled our blankets tightly about us in the bitter cold that precedes the dawn. Presently the darkness cleared, and the mountains of Matto Grosso peeped through the mists of morning. A thousand and one noises broke into the silence, fireflies extinguished their lamps, while a little wind ruffled the water, causing it to slap against the gunwale. From far to the right came a sobbing, roaring cough, repeated three times, which we took to be the breakfast call of the jaguar, and was actually an alligator emerging from the warmth of the river. Dozens of water birds clattered out of the rushes, and sent their shrill cries echoing across the marshes. To the westward a blue and yellow macaw lectured his wife on her morals, only to be promptly countered in a higher key with tales of an erring love-bird. The world was awake.

Rather curiously we stared at each other. Bee-Mason was crumpled and wide-eyed, with a stubble of silver hair showing on his chin. I felt, and looked, dirty; but Urrio might have emerged from a late night at an Embassy. His long, Spanish face was entirely unperturbed, his eyes were tired, but not bleary, and not a trace of a crease appeared in his immaculate clothes. Always the diplomat, he reached for the breakfast and put heart into a number of empty bodies.

Suddenly the mechanic, munching a biscuit which he held in one hand, and turning the handle of the engine with the other, gave a squawk of applause, and the motor started. Slowly we blundered northward, more firmly convinced than ever of the evil temper of the launch.

The cattle land of Matto Grosso was now tapering to a close, like the thin end of a duck-net. Gone were the wild plains and saber-sharp grass of the country below Corumbá, and in their place was a long, thin strip of marsh-land, wedged between the river and a line of wooded hills. In the dry season the animals live in the sedge, eating and sleeping in the swamps; but in the rains they feed by day up to their breasts in water, and retire to the warmth of the highlands at night.

It was just about here that we had a lesson in practical geography. The whole way from Tilbury, Urrio had stressed the unfortunate difficulty of his country, but it was only when we saw it with our eyes that the full enormity came home to us. Back in the last century the Bolivian politicians cared nothing for the eastern forests, and less for the giant waterway that swept her shores. Minerals were the order of the day, and all eyes were turned to the silver mines of Potosí. One of these Statesmen, the bandit-president, Melgarejo, wishing to grant a favor to the Brazilian Ambassador, a personal friend, ceded Corumbá and the entire river border in return for a diamond star. Only now is Bolivia beginning to regret the action which causes all goods to pass through a foreign country before entering her borders.

Towards midday we drew abreast of a cattle ranch which lay back from the water up a long, green slope of grass. We were just about to pass, when an angular man in riding-breeches ran out from the verandah and bellowed above the noise of the motor.

Obediently we pulled in.

"I don't know you from Adam," said a strange, high voice, "but I guess you can stop the night. I'm lonely as hell, and"—a humorous eye swept our battery of weapons—"there's a duck or two in the marshes."

It would have been barbarous to refuse, so we trooped up to the white, one-storied house, and drank his coffee. Led by Urrio we stirred him with skilful questions, egging him on to speak of his adventures. At first he thought we were making fun of him, being unable to conceive that his daily life could be anything but dull, but once convinced, his face shone and he lay back.

"Gee, boys," he gloated, "it's great to hear the clack of me own tongue. I've been bottled for the last two months. What would you like to hear?"

"Anything—so long as it lasts till dinner," said Urrio.

Our host, an Australian, smiled rather charmingly. In a moment the care-worn creases fell from his cheeks and brow, and he flung an arm towards the interior, where the silent ranks of Green Hell rose out of the swamp.

"Back there," he said, "thousands of wild cattle roam through the bush. The missionaries brought them from Buenos Aires, but when a bum of a Spanish king hoofed out the Jesuits, they escaped. Since then they've bred like lice; the woods are stuffy with them."

"Do you catch them and add to your stock?" I asked.

"Yes," said the Australian, drawling his words and winking. "We keep them in a small corral near the tiger's nursery and the alligator farm. Every Sunday morning we tie 'em up with pink ribbon and take 'em for a walk."

Suddenly he sat bolt upright.

"I mean no offense, but you globe trotters have queer ideas. D'you realize that a wild bull is as nervous as a jaguar and a dozen times more dangerous? In a straight fight old sharp-horns will push spots into the river, and then jump after him to eat him up. You never see them except by moonlight, or by luck, and if you're not a darn good shot, take my tip and race 'em to the ranch. They're savage. Any one who tells you cattle is easy to take is a gawdalmighty liar. Yes, sir."

I smiled sheepishly and apologized.

"You seem uncommon keen to hear about the country," he continued, "and, sartingly, you have a lot to learn. I'll tell you of a hunt I had when I first came out. I was young then, like you; thought I should make

VILLAGE IN THE TROPICS IN BOLIVIA

a fortune roping wild steers. Never mind. It's all over and past, and we're only fools once."

He grinned ferociously, and reached for my tobacco pouch.

"There was a whole crowd of us ijits," he rumbled, "full of devil and joy de veever, with about as much sense as an expectant mother. Mad, we was, and nervy, strung on the end of a string, and ready to jump when somebody twitched the works. Waal, one evening we reckoned we'd earn a bonus by knobbling a bunch of wild beef, and it didn't take long for us to be lined up along the forest wall between the animals and their home. I told you they only fed by night, and we'd made sure of getting 'em by arriving early, before the moon rose. It weren't exactly a picnic that night, in the darkness. We could hear 'em all splashing among the marshes, not a quarter of a mile away, and we knew they'd charge us blind if they got our wind, so we sat tight in the saddle, wound our scarves round our hosses' heads, and prayed that the breeze wouldn't drop. Seems funny now, praying, but we did, every man-jack of us. Guess the blackness got on our nerves. Anyway we were screwed to breaking pitch when that old, yellow ball of iniquity popped over the sky-line and showed us where we stood. There, right in front of us, was thirty of the brutes, black as masks against the silver light on the water.

"An old bull, heavy in the shoulder and short in the

horn, stood between us and the herd, which was knee-deep in marsh. He was a mighty fine fellow, yes sir, with his switching tail and slowly-turning head, and the steam blowing out of his nose. I was so occupied in admiring his points and wondering what I'd do with the bonus money, that I forgot about my friends, and the first thing I knew was a blast on a whistle and a noise like a soft hammer tearing over the grass. Then I gave me hoss his head and we charged into the bunch.

"They was a bit slow on the uptake, being fuddled by the din, but when they ran there wasn't a saddle-beast in Matto Grosso to touch 'em. Off went the cows bellowing to their calves, while the bull stirred up their behinds, impartial-like. Luckily, we was into 'em before they broke, or we'd never have caught up, especially in that queer, green moonlight. I swung my lasso, and saw it fall where it ought to fall—over the horns, when my moke put his foot in a hole and planted me in a thorn-bush.

"That old bull fought like hell. My friends were busy roping the cows, and didn't see what had happened, so he pulled my hoss a hundred yards on its side before we caught him. My leg was broken in two places and we had to shoot the hoss. Great times, *amigos*, great times!"

"What become of the cattle?"

"Oh, just what you'd suppose. Died of broken hearts in captivity. They was as wild as monkeys and you can't shut 'em up in sight of their homes and expect 'em to live."

The rancher grew grave.

"So if you gentlemen were thinking of making a fortune that way, forget it. Leastways you won't do it on my hosses—they're too expensive on the Rio Paraguay."

That evening, just as the sun descended over the rim of the river, he gave us a savory stew of goat's flesh. He had been talking for six steady hours, and I thought it time to learn something of camp life.

"By the way," I said, "how does one sling a mosquito net?"

He turned slowly in the light of the candle he had lighted. His lean jaw fell; his eyes summed me up and cast me into the limbo of unfledged things.

"Mosquito net?" he spluttered. "Suffering snakes, what are you, anyway?"

We told him we meant to explore, and his face broadened with astonishment.

"Explore! You?"

His tone was more than doubtful. It was the lash of a well-tried nature on a raw colt.

"God!" he managed to say. "You have got a nerve. If you wasn't my guests, lugged in by the seats of your breeches to listen to a lonely man, I should say you were the biggest bloody fools in South America."

"We'll get through," said Bee-Mason with the calm of an old explorer.

"I shall expect the news of your deaths sometime in the New Year," said the rancher pleasantly.

Nevertheless he helped us with our nets, advised us not to scratch, and bade us good-night. Indeed, from that moment his attitude became attentive, almost motherly, as a warder's might who was in charge of the condemned cell. Next morning he examined us afresh.

"What about a ride after duck?" he asked. And then, "Do you ride?"

A horrid silence was followed by one of those tiny incidents that reveal the spirit of a party. Bee-Mason and I had scarcely ridden in our lives, and said so, whereupon we were mounted on a couple of cowed, white country-breds, warranted fool-proof, which were too lethargic even to resent the spur. When Urrio's turn came he was offered the choice between a spirited, sleek-coated roan and a crock that was even more dilapidated than ours. Without a murmur he ranged himself with us, and thereby laid himself open to the penalties of loyalty. It was a noble art, calculated to bind the expedition together, but must have cost him a sigh, for he delights in horse flesh and revels in polo.

As we jogged along, ankle-deep in marsh we had leisure to appreciate the loneliness of our host. On our right the river wound a lazy, crawling course through a scene that was immeasurably desolate. The horizon of swamps and hills and swamps again, picked out in a medley of green, loomed up in such a hopeless similarity that one felt as if it must stretch into the next world. Nothing stirred in the brazen sunlight, no passing cloud flecked the hard blue of the sky, only the rank and bitter

GREEN HELL

smell of water weeds told us that we were riding in reality. A man would have to be unusually gifted or unusually empty to live sanely in such a waste.

Suddenly, in the midst of nothingness, the air was full. One moment we were gazing somberly across a dozen miles of flat, lifeless sedge, the next, the sky was choked with wild fowl. A screaming, swirling block of black wings and white breasts that looked like a snowstorm in the glare of the sun's rays. The shock was so physical that we did nothing, just sat like a lot of boobies with our mouths open, and wondered if this were another of Green Hell's illusions. After a while our thoughts returned to us, and I was able to notice some details. Great, black geese, heavy and lumbering, rose out of range with a noise like tortured leather and kept their distance. Swarms of snipe leaped up, whistling, zigzagged for eighty yards and settled. Small brown waders, spindle-legged and long-billed flew delicately and without fear. Spur-winged plovers cried distressfully, sweeping low above our heads. While, circling and quacking, rising in tiers and companies, were as many mallard as the air could conveniently hold. Indeed, had there been a few more there must have been a collision. So great was the concourse that out of six revolver shots fired at random into the sky two duck fell with a bump at our feet.

It was then that we understood why the Australian had not gone melancholy mad. He had company.

CHAPTER VI

AT eleven o'clock next morning Bee-Mason lay sprawled beneath a tree. His bony legs, which were sharply visible through his riding-breeches, rose like a gigantic peak out of the plain of his body. His mouth hung open, his hat reposed saucily against one ear, and an outrageous spotted handkerchief concealed all but the tip of a raw and peeling nose; while the heavy silence of Green Hell was desecrated by a slow musketry of snores.

Overhead a bright, persistent sun was engaged in soaking up the moisture from the marshes, so that a veil of heat mist danced over the land. Plovers swooped lazily in the shimmering atmosphere, and uttered their rasping screams in a manner which suggested that the lethargy of the tropics had taken possession of their spurred wings. From the far distance came the dim pop-pop of Urrio's shot-gun, for it had been arranged that he should presently drive the monstrous company of duck over the cinema. Meanwhile, the insects droned through the silence, the swamp gave forth its pungent odors, the world and Bee-Mason slept, but Urrio seemed to be in no hurry.

By and by, oppressed by the heat, I sought about for some shade. I wandered carelessly through the trees, trying this place and that, until gradually it dawned on me that there was no such thing. At first I thought that my senses were cheating me. I had never met a wood so destitute of shade, and indeed, the only creatures which I knew to consume their own image were ghosts. Rather stupidly, for the glare had dulled my brain, I looked up into the branches. Nothing stirred. Each trunk stood rigidly by itself, contributing nothing but its stature to the scenery. Then it was that I realized that, the sun being directly overhead, the shadow was slithering down the stems, after the fashion of lightning.

My first thought was for Bee-Mason, and I ran back to where he lay noisily in the sunlight. I knew of the terrible power of the African sun, and concluded that the South American would have a like effect. In this I was wrong, for the New World is in all things a law unto herself, and Green Hell has decreed that sunstroke shall not disgrace her boundaries. In point of fact it is unknown. Still, I roused Bee-Mason with my boot, mentioned the headache that would be his lot if he lay there much longer, and brought him to his feet. Together we sauntered off into the marshes, partly out of idleness, partly because there was nothing else to do. So we picked our way gingerly through the water and came upon a stretch of land that ran away to the river. Small, deep pools studded the surface and gleamed like crystals on a background of green lacquer. A few wild duck flapped up at our approach. Suddenly, Bee-Mason touched my arm and pointed across the sedge.

"There's something moving near that pool," he said in a strange voice.

I followed his fingers, and saw a queer movement in the grass. It was peculiar in that it seemed to be happening over a large number of feet at the same moment. Slow, unhurriedly regular, it swayed the green stems with a gliding, undulatory movement, and approached us steadily.

"I believe it is a water-snake," I said.

Instantly Bee-Mason became alive. His eyes shone with the glory of a fanatic, his face twitched, and a man who lived for his art stood transfigured before me.

"My camera!" he said. "Keep the brute in play until I return," and he was gone, splashing like a deer through the marsh land.

I was now left with a probably hostile water-snake, and a few dim memories of books of travel. I had heard that a constrictor needs an anchor for its tail before it can contort its huge muscles round the body of its victim. I also knew that the prick of a knife has been known to work marvels when applied with science and agility; and that if one stands with arms akimbo while the reptile is crawling to its grip, a sudden drop of the arms and a quick jump back will disengage the coils. At the same time I was not eager.

It was pure fear that kept me in that swamp. Bee-Mason is a roaring monomaniac on the question of his camera, and will go to inhuman lengths to get just that look of agony which appeals so greatly to audiences. I knew that he would rescue me if I were in real danger, but I was also certain that he would leave it to the last possible moment, probably until I was half way down the throat. Still, I was considerably more afraid of the biting contempt that would transfigure his priest-like features in the event of my failure than I was of any water-snake, so I cleared myself for action by loosening my hunting-knife in its sheath.

Meanwhile, the anaconda had advanced to within twenty yards of me, and was paying no attention. Keeping its spade-shaped head an inch or so above the ground, it shuffled its curves through the grass in a bored and supercilious manner. From the extreme grace and lack of self-consciousness with which it drew its fifteen feet of spotted, brownish-green elegance towards me, I should think it had never seen a human. Certainly it had never been frightened. In every way the meeting was a courteous one, and had it not been necessary to secure a picture of the creature I should have admired its beauty from afar. As it was it would have been lost in the bushes long before Bee-Mason could return. And in case any one should imagine that I was in danger of death at any minute during our encounter, let me hasten to deny the fact. Nevertheless I was a tenderfoot, it was my first large snake, and I was suitably nervous.

With a last jerk of my belt I looked back to see how Bee-Mason was faring, and spied him about half a mile away. He was behaving like a gallant old Conquistador under the heat of that implacable sun, for he staggered and stumbled and tripped as he ran with the camera and tripod over his shoulder. On a track in a cold country the record for the half mile is something inside two minutes; what it is in riding-breeches through marsh under a heavy load I do not know. It seemed like twenty, for with a last pathetic glance at my companion I stepped up to the snake and caught it by the back of the neck.

In the wink of an eye its air of boredom vanished, its jaws snapped open and I had a quick glimpse of white teeth. The small, dark eyes went black with fear and fury, and it lashed like a whip with its tail. So must the first slave have looked when, unsuspecting, he ventured too near to Sir John Hawkins. Even at the time I was quite convinced that the creature meant me no harm. It was in no need of a meal, and would have been perfectly content to pass me by, but for all that it had no intention of submitting to treatment of this ungracious kind. Stubbornly it fought for its liberty.

It is a curious sensation, slimy, and beyond doubt unpleasant, to feel a constrictor wrestling for freedom in one's arms. Muscles appear from nowhere and play beneath the skin, rising into knots and dissolving into jelly at the command of the small brain within the spade-shaped head. Moreover, these muscles appear to be entirely divorced from every other portion of the body. My feet were planted wide apart, and my hands were grasping the anaconda with what in any other animal would have been a half-nelson. My left hand held the neck, and my right, after passing under the throat, attached itself to the left wrist. In this way I was able to regulate the passage of air. Unfortunately, a constrictor, usually a sluggish creature, is at its most active when short of wind. It strained and leaped beneath the pressure, and I could feel, rather than see, the blind frenzy of the tail, which was searching for a tree-trunk behind me. On that score, however, I was safe, for I had taken peculiar pains that the affair should take place in the open.

After a period of silent struggle I heard a noise of panting and looked up. Bee-Mason, crimson with exercise, was straddling the camera over a small spit of dry ground. His hat was tilted over his neck, his peeling nose added a touch of the grotesque which the spotted neckerchief did little to dispel. He was blowing so hard that the professional part of the business was shaky beyond belief. He peered at his lens, wiped it with a rag, produced a tape measure and strode over to me. "Eight feet," he gasped, "must get it exact."

"You won't get anything," I retorted, "unless you hurry. I can give you just two minutes before my arms crack."

That moved him. He dropped the tape into a puddle and flew to the handle. To the whirr of the machine, he added a variety of instruction.

"Don't look at the camera," he urged. "You've got to seem natural. Loosen your grip, or you'll strangle it. Now, more movement. That's good! Hold it!"

"I am," I said stiffly. "By the neck. I thought perhaps you'd noticed."

"The pose, you fool. Shift your head so that you stare into the lens without seeming to know it's there. Can you force its jaws open? Splendid!"

Those two minutes were the most strenuous I ever spent. Not only did I have to act myself, but I had to coach a bitterly hostile anaconda in its lines. Gradually, the fingers of my left hand grew numb, and my pupil, sensing my approaching weakness, doubled its activities. At last I could stand no more. I dropped it and jumped back. Once free, the unwilling actor seemed to bear no malice. With a shake of its head it made straight for the deepest part of the swamp, and we cheered it on its way with a loud hallo. From first to last there had been no bad blood.

"H'm," said Bee-Mason, mopping himself and at the same time deflating any pride I may have felt, "it must have been distended and sleepy. You could never have held it, not fifteen feet, if it had been all there."

Later in the day he relented, and said that even if the anaconda had been dying of dysentery, the picture would be a lively one.

CHAPTER VII

ONE evening our host suggested a flighting expedition in the launch. It was only half past four, yet already a slight heaviness in the corners of the sky, and a flushed richness where the sun smote the clouds, hinted at the approach of night. From the verandah of the ranch house we could see strings of duck, the vanguard of a mighty army, winging low above the marshes, and could hear the trumpet-call of the great black geese as they honked mournfully across the flaming river. An increasing, tinny hum, rising into a *crescendo* of metallic abuse, testified that the brotherhood of mosquitoes was sharpening its stings against the arrival of darkness. Presently there was a movement at the further end of the house, and a queer little, ragged figure stepped into the open. It was obviously a man, because no woman could have looked like that. It seemed to be more wooden and Chinese than anything we had yet seen in South America. An intensely yellow skin, polished like a boot, gleamed over prominent cheek-bones; a pair of dark expressionless eyes that ran away at the corners like those of an Oriental, regarded us as if we had been growing there for years, while at intervals all over the stolid face a crop of cat's whiskers, rank and black, sprouted from the flesh. The creature was clad in an old, patched shirt, some unmentionable trousers, and a pair of hard, yellow sandals. Our host introduced us.

"This," he said, "is José Vaca, a native hunter of renown."

The mask before us creased into a smile that somehow left out the eyes, and suddenly was still.

"He uses the lance when he fights his jaguars," continued the Australian, "because he says that powder isn't to be trusted in this climate."

Once again the soulless smirk came and went like a wind-eddy on a pool.

"Seventy-eight tigers have fallen to his steel, eh, Vaca, my boy!" He hunts quite alone, and is only equaled by a Russian engineer who learned the trade from him.

José Vaca, which means Joseph Cow, turned towards the west.

"If the señores wish to shoot in my marshes, they should hurry," he said with no emotion whatever in his face.

"I have enough duck pictures," said Bee-Mason. "I will stay here and make a film test to see if my exposure is right."

So Urrio and I and José Vaca taking a rifle as an afterthought, joined the mechanic in the launch. Two miles upstream, on the advice of the Indian, we tied up to the eastern bank so that the birds flew at us out of the glare of the dying sun, and we fired as each dark outline came over our sights. This was a necessary precaution because the *piranhas* were there in shoals, eager to chew into ribbons anything that did not fall on dry land. Those that were bungled disappeared instantly in a worry of feathers and heaving water.

After a while I chanced to look towards the north, whence the river came. There, about three hundred yards away, was a large, black object that looked like a footstool as it forged its way through the burning river. I thought it was a water pig, and touched José Vaca on the arm. The effect on that gentleman was astounding. His air of detachment fell like a stone, his eyes shone, and his voice clattered across the flats. "*Tigre*," he called.

There followed a scene of some confusion. Urrio clutched his rifle, José Vaca stole Urrio's shotgun, the mechanic drew an ancient, rusty pistol, and it was left to me to start the engine. That mysterious piece of mechanism seemed to revel in the chase, for it sprang to life at the first essay, and bounded through the water like an otter hound. From the start it was obvious that the race would be a close one, especially at two hundred yards when it looked as though the jaguar might win. The great, round head never turned from its course, never faltered at the thunder of our approach, even when we were clearly going to intercept its passage. Possibly it took us for a new breed of alligator, and being accustomed to scoop the brains of *jacaré* with one sweep of a steel-shod paw, saw no reason to hurry. At fifty paces the strain overcame the mechanic, who with a whoop of ecstasy sprang into the bows and fired six shots off the reel. In a moment six gouts of water jumped out of the river, at points so far removed from the target as to bear no relation to the little comedy. Once again the jaguar paid no heed.

We were now almost on top of it, with the snout of the boat aimed so as to cut it off from the bank. Out of the corner of my eye I took stock of Urrio, for I had never seen him in action, and I knew that the whole of the rest of the journey depended on his demeanor. Like all South Americans he is highly-strung and sensitive, and I watched curiously to see if he would fire at random, trusting to the rest of his magazine. Almost at once I saw that his diplomatic training had come to his assistance. His face, which was in profile, was cold and blank, studiously devoid of feeling, his hands were steady as he grasped the stock, and there was that in his bearing which showed beyond cavil how he would behave in a crisis. As we came within ten yards of the jaguar he threw the rifle to his shoulder, took careful aim, and pressed the trigger. The beast leaped under the impact of the bullet, which passed through its neck. Instantly the water grew red as the blood pumped from the wound, and I knew it was a matter of moments before the *piranhas* arrived.

Urrio lowered his rifle, for he was convinced, as I was, that the end was near. The prow of the launch was almost touching it, and we leaned over the bulwarks. There, within a few inches of the shore, was a splendid creature grumbling at its fate, its wide, round eyes

HUT MADE BY THE INDIANS TO ATTRACT THE ATTENTION OF THE TRAVELERS, IN ORDER TO ATTACK THEM AFTERWARD (ROUTE BETWEEN SANTA JOSÉ AND SANTA CRUZ)

ablaze with anger, and its spotted head quivering.

"Give it another shot," I said. "It might jump into the boat."

"Pity to spoil the skin," said Urrio, coolly reloading. "I want it for the President."

Nevertheless he raised his rifle once more and covered the dying king. Then it was that an amazing incident happened, and I understood the meaning of speed. The jaguar was treading water when suddenly it found a purchase on a sunken tree, and leaped into the forest. Urrio fired instinctively, but the pace beat him by yards. José Vaca sighed.

"That's the end of that," he said.

Urrio landed grimly, and pointed to the pools of blood that marked the trail into the jungle. A disagreeable smell hung over the bushes, a stale, musky odor that hovered in the air, and made us feel that we could follow by scent alone.

"I'm going after it," said Urrio.

José Vaca broke into noisy protests.

"Señor, you cannot be such a fool. We have no dogs, and the jungle is so dirty that you will have to crawl. Return to-morrow, for, see, the sun is about to set."

A blaze of glory emphasized his words, but Urrio, who can be as obstinate as a mule, turned to me.

"If I am not back in half an hour, fire a gun. If I answer, well and good; if not, go back to the ranch."

"And listen to that Australian skinning me alive," I retorted. "The smaller fear wins."

Later in the expedition we realized what stupendous fools we had been, but at the moment we were rather elated. The idea of a night in the forest with an angry jaguar without torch or mosquito net appalled us not at all.

Laughing at the distraught countenance of Mr. José Vaca, we set out, crawling and creeping through the undergrowth that was dark with years of disuse, and in which it was impossible to swing a rifle. The trail, as trails went, was easy to follow, blood was so liberally sprinkled on the deep green leaves that we expected to find our enemy behind every other tree. Neither was there any need for a dog; the scent was sufficient even for our smoke-fouled nostrils. Gradually we drew away from Vaca's noisy protests.

After half an hour in the posture of Napoleon's armies, we came into the open, and discovered that the bush through which we had passed was only a narrow belt that ran parallel with the river. The trail led straight across a small, clear plain towards a thick clump of trees about a quarter of a mile away. By this time something of the spirit of adventure had lightened our bodies, and we laughed aloud with the joy of living. We had both done a little running in our day, and we arrived breathless in a triumphant dead-heat, some sixty seconds later. Then, while we were stilll panting, the sun sank and we were in darkness.

"Our first camp in the open," said Urrio, beaming. "How do you feel?"

"Better than I should at the ranch without you," I answered, "but not much. What about a fire?"

Taking great care that our safety-catches were released, we gathered a large heap of dead wood and applied a match. In a few minutes there was an enormous blaze, which we plied with fallen trees. Soon there were ten-foot flames to warn the jaguar to keep its distance.

The stars came out, and the moon rose, still we sat smoking in the glare. Neither of us was sleeping, and we leaned back to back listening to queer, little noises that we could not explain. Like drowning men, the whole of our past lives flashed before us as we took it in turns to pull this incident and that from the passing show, as comrades do when alone with the mighty silences of nature. Fireflies played through the night, running races with mosquitoes, and switching off their lights to make the chase more difficult. A great peace stole over us, lulling our senses without sending us to sleep. In the gray dawn mists we were still awake, though stiff.

We never found that jaguar. The smell had vanished by morning, and the trail was lost in the mazes of Green Hell. When we reached the ranch our Australian friend eyed us, but though he did justice to his amazing mastery of language he confessed himself impotent to touch more than the fringe of our stupidity.

We did not care. Such nights leave memories.

CHAPTER VIII

LEGEND is winged on the Rio Paraguay. The ghost of a whispered secret in the hills round Cuyabá is within the day common gossip among the water weeds to the south. In a week the news is drummed through the streets of Corumbá. In a fortnight Asuncion is aflame with a new rumor, and before the month is out old gentlemen are chuckling in the clubs of Buenos Aires over the birth of a first-rate scandal.

This, of course, is an exaggeration; but not so much as a stranger might suppose. The great, slow-moving, *piranha*-ridden, muddy stream is a brilliant sound conductor, a whispering gallery that gathers the information of half a continent and distributes it in distorted forms to every ranch-house and village and town throughout the two thousand five hundred miles of its course.

For many days we had heard sensational tales of a Russian engineer who killed jaguars for a living. In a land where professional hunters are all Indians, he had taken the trouble to beat his rivals at their own game by mastering the use of the lance. In Corumbá his fame was solid, because the previous year he had roped four cubs to take south to São Paulo for exhibition, though

RUSTIC SUGAR-CANE CRUSHER USED BY THE CHIQUITOS INDIANS

his personality was tinged with mystery on account of the abruptness of his departures.

When we saw him first, he was paddling a dug-out canoe down the exact center of the river. A tall Stetson silhouetted against the sunrise at a rigidly upright angle towered out of the stern. Wide, powerful shoulders overlapped the slender lines of the craft, dwarfing it into an appearance of insecurity and three small terriers sat trembling in the bows. We promptly mistook him for a missionary.

The blunt nose of the canoe, slightly lifted by the weight behind, headed straight for the landing-stage of the ranch. Yelping ecstatically, the dogs leaped ashore and indulged in an orgy of exercise that told of a long journey by water. The newcomer picked up a rifle, secured the boat, and strode across the turf to the house.

Our host was punching cattle so, after the custom in wild places, we entertained the guest. At close quarters he looked even more like a missionary. Tall, brown, bearded, he had that curious isolation of demeanor that comes to lonely men. His bearing was frank and confident, neither bashful nor assertive, as though he had lived for close on forty years without human ties, and was perfectly willing to face another forty. Nevertheless, his large, blue eyes were very friendly and had plenty of laughter creases in the corners. He raised his hat and bowed.

"Alejandro Siemel, at your service," he said in English.

Bee-Mason took to him at once. His face lit up, and I could see him diving into his memory for pieces of religious salvage. Learned views on Anglo-Catholicism and native morals flowed from his lips at such a pace that Urrio and I were left gasping. Our new acquaintance, after one surprised glance, settled down to business. He talked fluently and well with a lack of orthodoxy that we attributed to his savage mode of life. He countered a question of vestments with a shrewd quotation from Schopenhauer, and cited Freud in defense of original sin. Finally, he asked point-blank for the name of Bee-Mason's pet tribe, and inquired if converts were scarce that season. Bee-Mason turned scarlet, the mistake was exposed, and religion, as a topic, lapsed.

Once the misunderstanding had been cleared up, we embarked on a talk that lasted for hours. Our Australian host had been so satirical about our trip that we were rather coy about confessing it to Siemel; but we need not have feared. He was far too great a master to jeer at a bunch of tyros. He discussed the possibility of our safe arrival with a balanced judgment and sane sympathy that restored our self-confidence without blinking the danger. When we told him of our hunt in the darkness he neither laughed nor swore.

"You were lucky, gentlemen," he said. "I have followed the game for fourteen years, and I should never dream of spending such a night without an electric torch."

"Wasn't our fire enough?" we asked.

He spread his hands and smiled.

"Put yourself in the poor beast's place. He was wounded and in frightful pain. He could neither eat nor drink and must have known that he was dying. He was very angry, the smell should have told you that; it comes from a gland under the tail and is released in times of emotion. Imagine him lying in the bush just beyond the circle of the fire, his head heavy with agony, the light failing in his eyes. He sees two men sitting back to back, quite still in an attitude unsuitable for springing; for remember he judges the other fellow by himself. He cannot imagine the power of a rifle. Do you suppose that a fire will stop him then?"

"Does a jaguar charge without provocation?" I asked.

"We call them tigers here," he told me gently, "and you cannot say that a tiger does this or that any more than you can of a woman. Most of them are cowards, but once in a while you get a killer; it is usually a female who when she had cubs, jumped on an Indian one day and, finding it easy, stuck to the game."

That was one of the secrets of Siemel's charm. The forest was his home, the birds and beasts his neighbors. He understood them perfectly, and knew that each animal had an individual brain acting on its own motives. One tiger will jump into a tree when tackled by dogs—all South American big-cat hunting is done with terriers—and sit unconcernedly like a great pet, quite calm above the clamor on the ground. Siemel knew the reason for this. The jungles of South America are full of large herds of wild pigs, which, in bulk, are the most dangerous animals in the world. They are quite fearless, and by reason of their numbers can pull down anything in their path. Wherefore, a tiger retires a few yards from the earth and waits patiently till they are gone. But his brain is not deductive, and he is unable to see that a few mongrels and a man are more deadly than a thousand pigs. Another tiger would refuse utterly to be bullied into a tree but would turn, charging the dogs and filling the jungle with furious abuse. Siemel would look at once for evidence of shot-gun wounds, where an enthusiastic native had let off the family blunderbuss filled with nails.

If Siemel had migrated to Africa instead of South America, he would certainly have made an international reputation as a hunter. In moments of peril his brain becomes quite cold, and I can imagine no circumstance that would shake his nerve. He has the temperament of a hunter, too. At base he is a solitary, a reader of deep books of philosophy; and the great fiction of the world is at his finger tips. There are times when he retreats into himself and stalks restlessly through the shadows, as though he wished to be far away buried in the recesses of a forest. Even yet, he has more than a chance of becoming famous. It is his ambition to film the life of a tiger and the various native methods of killing it. From what I know of his proud persistence he will succeed.

In the rainy season, when the cattle land is flooded,

the Bororo Indians set out in their dug-out canoes with a long spear and a conch made of bark. They wait until a tiger roars from one of the tree-covered knolls that stands out from the water, and then send the love-call of the opposite sex thundering over the flats. Soon, the tiger leaves the hills and comes swimming to its mate, when the Indians paddle alongside it and spear it as one would a fish.

Siemel has the knowledge and the photographic material to get this film. He has shown me still photographs of tigers and pumas taken at three yards range. His reply to the question of danger is always the same.

"Look at his feet. A tiger must have his paws free if he is going to spring."

A great man, Siemel.

We were so truck by his personality that, moved by a growing fear of our own ignorance, we asked him if he would join the expedition. With characteristic frankness he accepted at once. It was like a Rider Haggard romance all over again.

"We shall call you Alexander," said Urrio.

"More likely to be 'Tiger-Man,'" said Bee-Mason.

And he was.

CHAPTER IX

Our host came down to the landing-stage to see us off. He was heavily humorous about it, wiping his eyes on his leather apron, and sobbing his thanks for the amusement we had caused him.

"By the beard of your nurse," he cried, "I wish you luck."

Tiger-Man grinned.

"They would get through alone," he said. "I only go to make things easier."

"Tell that to monkeys at mating-time," retorted the Australian. "Babes in the wood get buried."

We parted with regret, for his verbal horseplay was often witty, and he had stripped more than one illusion from our eyes. As we pushed out into the stream, with Tiger-Man's canoe bumping behind, we shouted farewells, till a curve in the river masked his figure from our view. Time passed quickly in the company of our new friend. His mind was a granary full of ripe observation, the fruit of long communion with the forests. Under his big-hearted teaching we came to call the birds and beasts "he" and "she" instead of "it," to think of animals as living creatures with personalities and foibles of their own; and henceforward we never killed, except of necessity. Tiger-Man was most particular on this point.

"I find no pleasure in the killing of game," he would say. "I shoot for a living and when I am hungry; otherwise I let the beasts enjoy their lives."

He drew our attention to a huge, white bird swinging through the skies in wide, alert circles, while it searched the ground for carrion with its keen eyes.

"*Urubu Rey,*" he said, "the great King Vulture."

In his strong, deep voice, he told us of a scene he had witnessed in the midday heat when half a hundred vulture commoners had squatted patiently at a distance, while His Majesty pecked the first fruits of a dead calf. This raised an absorbingly interesting question of bird psychology, for the commoners can hardly have been influenced by the loyalty that causes men to deny themselves for their king. Tiger-Man was inclined to believe that the nature of each individual was so selfish that the idea of mass movement did not present itself. Singly they were no match for the arrogant, white monster that took its privileges so regally; collectively they could have mobbed it off the earth. Yet they withheld.

By and by *carpincho* or *cayubara,* as he is variously called, came boldly to the water's edge. A species of river hog, sired by evolution out of a sense of humor, he stood on a small eminence and goggled at the launch. His body was round and deep, dark brown in color, and of a shape which Cæsar would have approved. His legs were short and his feet cloven. His face was irresistibly comic, being composed of a pair of shrewd, piggy eyes and a snout that might have been carved by a novice out of a sloping tree-trunk. He was far too genial a personality to shoot, though his hide is reputed to be the softest in the world. With a grunt and a lurch of his fat person he disappeared.

Gradually it was borne into our European minds that the farther north we went the hotter it became. At first it seemed wrong that the cool, invigorating wind should bear up from the south, while the torrid waves of heat should swoop down from what, to us, had always been a cold quarter. Nevertheless we had cause to remember the vast zone of the Amazon with every day we traveled. The alligators that lay gaping on the banks were noticeably larger than those below Corumbá. The great macaws were more florid in their plumage, and even the tiny, green love-birds semed to shine with a more tropical splendor. Immense coveys of parrots spangled the air with their quick-winged passing, and challenged the noise of the engine with their clamor.

Toucan, the toy-maker's nightmare, as Urrio called it, usually escorted a bevy of wives to a solitary tree half an hour before sunset. Their flight was rapid, rather similar to that of a pheasant at full speed. They flew low over the launch with their gigantic orange and red bills poked forward, and their small black and white bodies trailing behind, as though it was as much as they could do to balance ends out. We shot one, and felt guilty for the slaughter, but could not resist a closer inspection of this remarkable bird. The beak is tremendous, very

SQUARE IN SANTA CRUZ

brittle to the touch, and when tapped echoes like a drum. The eyes were round and bright, ringed with a pale blue strip of flesh, but the marvelous colors fade within a few hours of death, and must be painted on to a preserved specimen. A long, white tongue, like a chameleon's, suggests a diet of flies, but whether *toucan* sits with his mouth open and pretends to be an orchid, Tiger-Man was unable to say.

In a clump of tall trees, set well back from the river, was a colony of egrets. They had built their homes after the fashion of a rookery, and were splashing their nesting glory in the sunlight. Dazzling white against a background of dark trees, they were amazingly magnificent. Strident croaks issued from their cruel fishing bills as they wheeled about their home. Tiger-Man was surprisingly scathing about the plumage laws. He explained that before egrets became illegal each colony was watched over by a hunter. To all intents and purposes it was his own property to improve or destroy.

"How would it help a man," he asked, "to kill off his stock by shooting the mothers before the young can fly? Why should he when the feathers remain on the bird until long after the squeakers can rout for themselves?"

He went on to complain that the same women who shrieked about cruelty wore trapped furs and lizard skin shoes, and are quite unreasonably shocked when a fox dies humanely by the bullet.

Round a curve in the river we came upon a sight

which caused Tiger-Man to throttle down the engine until we were barely making headway against the current. On a sand-bank near the sedge were two great birds which were behaving in the queerest possible manner. They must have been close on six feet in height, and belonged to the stork tribe, as we saw from the heavy, wedge-shaped beaks and the long, black legs splayed at the toes. The tips of their black and white wings were crossed behind, their shoulders were humped, and their dark heads sunk low on their chests. It only needed a pair of spectacles apiece and they would have been university professors meditating the meat of their next lecture on the lawn of an Oxford college. They are known by the native name *Tuiuiu* in recognition of the mournful, whistling note that they utter on the rare occasions when they can be seduced from their gravity. We were aching with laughter before they noticed us, and lumbered heavily away.

On the Upper Paraguay there are three lakes, Mandioré, Uberaba, and Gaiba, Indian names that echo the beauty of their tree-clad shores. From an African standpoint they are not large, but then there are only three products of South America that can rival in size those of the sister, and darker, continent—Amazon, Andes and Green Hell. Two of these lakes belong to Bolivia, while the Brazilian boundary passes directly up the center of Gaiba.

We reached the point at the bottle-neck of Lake Gaiba in the early afternoon. A desolate and rocky promontory with Green Hell to the water's edge, it is inhabited by a Brazilian, whose job it is to check the flow of liquor into Bolivia; for, even this wild corner of the globe has its boot-leggers. In the dead of night canoes shoot out from the shadows, creep past the Point, and convey their cargo to a garrison of Bolivian soldiers at Puerto Suarez far down the river. The distance is tremendous, the profit scanty, but the average Brazilian is a sportsman, and counts the danger as part payment. The spirit in question is *canha*, a raw, white drink distilled from sugar-cane.

Immediately we landed, Tiger-Man unshipped his canoe, gathered his dogs, and set off up river to his home to fetch his camera and plates. It was nearly to being the last we saw of him, as I shall tell later, and we watched his departure with inward misgivings. The country was such a large one, and in our increasing ignorance we imagined the difficulties to be greater than life-size.

The Customs Officer, if one may so call the grizzled, shaggy creature, whose sole weapon was a stiff and ancient pistol, was married to an Indian. Their daughter, *Café con leche*, white coffee, as her type is called on the river, is worth a word. Small, olive-skinned, delicately pretty, and possessed of a really admirable figure, she showed her birth in the yellowness of her fingernails, and the loneliness of her life in the plain cotton dress that was her only covering. When we arrived she was leaning against the mud and lath shack, and was fanning her legs with a palm leaf. She vanished at once, out of shyness we supposed, but we received the shock of our lives when she appeared ten minutes later. Gone was the simple frock, and in its place was a gaudy, green creation that clashed with the tint of her skin. Cheap Manchester screamed at us, but she was well content, for a grin of coy beatitude shone in her face, which was generously and unevenly adorned with flour.

The faces she made at Bee-Mason removed all doubt as to her choice. Urrio and I declared that it was politeness but our indignant companion said that the lady knew a man when she saw one. Moreover, he ascribed to jealousy our desire to be in the village of Gaiba that night which caused us to hasten the coupling of a great, flat-bottomed lighter to the launch. For those who live in Gaiba were short of stores.

Meanwhile, the mechanic had discovered a wife, an oval woman with negroid lips. She was desperately frightened by the appearance of the lake, which, under the lash of a westerly wind, grew more troubled with each minute that passed; but she sternly refused to be left. From where we stood we could see ridge upon ridge of foam-capped waves bearing down in monotonous fury from the head of the lake. We must have been close on a thousand miles from the sea, and the sensation of beholding many hundreds of acres of "white horses" in the middle of a great forest was curious and rather sinister.

Bee-Mason and I, the only Europeans present, were placed in charge of the lighter and half a dozen natives.

We pushed off from the Point at three o'clock under a barrage of smiles from the daughter, and at first all went well. The launch grappled easily with the extra tonnage, and we chugged out towards the rough water. These storms on inland lakes, as the inhabitants of Geneva and Galilee can testify, are apt to be dangerous. A sudden squall, and the local craft, built for mill-pond work, are lying broadside to the waves and wallowing in the trough. Here, too, we had the added danger of *piranhas*, which we knew would rip us to pieces if we capsized. There was a sharp-drawn, uncanny line between the waves and the smooth water. So abrupt was it that the launch was bouncing like an erratic tennis ball, while the lighter was riding easily in the calm. The next instant we had joined the battle, and the Indians, half crazy with fear, were preparing to swim to the shore.

Bee-Mason, hardy mariner of northern seas, took command of the lighter. He crouched at the tiller with a seraphic expression on his face, and addressed us in language that smacked of the days of wind-jammers. At his rather emphatic request I pushed the natives into a corner and unrigged the canvas awning.

The sea was now so rough that wave after wave broke over the launch, drenching her from bow to stern and suffocating the engine. Down wind came the terrified squeals of the mechanic's wife, who was praying at an amazing pace, calling upon countless saints in the hope of pitching on one who could repair the damage. The names of Joseph, and Mark, and Paul, Remigius, and

Mamertus whistled passed our heads, and vanished like spent bullets towards the Point. Others more obscure followed them at ever shortening intervals, until the whole of that sea of air was echoing with the burden of remembered saintliness. It was really rather appalling.

In the meantime Bee-Mason's fertile brain had evolved a scheme which my unnautical fingers were left to perform. The launch was out of action, rolling like a dolphin, so he decreed that I should turn the awning into a sail, and thus enable us to tow our friends to safety. I can recall very little of what ensued. Dimly, but with a certain joy, I remember tearing the belts from the natives' trousers that a sail might flap from the uprights, and not fail when the wind bellied. I remember a number of yellow faces pinched with terror, and myself holding on by my teeth and nails when the lighter bounced across the waves. A shout from Bee-Mason made me look up, and there was the launch bearing down on us at a distance of a few feet. I seized a bit of wood and yelled to the Indians to do likewise. Suddenly I burst out laughing, for six pairs of trousers slithered over their owners' thighs and settled glumly in heaps at their ankles. Luckily, the mechanic's wife was praying with her eyes shut.

By a fluke the sail proved efficient, and an orderly procession, in which the cart took the place of the horse, moved sedately under the shelter of a headland. There, in calm water, Urrio was assailed by an angry crowd of natives made bold by panic, who swore that they would prefer a dry death on shore, even at the paws of a tiger, to facing again the terrors of the "white horses."

Urrio is not a diplomat for nothing. He has a most persuasive tongue and a knack of putting his opponents in the wrong.

"Certainly," he said suavely, "it is a dangerous crossing, and I shall force nobody to accompany me. The trip will be so hazardous that the lighter must remain here, and every coward has my permission to sleep in it. There will be no mosquito nets," he added.

This speech was directed to the mechanic, though Urrio was careful to stand with his back to him while he spoke. The others for all we cared could shiver their souls out at the thought of a boarding tiger. The mechanic, who had a tithe of native blood in him, and was, therefore, contemptuous of the genuine article, muttered apprehensively that he would try once more. His wife, upheld in her faith in the saints, decided to join him. So once again, having dried the engine, we set out into the lake. This time Urrio and I took no chances. We stood in the bows on either side of the motor and filled the well with mosquito nets so as to absorb the water. We had removed the temporary sail from the lighter and held it upright as a screen.

After five hours we came, in the night, to Gaiba.

CHAPTER X

BOLIVIA was sired by a Peace Treaty out of a Rebellion, and the result is an unholy mixture of ice and heat. From the days of the Spanish Empire the eastern forest plain was part of the Audiencia de Charcas resident in Sucre; while the wind-swept mountain plateaux of the Andes paid tribute to Lima and was called Upper Peru. In reality it is two countries with utterly different outlooks, inhabitants and industries, and to realize the difference between them one has only to listen to the member of Parliament for the Beni discussing matters with a deputy for Potosí, for in no question do they touch one another.

The Chiquitano Indians of the east are an idle lot, sun-soaked and complacent, content to allow the seasons to roll over them and to live simply on the fertility of the soil. They have never seen a mountain higher than 1,500 feet, the forest is their home and their dwellings are palm hovels of a primitive and noisome type. For a century or so the Jesuits gave them a soul but that has long since vanished in the murk which fell over the Chiquitos after the expulsion.

The Quechuas, on the other hand, over whom the Incas reigned, and the Aymará with whom the Incas fought, are virile, fighting races not unlike the High-

AN INDIAN MARKET, NEAR COCHABAMBA

land Scot in the obstinacy with which they wrest a living from the stony soil. They have never descended below 9,000 feet, have scarcely seen a tree, and when they want a fire use llama dung.

When the soldier-philosopher, Marshal Sucre, conceived Bolivia he intended that a smelting furnace and a granary should rest under the same flag. It was an admirable idea, a self-contained empire defying the buffets of fate and the jealousy of the rest of South America; but like many another genius he relied too much on the intelligence of his successors. Himself a great traveler, knowing well the vast possibilities of the Chaco, he took it for granted that others would make a point of seeing for themselves. In this he erred.

I can only suppose that a few timid souls climbed down the Andes, descended the Madre de Dios into the Amazonian Province of the Beni, discovered the stinging fury of mosquitoes, shivered and burned alternately with fever, and returned with travelers' tales. Moreover, until our expedition went across the eighteenth degree of latitude, the politicians in La Paz were admittedly hazy about the possibilities of Chiquitos.

This was the main reason why, one stormy night in September, Urrio, Bee-Mason and I landed in Gaiba.

At our first meeting in London Urrio had told me of Nuflo de Chavez' expedition up-river from Asuncion. I was now able to see for myself just the bare fringe of what it had meant. In those days Green Hell in all her terrible austerity came down to the water's edge. Chavez himself must have landed the gallant ladies of his company straight from the boat into the jungle. Their Castilian complexions must have been blotched by mosquito bites, and their delicate ankles swollen beyond knowledge before they had been on shore an hour. For a mosquito of the Upper Paraquay, though free from malaria, works in the day time as well as at night.

What drew these women from the cool courtyards of Asuncion? A courageous wish to die with the men they loved? Boredom, wanderlust, or the sheer blessed cussedness of their sex? Whatever their reason they must have trembled to themselves as they sat round that first campfire and watched the mountains of Brazil fade with the sunlight across the lake. And in all the thirsty leagues to the interior that last vision of a sparkling sheet of water must have mocked their weary stumblings. God rest their souls. They were brave women.

We were most courteously received in Gaiba. An English company has obtained a concession from the Bolivian Government for the exploitation of the Province of Chiquitos, and the management allowed us to remain while we made our final arrangements for the trip into the interior. Gaiba to-day is rather different from the pathless jungle of Nuflo's time. There are houses and beds and a wireless station, and Green Hell has been pushed back in a semicircle that is about a mile across at the horns. The clearing in itself was a romance, for it was done by a revolutionary army which, starving and ragged, stumbled into Gaiba after eighteen months of hardship in the forests of Brazil. Their leader, General Prestes was a military genius, a high-souled visionary who resembled Christ in something more than his beard, though he has since lost his prestige by taking to a razor and a commission agency in Buenos Aires. He was, perhaps, the politest bandit in South America, and it was his proudest boast that he stole neither horse nor provender by the way. It was his invariable custom to ride up to a ranch, ask for the host in terms of friendship and after a meal, at which he was the soul of good humor, he would mention quite casually that his animals were feeling the strain of a long campaign. The host, with one eye on the bivouacked troops outside, never failed to take the hint. It was the most peaceable revolution for centuries.

Danton, his lieutenant, a gaunt, hawk-nosed desperado, with the face of a fanatic who has recovered his sense of humor, lives to this day in Gaiba. He has much the same outlook as his French namesake, and satisfies his passion for dangerous living by driving a Chevrolet over forest paths at fifty miles an hour. Otherwise he has become domesticated. During my stay I came to know him rather well, and he told me this story of Prestes' genius one evening after dinner between the Port and the Administration Buildings.

"It is a curious fact," said Danton sadly, "that whenever one sets out to improve a Government, the President always objects. Our great and beloved leader, General Prestes, would have made an admirable President yet an army was sent to arrest him. Now, one day we were resting from the heat by the side of a stream. Everything was quiet, most of us were asleep, when suddenly from the forest came the crackle of rifle fire. Bullets began to whine through the leaves and to thump against the tree-trunks; a horse squealed and lay kicking on the ground; there was a hollow plop from somebody's water gourd, and a loud groan as a man pitched forward on his face. In a moment we were awake and standing to arms looking to our commander for the order to charge.

"Prestes sat with his back against a tree. He was reading a holy book and seemed in no hurry to engage the enemy. His face was quite placid, and before rising to his feet he carefully placed a marker between the leaves. I, who knew him well, was aware that his brain was going at racing speed, but a mask was over his face to encourage the others.

"All at once fire broke out from behind, and something like panic settled over the hearts of our men. Government troops in front and a strong body of police behind. All seemed to be lost. A lesser man than Prestes would have surrendered; a more foolish would have tried to keep both forces at bay, but our great leader did neither. He was a man of imagination and knew that although the firing was fierce no man could see another at thirty paces in a forest of that thickness. So he motioned us to draw near, and in low tones told us his plan. Eight men were to be left behind with orders to fire at random as hard as ever they could, while the rest of us just went quietly down the bed of the stream and withdrew from the encounter." Danton smoothed the long hair from his forehead and laughed.

"Never has there been such a fight. It lasted till sunset and when darkness descended the Government Force and the police had killed nearly three hundred of each other."

One day, like Brother Johannes of Glastonbury, we went a-fishing. We crossed Lake Gaiba in the launch, while the sun played ducks and drakes with gold-doubloons, and landed on the narrow beach under the mountains where Green Hell reaches almost to the water's edge. We were accompanied by José Vaca who, dressed in ragged shirt and wide trousers, was keen to initiate us into the mysteries of native fishing. Done properly it is a thing of supreme, rugged beauty, and looks childishly easy in the hands of an expert. José grasped a long coil of line in the manner of a lasso and settled his feet firmly in the sand. His skin gleamed rich and deep through the torn places of his shirt, and his muscles stood out in ridges as he flexed his body for the effort. Slowly at first and then faster and ever faster he swayed from the hips in a peculiarly graceful, india-rubber-like manner, while the line whirled and whistled round his head, till, with a little jump and a jerk of his wrist, he sent it humming forty yards over the water. Instantly there was a swirl and a tug and, with incredible speed a silver streak appeared in the shallows. A moment later a *piranha* was gasping out its life on the bank. José looked round smirking at our approbation.

"Would the señor like to try?" he asked Urrio.

Urrio, with a slight touch of condescension due to such a simple affair took his stand by the water's edge. Apparently, he went through the same motions, but Bee-Mason and I, gazing at the place where Vaca had dropped the bait, were surprised to hear a loud plop almost at our feet.

"I let go too late," said Urrio, grinning.

We helped him to disentangle the result from a bush, and he tried again. This time he let go too soon and the entire tackle, hook, line and bait, shot whistling out into the lake. With singular loyalty we waded after it, but as a fish just at this moment chose to swallow the meat, we could only stare at the wake of a rapidly disappearing piece of string.

"Better take a lesson from the pro," said I. "You drove that one out of sight."

Urrio wisely overlooked the wicked gleam in Vaca's eye, and humbly started again. Once more the native whirled the line, once more the coil shot out over the lake, and, observing closely, I saw where Urrio had made his mistake. He had used the whole of his arm, whereas José Vaca moved only his wrist. As the day slipped by we became more proficient, *piranhas* snapped the bait like tigers and were amazingly full of fight even when landed. One bit a piece of stick in two with scarcely an effort.

After a while our guide suggested that we should try for something more appetizing, for *piranhas*, though edible, are a mass of small forked bones. So we anchored off the large swamp at the head of the lake and cast our line towards the weeds. It is extremely difficult to throw accurately from the slippery turtle-deck of a launch, and the presence of *piranhas* made us cautious; still we managed to procure a dozen *pacou*, which is the most agreeable fish in South America. About two feet long, they live on the juicy water plants in the fresh current that flows from marshes, and are deep-bellied. The Bororo Indians to the north spear them from their dug-out canoes.

We caught, too, an extraordinary fish called *pintado* that never leaves the lake bed. It is three feet in length, deep green in color and has an arched head and snub nose not unlike a dolphin, on which, like water plants, grow two wavy stalks. On the way back we saw a sting-ray floating on the surface. These creatures have a gray, unhealthy looking body shaped like a diamond, and gaze sardonically out of an obscenely evil eye. They have long flexible tails to which are attached barbed pieces of bone that whip round and bite deep into the body of an enemy. They are terribly painful to extract because of the array of microscopic teeth, set backwards, which lie on their edges. We removed the smirk from that particular ray with a revolver bullet.

During dinner that night Urrio was terribly distrait. He smiled mechanically and answered at random, while his hand kept stealing behind his back and he rubbed his shoulders against his shirt as though they itched. Afterwards he took me aside.

"I wish you would come and examine my back," he said. "I am so irritable I can scarcely sit still."

I took him to his bedroom, and so made the acquaintance of the common *garrapata,* a scallop-shaped tick with six legs and two blood sucking claws. Urrio, if I remember right, had thirty-seven sticking to his body, and when I undressed in sympathy he found much the same number on me, though neither then nor later did they cause me any discomfort. For some reason they never touched Bee-Mason. He maintained that he had been stung by so many bees that his blood was full of formic acid and the taste disagreed with them. Hereaftei a *garrapata* parade morning and evening was a recognized part of our toilet.

With them as with mosquitoes, the question of diet is a mystery. They live in palm-trees, large balls of them in the crook of the leaves and batten on to anything that shakes their abode. At the end of three days they swell to the size of a hedge sparrow's egg and, sated with blood, drop off into the grass. Dark brown and insidious they may be found wherever a palm-tree grows, yet they seem to exist where there is no possibility of food. We found them in places where no man had been since the days of Nuflo de Chavez, in places moreover where game was rare.

One morning Bee-Mason strode into my bedroom at

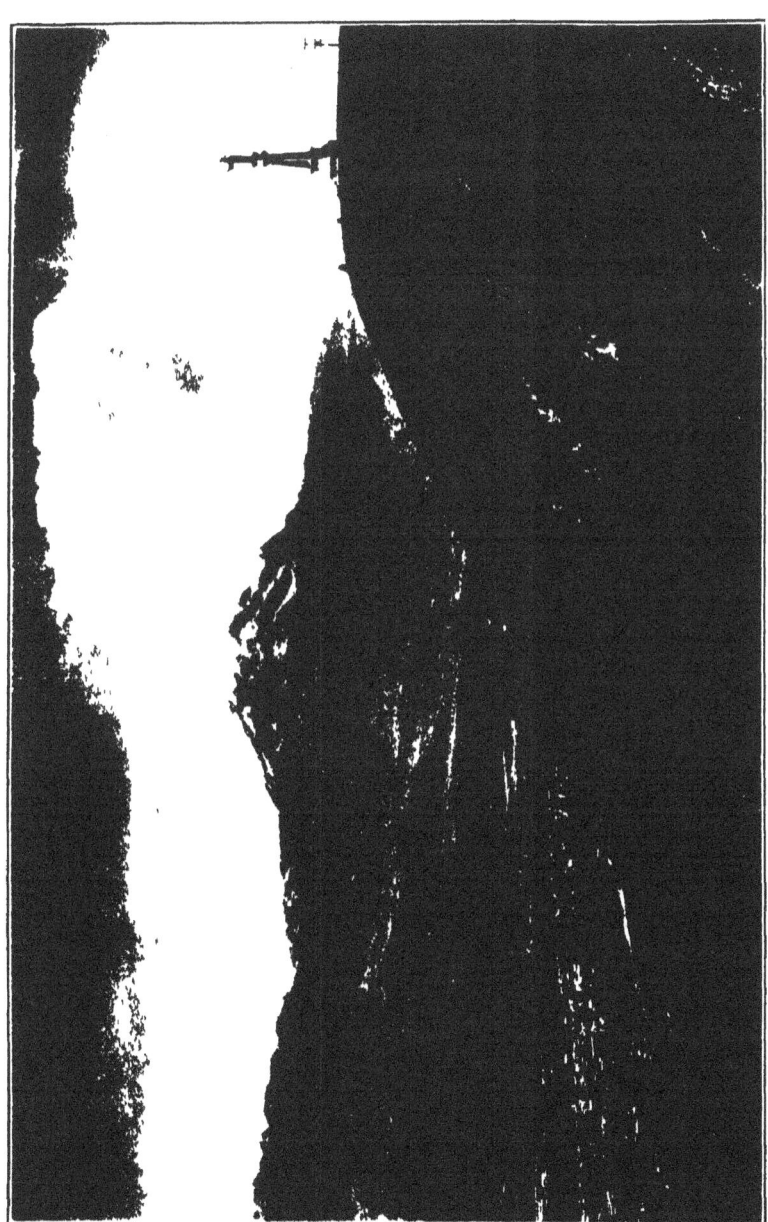

PANORAMIC VIEW OF LA PAZ WITH ILLIMANI IN THE BACKGROUND

dawn. He placed a sponge on my forehead and squeezed gently until I awoke.

"You like snakes," he said.

"Eh?"

"I said you liked snakes. There is a tame viper in the store, a sort of pet."

"What!"

"Yes, very poisonous. I want you to hold it over the gramophone while I register its emotions on the cinema."

I sat up in bed.

"Last time I performed for you," I said, "you told me the brute was half asleep and incapable of defending himself. Go and get Urrio."

Bee-Mason began to wheedle.

"It isn't given to many men to show their heroism to typists. I'll put on the big lens and you'll fill the screen."

I closed my eyes.

"And," he continued in triumph, "you can have a cutting for your book."

So it was arranged.

It was a black snake, rough skinned and sluggish like all the poisonous snakes of South America. It lay in a box covered with mosquito-wire and ran its head angrily against the top, flickering its tongue among the shadows. The store-keeper, its master, dropped it hurriedly on an open sandy patch and looked expectantly at me. I approached it gingerly and was amazed to see a large number of *garrapatas* wedged between the scales and already half blown-up. I did not, however, offer to remove them.

We chose a Spanish tune so that the snake might feel at home, and awaiting a moment when its head was buried in a bush I seized it meanly from behind and swung it round in the hope of making it giddy. Nevertheless it was quite impervious to music, and refused to be put off even when suspended close to the whirling disc. Slowly, but with infinite persistence it started to climb its own body.

"Good," said Bee-Mason turning the handle of the camera.

During the next three minutes I blessed the sluggishness of snakes, for I soon discovered that its mountaineering efforts were slower than my wrist. This restored my faith in the powers of charming and I was able to make pleasant faces into the mouth of the camera.

Meanwhile the problem of transport was hanging over our heads like a cloud. With four servants, ourselves and our baggage we should need eighteen animals, but as Urrio had told me on the liner, mules are scarce on the Upper Paraguay. We could, at a pinch, fill up our ranks with horses and bullocks, but, in a journey of over five hundred miles, mules are the only creatures that can be trusted to last. Again and again it was impressed on us by those in Gaiba that our chances of success would be very severely limited if we could not obtain our full quota of mules. There were only five to be had on the spot, so with a view of purchasing more Urrio took the launch and a lighter down stream. He returned inside a week with distressing news and four animals. It was apparently quite impossible to buy more. Nobody wanted to sell. Each rancher had as many as he could employ and no more, and no amount of money could seduce these lonely men to part with their animals. The value of money to the person who rarely sees a town is surprisingly small. So we were forced to take six small country-bred horses and six skittish bullocks.

As the days passed we began to give up hope of Tiger-Man. We had heard no word of him since we had seen him at the Point, and as there was no method of communication we had to assume that he would not come. October was drawing in and if we were to reach Santa Cruz before the rains there was no time to lose. Already there had been mutterings and thunder, and experienced men in Gaiba had told us that they might start at any moment. So, reluctantly, we decided to push through on our own.

We were, I believe, regarded by the inhabitants as a kind of traveling circus, and odds of five to one were freely offered and refused on the question of our safe arrival. This served to stiffen our resolution and send us about with the haughty air of those who will get through or die in the attempt. One evening we held an indignation meeting and swore a mighty oath that rather than return to the laughter of civilization we would invite the vultures to a cheap lunch off our carcasses.

On October 18th all was ready. The animals were loaded, the mule trunks filled with food and clothing, the saddlery was as good as we could make it. A large throng had come derisively to bid us farewell, and our cook was taking tosses off a bullock all by himself in a corner. Suddenly Urrio shaded his eyes and pointed across the lake. The water was rough, almost as rough as when we had arrived, and the sun was gilding the wave tops. About two miles away was an object about the size of a pencil, and from the stern there stood up rigidly erect a miniature Stetson.

Filled with wonder at his skill and daring we crowded to the lake's edge and watched his progress. Any one who has attempted to propel one of these dug-out canoes on the bosom of a dead calm river on a dead calm day will know what courage, balance and endurance are needed to govern it in a storm. Showers of spray broke over the bows which were lifted high above the surface by the weight in the stern, and we could hear the slapping of wood on water while he was yet a great distance off. With immensely powerful strokes of the paddle, now one side, now the other, he kept the canoe head on to the waves while the foam creamed round the nose. He landed amid enthusiasm.

"Sorry," he said, "an Indian stole my canoe."

An onlooker who had been gazing hard at the craft stepped out of the crowd and lifted one end. "This is hard-wood," he said.

"Yes," replied Tiger-Man, "but I only found out in the middle of the lake."

"What difference does that make?" asked Bee-Mason.

"Hard-wood sinks," said Tiger-Man.

Behind him the "white-horses" reared and sported, living warnings to those who travel the waters in other than soft-wood canoes.

It was then that we began dimly to know what sort of man we had with us.

CHAPTER XI

THERE are two roads out from Gaiba and they meet in the forest a mile or so inland. This simple fact led to a personal adventure, which for weeks to come cheered the spirits of my companions whenever they thought of it. Indeed Urrio went so far as to compare me to Tartarin de Tarascon. This was how it happened. When Tiger-Man landed from his canoe he ran his eye rapidly over the equipment and pronounced it good enough to start. So we mounted once more and looked at him expectantly.

"I can't come yet," he said. "My camera and plates are over at the Point. The weather was too rough to risk them and I must borrow the launch."

"Can you catch us up?" we asked.

He gazed solemnly at our well-loaded animals, at the heavy-shouldered pack bullocks, the small country-breds and the mules.

"You will be lucky," he said, "to do an average of three miles an hour. I can do five and ride longer hours. In two days I shall have overtaken you."

Urrio turned to the population of Gaiba which had resumed its patient attitude of farewell.

"Good-by," he said. "I know you consider the odds

to be five to one against us, but if the worst happens we shall walk. You will not see us again."

Urrio is constitutionally incapable of bombast. He said this with a charming mixture of diffidence and amiability and there was a roar of laughter.

"I'll take three to one now your Russian friend has arrived," said a voice from the crowd.

"Done," said Urrio promptly.

Suddenly the Bolivian representative of law and order in Gaiba trotted up from the Port and came up to me. He was a genial ruffian whose revolver looked very much at home on his hip.

"I have discovered who stole your belongings," he said.

For some time past various small oddments had disappeared from my room, a tobacco pouch, handkerchiefs, a couple of knives and so forth, and I was glad to hear of their return.

"Go with him," said Urrio, "and take Tiger-Man to interpret. We will see you later."

So Tiger-Man, the *Intendente* and I went down to the port, leaving Urrio and Bee-Mason shaking hands all round. We found the culprit, a moon-faced yellow creature, sitting moodily and uncomfortably in the stocks. A number of children were causing him to regret his indiscretion by pelting him with garbage. The *Intendente* eyed him severely.

"Have you anything to say for yourself?"

The fellow looked up with a surly expression on his flat features.

"The señor had more handkerchiefs than he could possibly need."

This excuse, typical of the childish minds of Indians, was not sufficient to get him off another twenty-four hours of discomfort. As we walked away Tiger-Man held out a large horny hand.

"If you are going by the short cut you should meet Urrio at the junction of the roads," he said.

Then he grinned and a more cheerful, bearded countenance I have never seen.

"Do you mind if I give you a bit of advice?"

"Of course not," I answered. "That's what you're here for!"

"Well, don't go about so heavily armed. You've got a rifle slung over your back, a pistol at your hip, and a shot-gun at your saddle-bow. You'll get terribly tired if you always ride like that. Take my tip and lend the shot-gun to the cook."

I thanked him and trotted away up the dusty road after a last look over the lake to the mountains beyond. The water was still choppy and foam-capped, fleecy white clouds were bearing up from the south, and the air was cool. I thought of Nuflo de Chavez and his ladies who had started from the same point and were going to the same destination. Had they, I wondered, been wave-tossed on the lake or had they set out in the damp heat that precedes a thunderstorm. At any rate we were better off than they for we had animals and good firearms, and knew at least the general direction which we must take.

Then as I passed out of sight of the Port and entered the jungle road, the spirit of the old explorers took charge of me and I felt myself moving in distinguished company. On either hand the tall trees stretched soft fingers towards the skies and I seemed to be riding on a bright carpet up a dark green canyon. By my side were men whose histories I knew, men who had been dissatisfied with the comforts of civilization and who had taken to the wilds in the hope of fortune certainly, but more I suspect from the terrible regularity of meals. Much might be written on this subject. I know more than one man who has fled from the lights of town simply because when he has asked the time, he has been told, not twelve o'clock but an hour and a half till lunch.

When I reached the cross-roads, if I may so call a spot where two jungle paths converge, I found a number of hoof marks on the red surface of the soil. I was not sufficiently experienced to be able to tell whether they were fresh, but I trusted to luck and pushed on. An incredible stillness had fallen over the woods, for the wind had suddenly dropped and the evening hour for bird chatter had not arrived. It was about four o'clock, the sun was still hot but on the wane and I rode straight into its fiery eye towards the west. My horse was a little brown animal, tame as a cow and willing enough, but I did not trust its stamina over a long ride. That is the worst of horses on the Paraguay River. The country is not sufficiently cleared for grass to grow in any abundance and alfalfa has not ventured north of the Argentine. Wherefore mules are essential for a prolonged trek and they are practically impossible to buy.

After a while I came to a clearing in the forest. A small wood shack nestled under the shadow of the trees and two figures were seated at the doorway. As I rode up a gigantic Negro with curly hair and shining teeth rose and saluted me. There was a white woman by his side and I thought that he was probably her servant. The man spoke nothing but Portuguese but the lady was an Austrian and spoke French, so I was able to gather some information as to their manner of life. It seemed that they had been married for ten years and had settled in this forest some year or so back and had cleared a large patch on which they were growing mandiocre, a long-rooted vegetable that looks like a parsnip and tastes like a potato. Let me say at once that in civilization the sight of a black man and a white woman in close companionship moves me to a nausea that is almost physical. But somehow in this far place it was different. To begin with they were friends; it was evident from the quiet smiling way in which she looked at him when she spoke; it was more than evident from the tenderness of his expression when she asked him for a glass of water. Their attitude to each other was the tried and intimate fellowship of two people who laugh at the same jokes and have learnt to sympathize with each other's failings. Moreover they had wrenched a joint living in the very teeth of Green Hell and were perfectly happy enjoying the fruits together. They told me that Urrio had not passed and begged me to sling my hammock among the trees and take supper with them. I refused, I am not sure why, but I think it was because I had never been alone in the forest and wished to savor the sensation. So after a cup of coffee I mounted once more, and whilst the sun raced down the sky, set off alone.

Soon it was dark with the sudden velvet blackness of the tropics. The air was remarkably pleasant and conducive to the luxury of history re-lived on the scene of action. I thought of the times in my club when academically I had discussed the Jesuits, of the hours I had spent with books reading of their adventures. The missionary Jesuit has always aroused my enthusiasm and admiration with his habit of departing to the utmost ends of the world at the command of a superior officer. But the heroism and single-mindedness of these great men had never come home to me as it did that night in the forest. I pictured the black-frocked brethren setting out on foot through a jungle that was pathless, towards water that might or might not be there. An easy prey to a prowling tiger, an object of hope to the sweeping, bright-eyed vultures. Absolute rulers of the province towards which my horse's nose was turned, so absolute indeed that the monarch in Madrid feared for his own influence and caused them to be expelled. Whereupon these same men, after many years of beneficent rule, laid down their charge without a word of bitterness and prevented the natives from rising in fury. A century of hardship wasted, and no bitterness! What a record!

The night was clear; the Southern Cross, much less majestic than I had imagined, hung aslant the star-strewn sky. The ink-black outline of the trees reared up into the deep blue of the heavens and the underbrush, mere ill-defined gradations of shadow swallowed the trunks. Silence is comparative. A city worker returns to the silence of Kensington. A town dweller is unable to sleep in the country for the noise of the farmyard. Only a forest can be really and finally silent. The shock of an unshod hoof against a stone sent the echoes thundering through the trees; the clank of a spur against a stirrup rang like a hammer on an anvil; the ruminative cough of an uninterested horse crashed through the silence like a clarion, and after each immensity of sound the silence dropped back into place.

There are silences and silences. There is for instance the silence of a man who drops into an armchair after a successful meal; or the not quite comprehending silence of a murderer when the chaplain has droned "Amen"; or the peaceful unruffled silence, with a touch of learning in it, that comes to a library when the owner is undisturbed. The silence of the forest is like none of these. It is alert, watchful, awake. It is the silence of the tiger's paw; the silence of the darting bat; the silence of the snake. It is not a bit restful, nor does it induce sleep. Rather it brings out all that is self-protective in man. It is the kind of silence that causes those that hear it to refrain from glancing over their shoulders; the kind of

CROSSING THE RIO GRANDE IN FULL SWING

silence that makes one cock a pistol in the sure knowledge that whatever comes will come too quick for thought. That night I entered into the spirit of Green Hell.

I had seen her from the river and had ventured through her shadows by daylight, but in all those excursions I had been within hail of man. Now I was alone, riding into the distance, abnormally conscious of all that seemed to be still. Presently the moon rose, gaudy and yellow, climbing through the trees. On the outstretched branch of a bare *lapacho* were a pair of macaws, their tails hanging down like monstrous brushes. They paid no attention as the horse and I rode beneath them, but sat quite still. An owl swooped across the moon masking it for a moment, then freeing the glare to shine more brightly for the eclipse. Fireflies danced and played through the obscure aisles of the forest. Green Hell was as silent as a mother watching the sleep of her child. Presently the moon sank and a soft, cool darkness fell over the world. My horse, which hitherto had been marching cheerfully, began to feel the uneasy element in the silence. It whinnied and shook its head till the bit rattled at the echoing force of the reply. It edged past shadows and lay back on the reins when a night bird fluttered through the trees. It stood in trembling indecision for a good five minutes, oblivious to spur or voice when the stench of a dead companion was blown across the path.

I had now been in the saddle for seven hours and was

beginning bitterly to regret my impulse to ride on alone. Later in the expedition I should have known what to do. I should have pitched my camp when the moon sank, lighted a fire and slept till dawn; but I was too raw for that. I knew that I must make for the camp of a water-prospector some twenty miles from Gaiba and I was determined to get there somehow. I had no means of knowing how far we had come, though the horse owing to my inexperience of "pushing" an animal had been moving literally at a foot's pace. I was chiefly perturbed by the unwieldy nature of my equipment. It is no easy task for a greenhorn horseman to mount a playful steed when he is holding a rifle and a shotgun. So I refrained from dismounting at all.

As the hours passed the horse and I began to grow sleepy. It was an adaptable creature and willing enough, for it trusted to a mechanical placing of its feet and simply dozed off on the march. This was simple on the soft, level plains which constituted most of the road, but at times the track ran steeply among rocks and I was forced to jog its head and apply my spurs. Even this, however, was not really successful. The sleepy beast just grunted, closed its eyes and stumbled forward.

Gradually, for I had started packing at four that morning, I dropped off to sleep myself. Suddenly just as I was in the middle of a pleasant, drowsy dream I felt the horse heave up and I nearly lost my seat. I clutched my shot-gun firmly, gripped tightly with my knees and looked about me for the cause of the disturbance. By the color of the sky I judged it to be about two o'clock in the morning and a distinct chill crept through my clothes and raised the goose flesh on my skin. The forest if possible was more silent than ever and I saw no reason whatever for the queer antics of my tired beast. There was no doubt at all that something out of the ordinary was happening. The horse was on its hind legs, snorting with fear and trembling like a frightened girl. It was only with the greatest good fortune that I was able to sit on at all. Driving my spurs in deep I cursed the brute with commendable fluency but no result, at the same time peering through the darkness on both sides of the road.

Then the most extraordinary thing happened. On the right hand border of the forest about five yards away and a foot or so from the ground, a couple of yellow lights blazed into being. They were steady and unwinking, a few inches apart. The horse appeared to see them too for it turned tail and would have galloped away if I had not jerked its head with more strength than good feeling.

I was now fairly certain that a jaguar was crouching in the shadows. The extreme reluctance of my mount and the sudden light, as though an animal had turned its head, convinced me that this was so. Green Hell, having weighted the dice in favor of her servant, seemed to sit back and grin.

The familiar inquiry as to what Napoleon would have done was not too helpful, because by no stretch of imagination could I visualize that portly megalomaniac in a forest without Ney or Masséna. He might have turned tail and trusted to the tiger resting content with the hind quarters of the horse; he might have glared at the yellow eyes and hoped that the beast would be able to see the directness and power of his own. On the whole I think he would have done what I did—drop the reins, spur incessantly and cover the supposed wild beast from the left shoulder with a shot-gun. At any rate I could think of no more appropriate action, and the spurring, if it did not advance the horse, at least kept it from retreating.

In this uncomfortable position of stalemate we remained for a considerable time. To make matters worse the eyes now and again blinked and my heated imagination told me that this was a voluptuous gesture on the part of the tiger, indicative of a desire to savor the full sensation of the encounter before sitting down to a meal. Suddenly I had the kind of inspiration which I am sure would not have occurred to Napoleon. I began to sing, not that I have a beautiful voice, but it is powerful, and has a terrifying habit of changing into low gear when ascending the gradient of a song. So with a certain heartfelt feeling I gave the tiger two verses of "Show me the way to go home."

At first these raucous noises did nothing beyond startling Green Hell, who laughed, and the horse, which reared. The tiger went on blinking. However, towards the end of the second verse, the lights disappeared quite silently into the forest and the horse for obvious reasons stopped trembling. Once again we proceeded on our sleepy way.

Towards six o'clock, when dawn had broken in a riot of pale blue and a profusion of fresh smells, the horse gave out. Quite simply and firmly it refused to budge, and I dismounting, laid myself in the dusty path and slept whilst the soft, fluffy bodies of innumerable moths brushed my face.

This story I regret to say has a sequel which denudes it of most of the heroics. It earned for me, however, as I said before, a reputation with my companions second only to that of the great Tartarin.

CHAPTER XII

INLAND from Gaiba is a belt of forest thirty-five miles across in which water has yet to be discovered. To that end an American well-digger from Buenos Aires had taken up his abode in a clearing with a white bell tent and a triangular steel derrick. I came into his camp at nine o'clock in the morning and demanded food, for I had touched nothing but a cup of coffee for the last twenty-two hours. Whereupon he ministered to my needs and I spent the rest of the day revising my opinion of Americans.

To a man who has listened to fat Yankees haggling over the exchange in a poverty-stricken Europe the breed that goes into the wilds for a living comes as a great shock. Bluff, kindly, terribly efficient and tough, he looks his neighbors straight in the face and will share his last biscuit with a complete stranger. I am writing, of course, in the light of my experience with the Standard Oil men later on, but even in this tiny encampment I realized that my previous judgment had been terribly inadequate. I had been accustomed to say "American women, yes, charming. But the men—not on your life." I take this opportunity to apologize for being misled by a bombastic minority.

After my meal was over I watched the American, Harris by name, as he dealt with his men. Now the pure-bred Bolivian who lives in the sun is that difficult proposition, the lazy man with brains. Very quick in the uptake he is equally rapid in downing tools when he feels he has digested the marrow of a subject. Such a person is usually sulky when tackled. Harris, who had no other labor at his disposal, was handling his little team to perfection. With a battered soft hat on the back of his head, his face grim and unshaved, he stood on a packing-case by the derrick and spoke winning words to his disciples. To begin with he addressed them as *"compañero"* a fact which immediately raised them above the *café con leche* Indians and stamped him in their eyes as a leader of discrimination. Then he laughed with them and did not hold himself aloof as so many foreigners do. He praised their intelligence and was not too scathing over their offenses and took care to tell strangers in a loud voice what excellent fellows he possessed. In consequence they really came to believe that their laziness was a thing of the past, a youthful foible that they had outgrown. The well increased in depth.

At lunch time he came across.

"How long are you going to stay here?" he asked.

"I'll go at once if there is any difficulty," I said. "I can easily wait by a stream fifteen miles from here."

Harris made an emphatic gesture.

"Certainly not. Our drink will hold out till the next

water-cart comes from Gaiba, but we *are* a little short of food."

"Then I shall certainly move on."

Harris laughed.

"Oh no you won't. You've got nothing to do, so you might take your gun and scout about for game."

Just then Danton, the revolutionary, rode up on a raking mule. His long legs dangled near the ground, his hawk's features were distorted by his most genial smile, and when he removed his great white hat, a lock of hair fell across his nose. His pale, keen eyes blazed a welcome.

"All Gaiba thinks you dead," he said.

"I met a tiger," I replied, "but not fatally."

"Why did you ride ahead? It was a fool's trick."

"I rode with the spirit of Nuflo de Chavez," I answered. "He is great company."

"Señor Urriolagoitia and the Englishman spent the night at the Port. I think they prayed for your safekeeping. Certainly they cursed."

"There is not much difference except in expression," I said. "But I think the second more likely."

Danton grinned.

"There are elements of a bandit about you," he said. "Next time there is a revolution you shall come too."

Which was the greatest compliment I had ever received.

Between the hours of one and four we lay beneath the small bell tent and suffered. A pitiless white heat flamed down from a sky that seemed almost gray with

NATIVES ADMIRING A MOTOR-CAR FOR THE FIRST TIME

the intensity of the sunlight. A heavy wall of haze hung above the ground and danced about with a shimmering perseverance which made it an effort to move. A swarm of tiny, stingless bees buzzed through the silence and sucked the sweat that poured from our wrists whenever we permitted ourselves a drink from the tepid water in the tank.

"Is it my imagination," I asked, "or is it hotter to-day than usual?"

"I have been in the tropics for twenty years," replied Harris, "and I cannot remember a single day that could compare with this."

Certainly, during the next five months, we had nothing to touch it. And, if I describe the purple patches in some detail, it must not be forgotten that the vast majority of days are mild and sunny and the vast majority of evenings fresh, with the coolness of night breezes. For the climate as a whole I have nothing but praise.

Towards five o'clock Harris shouted from the derrick, telling us to bestir ourselves if we wanted an evening meal. So I took my shot-gun and Danton his pistol, and we walked through the rapidly cooling evening in search of game. The trees were sparse, an apparently open stretch of parkland whose thickness one did not realize until one came to search for a fallen bird. Such country is probably the easiest in the world in which to get lost. In true forest even the novice takes care to blaze the trees or to notice the direction of the sun from the camping-ground. But this low open bush looks ridiculously, sometimes fatally, familiar. It seems as though one could see for a mile through the thin trunks and rough grass, as though one might find one's way blindfolded to the place at which one started. In reality two hundred yards is good visibility and it is extremely difficult not to walk in a circle.

Danton and I wandered deep in undergrowth for a long time. We hoped that we might find some pigeons because Gaiba had been full of them, but there seemed to be a distressing lack of game. We walked intentionally in a large circle that would bring us back to camp about sunset, and we had almost returned before we saw anything at all. Then Danton drew his pistol and pointed. At first I saw nothing, but after a while I made out a couple of large green parrots sitting close together on the branch of a tree. Danton took aim and the echoes leaped. One parrot fell and I brought down the other with my shot-gun.

Never before had I regarded parrots as fair game. They had been connected in my mind with old ladies and steel cages; but when one is hungry one forgets one's scruples. Really, when relieved of their tough outer skin and boiled for twelve hours in a jacket of herbs, they are very good eating. That night, however, cooked hastily over a fire, they were far from tender.

"By the way," said Harris, lifting a roast wing to his mouth, "where is your horse?"

"I tied it to a tree quite near. Why?"

"Only that I did not see it when I looked just now."

I rose guiltily and ran to the place. There was no doubt as to the tree because the coarse grass had been eaten flat in a wide circle; but the horse itself had vanished. The trail of a long rope leading towards Gaiba showed where the beast had gone. Bitterly conscious of my failure as a campaigner, I returned slowly to the fireside where Danton and Harris eyed me with amusement.

"What knot did you use?" asked Harris.

I demonstrated with a piece of string on a stick and he laughed.

"You are a lucky man," he said. "If this had happened later in the trip the loss would have been irreparable. As it is, I can lend you a mule. Come, don't look so sad, but give me the string, and I'll show you the right knot."

"It won't happen again," said Danton. "Men learn by their sins, only women are born with experience."

Thus did two chance friends comfort me for a piece of unutterable stupidity. Men have died for less, but as Harris said, I was lucky.

We arose with the dawn as men do in the tropics. It is an exquisite experience, that dawn uprising, cool as a mountain stream where heat is the order of each blazing day. At five in the morning the world is untouched, innocent of those passions through which it must pass before the winds of sunset bring it to a close. Flights of parrots come screaming out of the eastern sky so as to drink their fill before the midday sun drenches the forest; for the sun when directly overhead, casts no shadow whatsoever and the only possible shelter is a thick canopy of leaves. Blue and gold, delicate and fresh, like pale enamel in an aura of sharp scents—that is the everlasting miracle of a tropical dawn.

Harris and his gang set to work immediately while Danton and I went out in search of lunch. We spared a gigantic couple of blue and scarlet macaws, not from esthetic reasons, but because we feared for our teeth.

Some way down the road we ran into my companions. A small fire burned by the side of the path and a small saucepan bubbled on the top. It was a merry bubble, a cheerful greeting to a couple of thirsty sportsmen, but it was the only joyful thing about the group around it. Urrio and Bee-Mason, booted and spurred, sat glumly with their backs to a tree and did not look up when we approached.

"Good morning," said Danton and I politely.

"Wumph," said Urrio.

Bee-Mason did not reply.

I stared at them in astonishment, for it seemed impossible that a twenty mile ride should have frayed their tempers to such an extent. Yet they continued to glare at a quite uninteresting section of forest and showed by their demeanor that they had no interest whatever in either Danton or me. Nor were our servants one whit more demonstrative. Tiburcio, a large half-caste with a sulky face stood with his hands in the pockets of his blue cotton trousers and glowered at the fire. Cosmé, a thick-set Negro, flipped the back of his legs with a *chicotte*, a villainous short whip comprised of three plaited leather thongs joined by steel rings, a weapon that he was rumored to employ with equal enthusiasm on his bullock or his wife. Adolfo, a meek Indian, smiled sheepishly at me, as though I were a criminal whom he dare not reprove. While Suarez, the cook and the only educated member of our staff, poured coffee from a grimy hand into the saucepan. Over everybody hung an air of gloom and despondency which I was at a loss to understand.

Since the majority of those who read this chronicle will never have been on an expedition it might be as well to explain something of the atmosphere to which wanderers are subject. When three or four men go out into the wilds for months at a time with no change of companionship and few interests outside the immediate circle that bounds them, something is sure to happen. Tiny incidents assume gigantic proportions, little tricks of character or manner stand out in such bold relief that a new perspective is essential if irritation is not to set in. Every man sees his neighbor as he is, shorn of all pretence, naked in soul, as a child sees his elders, with the pitiless, white gaze of youth. It is as though each member of the expedition were separated from the others by an immensely powerful magnifying glass.

We realized this quite early in the expedition, for Urrio, Bee-Mason and I had been almost alone together since Tilbury, and were beginning to know where our respective corns lay. Further we realized that if we would continue the good feeling throughout the trip we should have to see about it ourselves. Friendship is not static. Like every other emotion it has to be fed with kindness and nourished with care. A willingness to die for one's companions is a basic assumption in such cases, but it is of far less value than the timely courtesy of a glass of water. An undigested dinner may lead to a hasty word, and a bitter retort, born of a headache, may very seriously threaten a friendship which has taken months to build. Consequently before we left Gaiba, we met together and codified a set of rules that should sustain us under the whip of circumstance. This idea may sound cold and priggish, calculated to rub the varnish off any human relationship; but it held true. I do not say that we should have quarreled without it, but I do know that it diminished the danger and that we were able to say proudly at the end that bitterness never ruffled our small but sporting expedition. The rules, inspired by each of us in turn, were as follows:

(1) Never discuss a knotty or contentious problem until after a meal.

(2) Never press a fellow to food. We are all greedy enough to ask for what we want and are entitled to go without a meal if we wish.

(3) Never bite back at a hasty word until the speaker has had time to show that he is sorry.

(4) When a fellow is out of sorts hand him the Eno's and leave him alone.

With these injunctions fresh in my mind I gave one look at the faces of Urrio and Bee-Mason and took Danton by the arm. An hour later, when we returned with half a dozen parrots and an appetite, the atmosphere was appreciably clearer. The cargo mules were loaded and my companions had saddled the riding-animals. Urrio, urbanity itself, was just about to place his foot in the stirrup. Bee-Mason, grinning like a monkey, was aloft.

"Hullo!" said Urrio. "It's time we were away. We have fifteen miles to go for the next water. Is your horse saddled?"

To my suspicious mind Urrio was too smooth to be quite natural, and there was a mischievous look in his dark eyes which made me wary.

"My mule will take five minutes to saddle," I said.

Bee-Mason swung round.

"Mule! You rode out from Gaiba on a horse."

"Yes," I said icily, "but he ran away and I have now got a mule."

"Ho! Ho!" he shouted. "You careless devil; and you hadn't the courage to own up."

During this interchange of compliments my eyes had been roving in a desperate attempt to turn the tables. They rested on a large 6 branded on the buttock of Bee-Mason's horse.

"By the way," I said, interested, "where did you get your branding-iron?"

"Don't be silly," said Urrio.

"That horse is not the same," I accused. "You started on a white animal with no marking at all."

Bee-Mason's face fell. In a flash I saw the reason for the morning's glumness.

"I am sorry you were done out of a sneer," I said. "Where did you find the other?"

"It was wandering among the trees," replied Urrio. "We had thought of some wonderful things to say about your carelessness. It was a pity we couldn't use them."

Bee-Mason sighed.

We left Harris and Danton and went our way. Harris we never saw again but the genial revolutionary overtook us a fortnight later. It is one of the tragedies of travel that friendly personalities flash across one's path, and like shooting stars vanish forever in the darkness.

As we rode down the sunlit track through a green lane of forest we learned something of the art of the muleteer. It can be said at once that our servants taught us nothing, for they knew nothing and were in addition as sulky and incompetent a lot of men as ever I saw. We learned bitterly and by experience, and Bee-Mason shed his few remaining hairs in yearning over his camera. It is no easy matter to drive eighteen animals in a straight line. Mules are difficult enough by themselves, but when bullocks and horses are added to the train it becomes a matter for high diplomacy.

The first sign of trouble was the rasp of an oath from Cosmé and the crack of his formidable *chicotte*. I looked up at the sound and saw the horns of a bullock prick the posterior of an elderly horse. Instantly the line was in an uproar. The horse, indignant at the liberty, plunged into Green Hell and bumped the *bouraccas* against the tree-trunks in a frenzy of resentment. The mules pricked up their ears and, hearing the noise of tin plates racing round a wooden box, decided that it was a good game and joined in. Soon the undergrowth was full of an infamously happy family that kicked its heels and snorted with the joy of living. The men became hot and blasphemous. Cosmé rolled his black eyes and whirled his *chicotte* as he rode in pursuit. The animals ran farther and farther from the path until all idea of a procession had vanished and there was nothing to be seen but a number of irritated men chasing a number of ecstatic and jubilant beasts of burden.

It was half an hour before we were able to move on.

That night we pitched our camp by the side of a rattling brook. By the light of a roaring fire we ate our rice and discussed the transport problem.

"What we want is a bell," said Bee-Mason.

Now as luck would have it we had bought a dinner bell in Buenos Aires in the hope that it might amuse the leisure moments of Indians. So with Bee-Mason's *machete* we cut off the handle and tied a string to the top. Then we looked about for a victim.

"The leader," said Urrio, "should be a mild-mannered horse. They tell me that a mule will follow a horse and disregard a bullock or another mule. Which shall it be?"

The moon had risen in pale, still glory and our animals were cropping contentedly just beyond the glare of the fire. We chose an elderly fat, white country-bred, noted for its good temper, and tied the bell to its neck. Then we retired to the fireside to await results.

At the first harsh note of the clapper, sixteen heads were lifted from the grass, and the bell-horse immediately became the center of attraction. Pleased by the subtle flattery, it shook its mane and sent a soft whinny echoing through the stillness. Whereupon the bell raised its voice and the woods resounded. Urrio sprang up, afraid lest they should vanish in tumult, but sat back at once when he saw what was happening. The mules and bullocks approached from all sides and stood in a circle round the new leader. Their attitude was both curious and unexpected. Their intelligent faces seemed to be saying in a mixture of congratulation and jealousy: "My dear, how too becoming! Of course we shall never stray after this."

If ever a horse purred that white animal did that night.

CHAPTER XIII

On the bright blue official map of Eastern Bolivia a little row of dots runs away into the distance. They are a pompous high-sounding brood called after the saints or some natural peculiarity, and would cause a stranger to think that the country is highly populated. To one such dot we made our entry in the cool of an evening and there resolved to await Tiger-Man. The dinner-bell clanked dolefully on the neck of the old white horse, the procession wound its way through the wooded parkland and the inhabitants of the boldly marked San Lorenzo turned out to welcome us.

"What do you think of our first town?" asked Urrio.

I stared, uncomprehending, at the single rickety house that stood by a broken down cattle corral.

"When do we come to it?"

Urrio laughed.

"You must adjust your scale of values. That shack is San Lorenzo."

"Good Lord!" said Bee-Mason. "Your map makers *have* got nerve."

"One must fill in the country somehow," said Urrio.

San Lorenzo had a population of nine and a falling birth rate. A man and a woman with five girl children, a servant and his barren wife. That was all. The father was a gnarled old Indian in a pair of blue cotton trousers and a shirt. A few long hairs, separate and wiry, like cat's whiskers, stuck out from his yellow face; and his high cheek bones and narrow slanting eyes had more than a touch of the Mongolian.

His arm was passed affectionately about the scraggy waist of his wife, who, bony and cheerful, grinned out of a forest of coarse black hair that fell around her shoulders. Of the five children, two were blind.

The house was a gem. It stood in the midst of palm-trees of the tall, thin variety that is topped by a rustling crest. This tree is peculiar in that it has an intensely hard fibrous rim and a hollow interior. Consequently when sliced up the center it provides two durable curved logs which are invaluable for building purposes. San Lorenzo was fashioned entirely of palm, and looked more like a thatched stockade than a dwelling, for the posts had been driven into the ground at regular distances and were not joined together. The roof was made from the leaves of another brand of palm, a gigantic affair which grew the wrong way up, like an inverted shuttlecock.

The floor was of earth, scratched into sand baths by a wiry breed of chicken, and glazed at intervals by the perpetual tramp of hot feet. The master of the house bade us welcome and make free of the building for the slinging of hammocks. Bee-Mason complied joyfully, and it was not until he discovered that there was a hen-roost above his head that he voted the project too dangerous and joined us in the open.

A glorious, cold stream sang and gurgled near by, and we recovered from the heat of the day in its sandy pools. Men speak of the luxury of a grand hotel with a telephone in every room and a bath next door, but to me there are few sensations comparable to the feel of a brook when day is dying in flaming splendor and brilliant birds are wending their noisy way home. In these circumstances one draws very near to one's companions and comes within measurable distance of the "peace that passeth all understanding."

During the two days in which we waited for Tiger-Man we inquired into the lives of these people. As near as may be they are cut off from the world. Puerto Suarez is a hundred miles away, Gaiba fifty, and though the business at the port has latterly brought more people through, the sight of a stranger is still a signal to knock off work.

They live in the simplest manner conceivable, and are almost self-supporting. A few dozen cattle roam through the parkland and wax fat on the long grass. Chickens wander about the house and increase wonderfully, scratching for insects in the sliced-bark floor of the corral and snatching at flies where the meat hangs drying in the sun. It was here that we first saw *charqui* in the making. A scaffolding is set up low enough to handle but high enough to discourage the flea-bitten curs, and on it is stretched a number of blankets of meat. Under the intense heat the bright red soon fades. Thousands of flies help to absorb the moisture and in a few hours a dried sheet of pemmican is ready for the cook-pot.

At the back of the house is a maize field, about half an acre in extent. The dark green, spear-shaped stems creak and sigh in the evening breeze. A working minimum is made into meal or given in husk to the undersized horses, but I regret to say that the vast majority is made into *chicha,* an alcoholic drink that tastes like barley water. Their clothes grow on the bushes. High, thick shrubs clustered about the stream and looked as though a number of rabbits had hung up their tails to dry. This is the native cotton, and by means of a spinning bobbin and a small hand loom they fashioned the rough dresses which the ladies wear. Occasionally a Turkish pedlar—Turks are surprisingly numerous in Matto Grosso—passes through, and exchanges a suit of dark cloth or some gaudy trinkets for a few cattle.

Life in these conditions becomes the most simple affair in the world. Ambition is either dead or was never born. From year's end to year's end, through rain and heat and storm these people lead their unassuming, placid lives in utter ignorance that there is such a place as Europe. We told the owner of San Lorenzo that we came from beyond the sea.

"I know the word," he said, "but what does it mean?"

"Have you seen Lake Gaiba?" we asked.

"Once, many rains ago. How beautiful were the mountains."

We racked our brains for a metaphor that would convey something to his mind.

"As the tick is to the jungle, so is Lake Gaiba to the sea," was Urrio's brilliant comparison.

The Indian gazed at us as the natives of San Salvador gazed at Columbus, with wonder and respect.

"I suppose your canoes were of soft wood," he said.

On the second day, in the evening, Tiger-Man rode into San Lorenzo. We saw him when he was still a great distance off, and walked out to meet him. His tall Stetson was planted firmly erect, and he sat his small horse like a cowboy. His long legs, almost touching the ground, seemed welded to the saddle, and his rifle stood upright in a leather case. When he saw us he pricked his mount and cantered between the trees with an immense smile on his bearded face, while his blue eyes shone at the meeting. A loaded cargo bullock lumbered along behind.

"This is great," said Urrio that night at supper, "d'Artagnan has joined the three musketeers who were badly in need of help."

"You might get there alone," said Tiger-Man simply, "but I think I can make it easier for you."

"Duguid wanted help the other night," said Bee-Mason. "He met a tiger in the forest, large yellow eyes and a buckling horse—most dramatic."

Tiger-Man became professional at once. "Sure the eyes weren't green?" he asked.

"Quite."

"Light or dark yellow?"

"Dark."

"Were you sleepy?"

"Very, I had only just awakened."

"You say you covered the lights with your shotgun?"

"Yes."

"And how did you hold your torch?"

I began to be a little irritated by this pointed questionnaire.

"Look here, Tiger-Man," I said, "what are you getting at? You know quite well I have not got a torch."

His bright, steady eyes shone with amusement. "I know," he said, "I know. I only wanted to make sure. You see tigers' eyes don't gleam at night unless they come into contact with another light."

Never so long as I live shall I forget Bee-Mason's shout of glee. It rushed through the moonlit shadows proclaiming his revenge for his lost sneer over the horse. Chickens jumped up with a squawk and clucked nervously in the loft. The Indian approached and asked whether somebody had trodden on a snake. Even the cattle in the corral raised heavy heads in dumb rebuke. As for Urrio, the whole of his long Spanish face turned into a gentle smile, and Tiger-Man grinned openly.

"You infernal liar!" said Bee-Mason as soon as he could speak.

HUT IN THE BOLIVIAN FORESTS

"Not necessarily," said Tiger-Man. "If he had told me that the lights were green I should have agreed with you, but he didn't. He said they were yellow, and dark yellow at that. Now fireflies are exactly that color, and often a couple of them rest on a stone at just that distance from one another which would make them look like tigers' eyes."

Bee-Mason was not to be lightly balked from his advantage.

"Do horses rear at fireflies?" he asked.

"No," said Tiger-man, "but a dumb animal is easily scared at night. A tiger-cat may have been lying nearby."

Bee-Mason turned to me. "I suppose we shall have to give you the benefit of the doubt? Jolly lucky you didn't choose green."

We led Tiger-Man to speak of the luminosity of tigers.

"Every travel book I have read," he remarked, "states that the author saw the eyes of wild beasts shining at night. Some are lucky or observant and only say so when a fire or a torch is nearby. Others are less fortunate; and they lie. Think what it means? In order that eyes should gleam of their own accord in complete darkness there would have to be a light, self-generated in the brain. In a completely obscured room no cat is visible at all, but flash a light in its face, or light a fire, and the bright glossy surface of the eyes acts as a reflector."

"Let this be a lesson to you," said Bee-Mason nodding in my direction.

Next morning, while the animals were being loaded, I lay in my hammock, and listened distressfully to the groans of a child at the other end of San Lorenzo. I could see the mother bending over it, patting the wiry hair, and making ineffective crooning noises. Tiger-Man approached.

"Can I do anything?" he asked. "I have a little skill as a doctor."

The woman burst into speech.

"My eldest child is blind, señor. Eight months ago the darkness fell, poor little mite, and see—her eyes protrude. Now my second is passing through the pain that has left the other."

Tiger-Man strode across the dusty floor and took the small face between his hands.

"One eye has failed already, señora, the other cannot last long."

His gaze swept the remaining three children who stood in a circle with open mouths, and he came quickly to a decision. His voice was soft, edged with a compassionate sternness which was devoid of all offense.

"One child is blind, señora, another cannot be saved. How are you going to protect those younger ones whom the scourge will afflict in a few years' time?"

The woman knotted her fingers in her dirty dress and whined.

"It is the fault of the señor, my husband. He would not bother."

"The fault is a grave one," said Tiger-Man in tones that said as plainly as light, "the fault is equally divided."

There was a short silence broken by the woman's snuffles.

"What can we do, señor? This terrible blindness descends on all who attain the age of eight. Nothing can be done."

"One moment," said Tiger-Man. "You yourself and also your husband have passed the age of eight. What did your parents do for you?"

"A certain white powder bought from a traveling Turk relieved us, señor."

"Do you know there are doctors in Gaiba?"

"Yes, but my husband will not bother."

"A hundred miles there and back. Less than a week's journey. Is it worth it, do you think?"

For a moment the woman frowned and then burst into a smile. She darted forward and fingered my signet ring. Radiant, she looked into my face. "Will you sell, señor? It is so pretty."

Tiger-Man shrugged his shoulders and turned away with a sigh.

"The disease is curable with boric acid," he said in English, "but what can one do when the parents are like children themselves?"

He frowned.

"Think what it means," he added, "when one has no pleasures except those of the eyes. I would kill a child of mine who was blind."

It was Tiger-Man who initiated us into two mysteries which brought a little domestic comfort into the camp. Their names were *maté* and *churrasco*.

Maté is Paraguayan tea and; even as there are sacred feminine rites pertaining to ordinary tea, so are there sacred male rites in the preparation and absorption of *maté*. To the hardened *maté* drinker sugar is a rank abomination (I have said it is a male drink) for it is the slightly bitter flavor that drives away that sinking feeling and puts an edge on the appetite. *Maté* is the best cocktail in the world. One morning I saw Tiger-Man boiling a tiny kettle on a wood fire. In his hand was a small gourd highly polished and shaped like a pear, into which he was pouring a quantity of green herb. Standing upright in the gourd was a long silver tube. Suddenly he filled it with boiling water and sat down on a mule-trunk.

"*Maté no tiene piernas*," he called.

I knew enough Spanish by now to translate, and his meaning puzzled me because obviously *maté* had no legs. Urrio, less stupid than I, seated himself close to Tiger-Man and awaited his turn with the gourd. Bee-Mason licked his lips.

"We must hold a *maté* party when we return," he said.

HOW WE CROSSED RIVERS IN THE BOLIVIAN TROPICS

"Then it must be a male party," retorted Urrio, "for I cannot imagine a number of ladies drinking out of the same tube."

"There is a proverb in Portuguese," said Tiger-Man, "which says it must be drunk so hot that if you spit at a dog the beast will run away howling."

Churrasco is even more of a manly affair. We bought a calf in San Lorenzo for 7s. 6d. and had it killed. Tiger-Man, lover of all natural things, came up after the death and stared at the skinned carcass.

"Nature is lavish with her paint," he said quietly. "What imagination! Look at all those wonderful colors *inside* the beast."

Meanwhile, a fire of palm logs had flared up and died away, leaving a red-hot bed of embers. On to this we placed the ribs, and in twenty minutes approached with our hunting knives. Tiger-Man used his bayonet, which, to my certain knowledge, has been used to stab tigers, carve leather, cut down trees, open tins, butter biscuits, scrape mud off his boots and kill tarantulas. Then we set to with fingers, teeth and knives and polished up that calf. It was not a pretty sight, but it was incredibly satisfying. This time Bee-Mason didn't suggest the presence of ladies at our re-union when we returned to Europe.

Just as we were about to start, Danton and the head policeman of Gaiba rode up. The revolutionary grinned as he saw our eighteen animals waiting in a row.

"Give me light traveling," he said. "For ourselves, we

go in search of a torturer, a barbarous man who racked some Indians in order to dispossess them of their land."

"Will you catch him?"

"The Virgin alone knows. Probably he will have taken to the forest. It is mostly farce, this police work. In a country so thinly populated almost everybody is a relation, and God help the police!"

He swung his long hair back from his forehead, and after a drink of water pushed on. We never saw him again, although we heard that the torturer escaped.

For the next few nights we slept in the open, our hammocks slung between trees, but one evening, just as the sun was sinking, we came to another high-sounding town, San Sebastián. As we rode down a dusty hill we saw two palm-houses nestling near the bend of a stream, and immediately a band of dogs came out to meet us. Every breed, from bloodhound to dachshund, from spaniel to Great Dane, interbred and crossed until nature had invented some new strains for herself, barked and growled and sprang at the horses' throats in a tempestuous medley of dislike. We passed by the apparently empty dwellings, and Tiger-Man raised his voice in the style of Matto Grosso.

"*O de casa*," he called. "Is any one at home?"

A brown, nervous face peeped through a window slit.

"Our men are away," said a squeaky voice. "What do you want?"

"Rest, and a little water, señora, if it please you."

"Very well, señor, but we cannot come out."

"That is to be deprecated," said Tiger-Man politely, and pitched his hammock between lime-trees.

It was dark before we could bathe, and we stumbled through some shrubs to where the music of a waterfall called to us in the darkness. We were all undressed and our feet in the water before Tiger-Man cautiously, as a hunter should, flashed his torch upon the pool. The bright ray disclosed a multitude of tiny fish, and as he moved the light, something gleamed red and ominous some yards from the bank.

"I shouldn't step in just yet," he said to Bee-Mason who was feeling his way amongst the fish. "There is an alligator basking on the surface."

Bee-Mason leaped back, and Urrio, who was pretending that he liked the nibbling of the minnows, suddenly changed his mind.

It seemed incredible that an alligator had found its way from the river, eighty miles distant, but there was no doubt of the evil arch of flesh and the red eye beneath. We threw stones and it disappeared in a swirl of water.

Next morning we rode straight out of San Sebastián into the most superb view that any of us had ever seen. Even Tiger-Man, who has fourteen years' experience in Matto Grosso to his credit, spoke of it with awe. Numberless rows of tall palm trees planted at regular intervals as though by divine plan, rose out of a dew-drenched plain. Their feathery heads, plumed like Zulu warriors pointed to a pale blue sky, while the green earth shimmered like jewelry in a world that smelt of dawn. For two whole hours we rode through this fresh-scented paradise.

Gradually the scene changed.

The open spaces closed in on us. The palm-trees vanished. The sun lost its early freshness and became fierce as a forest fire. We came into an Indian pathway, narrow and arched like a tunnel. It was just wide enough for a pack animal, and no more. High green walls shut us in and obscured the light, the jungle breathed a musty odor on us that is peculiarly its own, tropical parasites stretched out their arms from the trees on which they battened, while orchids and lianas and cactus fingered us as we passed. Immense macaws, blue and yellow, or red and blue, four feet from beak to tail, shrieked blasphemies on our heads, and set a like example to the lesser parrots and parakeets that glittered through the green dungeon. Lizards of every shade scuttled with quick, dry movements through the underbrush, and left us wondering whether we had ever seen them, for no one could see more than a few feet on each side of the trail.

That day we went waterless. It was our own fault that we passed a stream at nine in the morning and hoped for another by midday, but none came, and we paid the penalty for our fault. Towards evening we forgot our thirst in a phenomenon which we often met again, but of which we had been ignorant until then. We were still passing through the tunnel of jungle and were looking towards the mouth where the sun was sinking in a ball of red flame, when an extraordinary noise broke out. It was sudden and metallic, and Urrio, who had been almost asleep in the saddle, awoke with a jerk. It rose in waves and died away only to rear up again with a shrill whine as though somebody were idly tampering with a dynamo.

"What on earth's that?" I asked Tiger-Man.

"Insects," he replied through dry lips.

We were too parched for conversation, so I sat back on my mule and tried to understand the weird shriek of the insect bed-time hour. As I listened I realized that there were at least eight different voices upraised in a mad medley of sound and, as a musician picks out the oboe from the clarinet, the cornet from the cymbals when faced with a band, I tried to separate the noises that comprised that disturbing orchestra. A humming top, a train screaming through a cutting, and a factory hooter I detected at once, for they were the loud instruments that kept the time; while over and under this, intruding only at intervals, like a drum or a triangle, were insects that represented the small electric bell, a boy running a stick along palings, a man winding a watch, a Chinese gong and a prolific hen. The tunnel was vibrant with sound, and it is no exaggeration to say that at the top of each wave it was impossible to distinguish the words of a companion when he shouted quite near. The performance lasted for about an hour, and for many weeks we heard it each evening at, so to speak, closing hour.

We slept that night in Santo Corazón, an old Jesuit stronghold.

CHAPTER XIV

EVERY reader of fiction is familiar with the man who is dying because he has nothing to live for. There is nothing organically wrong. His ribs are mending nicely, and his leg is out of a splint, but with sublime self-indulgence he whimpers into his pillow and refuses to recover until a certain pair of hands has cooled his forehead.

That, briefly, is the way of Eastern Bolivia.

In 1767 there was no richer province than Chiquitos from Tierra del Fuego to Panama. Rich, that is to say, agriculturally. Maize and sugar-cane, bananas and mandiocre grew freely in the fields; wild cotton bushes studded the woods with their white tags; vegetable silk hung in balls from a tall, thin tree; and large herds of cattle roamed the parkland to the north. The men, according to d'Orbigny, the famous naturalist, were vivacious, gay, frank, naïve, sociable and extremely hospitable, fond of dances and addicted to games. They worked at their crops all day and returned to a pleasant, low-built homestead at night. The women, noted for their lovely teeth and high cheerfulness, pounded maize, spun cotton, suckled children, and carried water from the fast, cold streams. Life approached as near to the

Golden Age as is desirable on this side of the grave. The reason for this rustic felicity lay beyond doubt with the Jesuits. These noble and enlightened men cut themselves off from their kind and devoted their lives to the instruction and encouragement of the Indians. There were two priests to each town, and while Father Domingo taught the children to speak Spanish and to read and write, Father Miguel showed the men how to get the best results from their crops. It was no small sacrifice on their part, because a Jesuit is automatically an intellectual man, and they must have missed the high conversation to which they were accustomed in Europe.

By degrees they won their flock from barbarism, and set their feet in the way of the Lord. Churches sprang up and, instead of deploring the native passion for rude music, the best performers were pressed into service and became substitutes for an organ. Violins were introduced from Europe, and the Indians taught to play. Tribal dances were not abolished, but gradually the fierce orgies died away under the gentle influence of Mother Church and became religious festivals.

At first, of course, it was largely a matter of personality. The priests came to a village and started by curing the sick. Their habit of celibacy, strictly adhered to, raised them above common clay and added a mystic value to their teaching. They were a thing apart, divine, healing, and, most marvelous to the native mind, approachable. The Indian had never met anything like it before. His gods were violent beings, sitting aloft in the

FLOCK OF LLAMAS CARRYING TIN ORE IN THE MINING DISTRICT NEAR ATOCHA

majesty of a thunder-storm, vibrant in the flaming wrath of the lightning. No one had ever thought of making personal friends with the sun, nor of gathering agricultural knowledge from the wind and the rain. The stars and the moon were lovely and perfect, no doubt, but they didn't ease a boil or give comfort to the dying.

The new religion gave all that and more. It exemplified the doctrine of loving kindness in the persons of the priests, and enabled frightened souls to fling themselves on the mercy of a celestial court through the entreaty of an earthly friend. So Chiquitos grew rich, and the Jesuits were adored as young children adore their parents.

In October, 1767, the Spanish Government gave vent to a craven fear. Word had gone home from Lima that the Jesuits were all powerful on the great forest plains, and, since the King of Spain was only acquainted with the court Jesuits, he judged the Chiquitanos would revolt. Wherefore he sent secret orders to the Viceroy that every single priest was to be taken to the Pacific coast and shipped off to Europe. Moreover, it was to be a concerted move. On a certain fixed date a small band of troops was to invade each village, and at a certain fixed hour was to take the fathers into custody. It was to be a silent stroke in case they should raise the country.

Of course, it was nothing of the kind. The Governor of Santa Cruz was totally unable to hide the movements of his troops, and when challenged by the archbishop, yielded the terrible secret. Instantly messengers ran to the far-flung missions and the priests were warned.

Now, if the Church had really desired to raise its standard the expulsion could never have been enforced. In a country where Green Hell makes an ambush easy, where the native population adores its teachers, and the army is by no means keen to lift a hand against a priest, nothing would have been easier than a revolt. But the archbishop had no such wish. When his orders arrived the fathers, cut to the depths of their souls, packed their books and their belongings and had one last talk to their people.

"We must go," they said. "Our king recalls us."

"Do you wish to go?" asked the Indians humbly. "We have sinned, we know. But we have done our best."

"We would stay with you all our lives if God so willed, but we may not."

A martial light burned in the eyes of their flocks.

"Do the soldiers take you by force? If so, we will kill them and throw their bodies to *Urubu*."

This was just what the fathers feared.

"Certainly not," they said. "We go because the King has need of us. The good Lord will provide other teachers and you must obey them."

Therein, perhaps, lay the greatest insult that has ever been offered to a body of men. Boys, seventeen years of age, green beyond belief, creatures whom the colonel in charge of the expulsion described as being neither men nor women, were hustled through their theological course so as to take the place of these wise and seasoned fathers. The Indians nearly lynched them.

So the Jesuits departed, and a vast lethargy fell over the land. The Chiquitanos had been weaned from barbarism, and Christianity was in the hands of boys. Their black-coated teachers, so stern, so kindly, so bracing in their creed had left a yawning chasm that has never been filled. Thus befell the greatest disaster that has ever happened to South America.

For the results of this timorous and purblind policy one must rake among the archives of the times and compare them with the state of affairs to-day. To this end I have studied the admirable *Mojos y Chiquitos* by Señor René-Moreno, and, from the brilliance of its style, was able to visualize the social life of the eighteenth century in these outlandish parts. In this I was materially helped by a detailed census.

In 1768 Santo Corazón which I shall take as an example, both because my chronicle has reached that point, and because it is typical, had 2,387 inhabitants. Reading between the lines one can see that they married young, lived to a reasonable age, and had numbers of children, almost equally male and female. As there were few widows and widowers, and re-marriage was rare, it is fair to assume that the expectation of life was equal to both sexes.

One has, therefore, a picture of a small township not unlike an English village of the Middle Ages, self-contained, self-supporting, refraining from intercourse with other tribes, and so avoiding war. By degrees the native habit of piercing the lips and ears for adornment by feathers died out, and a kind of austere happiness descended on the place under the guidance of the priests. Unambitious, consuming their own smoke, the Indians lived their lives in an aura of husbandry and incense, and were content to dwell in the watertight compartments of their own *pueblos*.

Into this garden of happiness fell the bombshell of expulsion, and History has underlined the circumstance with indelible ink. Santo Corazón to-day is a living, or rather dying, rebuke to the Spanish Government, and a supreme though twisted compliment to the Jesuits. As we rode out of the forest into the huge, sandy square, the four-pillared face of the old church, silver and gleaming in the moonlight, gazed sadly at our caravan. It was as though, in the clanking of our dinner-bell and the soft pad of our animals' unshod feet, the spirit of a once vigorous army deplored the lethargy that had fallen. A gigantic crucifix stretching its arms against the dark blue sky seemed to mourn the glory that had departed. A stale aroma of decay, an atmosphere of futility that came perhaps more from our heightened sensibility than from anything tangible hung about us as we made our way in silence towards the deserted school. Long barn-like buildings whose thatched palm roofs had fallen into disrepair surrounded us, and the frightened figures of men crept through the shadows. In the doorways yellow blurs which we took to be the faces of women peered out, and when we glanced in their direction disappeared like startled wraiths. One

OPENING UP A MOTOR ROAD IN THE BOLIVIAN FORESTS

small child playing in the sand at the foot of a crucifix whimpered audibly as it fled from the noise of our approach.

Next morning we were better able to adjust our impressions. Under the sun's glare the square looked like a parade ground that no one had troubled to weed. A green scum of vegetation, thin but palpable, obscured the sand over three quarters of the area, only the cross and the steps of the church being free. The church itself was a squat erection of mud and earth, painted white. Four circular pillars of great girth supported an overhanging roof of hollow palm logs cut to resemble tiles. On one side of a horizontal bar hung two pairs of bronze bells. They were obviously of European casting, and inscribed *San Ygnacio Ora Pro Nobis*, 1723, and *San Miguel Oro Pro Nobis*, 1799. What a deep romance lies in their journey from Spain by sailing ship, canoe and bullock-wagon! If attainment goes for anything, their owners must have felt a profound pride in their arrival. As we stood before the rustic façade we heard a gentle cough. Turning, our eyes fell on an old Indian, bare-footed, wrinkled, with the usual straggling cats'-whiskers instead of a beard, who was viewing us gravely.

"I am the *cacique*," he said. "At your service, señors."

The Chiquitano Indians have a profound regard for age, revering it as they revere their time-muddled conception of God; and they choose the oldest member of the village as their headman. He has no authority save his own personality, yet he acts as priest in a priestless community. He is responsible for the well-being of the village, instilling a sense of moral obligation into the sun-soaked laziness of the young, marrying his flock, baptizing and burying them until a wandering priest shall arrive and set the seal of the Church on those ceremonies that cannot be postponed. This man is called the *cacique*.

Under his proud and reverent guidance we entered the building which was his especial care. It was cool and roomy, loftier than the outside view suggested, with stout wooden beams and an earthen floor. Bats hung from the roof in thousands, and hundreds more flitted through the nave into the vestry and out again, twittering with fright, skimming the altar with their wings and almost touching the dull, beaten silver of an ancient cross. This relic of the late sixteenth century came from the famous mines of Potosí, and was entirely hand worked. In the vestry was an intensely interesting incense casket which, from the roughness of the molding seemed to be of colonial work, while the subject and treatment were obviously Renaissance of the school of Benvenuto Cellini. Rudely carved angels and cherubs stood out in embossed relief, and Urrio and I had a long argument as to the possible history of the maker. A Spaniard, we gathered, who had been to Italy before emigrating to the New World under the followers of the Conquistadores. Probably somewhere about 1630, though the Jesuits were not properly settled in Santo Corazón until 1697. At the back of the church was a kind of musicians' gallery, approached by a narrow flight of steps. Music-stands littered the floor, and an ornate and clumsy drum lay in a corner. A number of old religious books, notably a prayer book from the private press of one Balthasar Moreto of Antwerp, and dated 1689, so obviously delighted us that the *cacique* sidled up with a protective look in his dark eyes. In order to try him, Urrio asked the price, and was promptly snubbed.

"The church does not sell, señor. She has no need. She has 400 cattle."

This indeed was a sidelight on the financial basis of religion. Santo Corazón to-day has exactly sixty inhabitants, poor, lazy and woman-ridden. The men, for the most part, are weedy, inconsequent, little creatures, muddle-headed from *chicha*, lacking that steel spring that makes a man realize that work is worth doing for its own sake. Yet the church has 400 cattle.

The present birth rate in Chiquitos is an amazing affair. Not only in Santo Corazón but in Santa Cruz itself, there are nine girls to every one boy. What is the reason? Asuncion was in a like state seventy years ago, but Paraguay had just lost her manhood in a bloody war. Chiquitos is at peace, and has been since the arrival of the Jesuits. Is the province so inert and lifeless that girls are produced because their gentler natures are more in keeping with the times? Is there so little manliness in man that Providence, tiring of the game, has adopted this method of ending it? Urrio and I talked it out on many occasions, and we came to the following conclusion:

It is a physiological commonplace that boys predominate after the carnage of a war, but there are at least two possible reasons for it. Does the expectant mother's mind become so agonized with anxiety for her man that by very suggestion the sex of the child is determined? Or is it that the world has gone mad for a space, and man becomes in truth the dominant and masterful factor that he seldom is in peace time? At first sight there seems to be little difference between these theories, nor is there in time of war. But apply the ideas to the somnolent province of Chiquitos and the answer is otherwise. There is neither anxiety nor agony, nor is there any strong feeling of any kind. Man is entirely useless and would have long ago died out were he not slightly necessary for the procreation of children. As a potent and dominating factor he is dead. Wherefore it seemed to us that he had so far failed to impress his personality on the women that they had given up heeding him, and in consequence it was in the nature of an accident when a boy was born.

The humorous side of the matter is the attitude of the men. They sit in the doorways of their mud and plaster houses, or lounge about the square and peevishly command their women to set about the business of the day. Theirs is the attitude of a conquering army, returning hot-handed with the loot of war, and too puffed-up to be bothered with the matters of the field. With a little wave of their hands they indicate the maize patch and the banana grove, and point grandly to the water-pots. In a warrior, bursting with ardor, the sentiment would be sublime; in an under-sized Indian with drink-bleared eyes it is apt to be ridiculous.

And the women take it in good part. They are not the least bit humble or subservient. They do not fear the wrath of their lords and masters. Why should they when physical labor has made them actually the stronger sex? They seem to accept the situation as a kind of grave joke, and treat their men with a good-humored toleration which is most entertaining to watch. The men themselves fail lamentably to appreciate the matter, and the female children toddle about in the dust, a veritable banner of shame which their fathers are too dense to see. There, if anywhere in the world, man is a kept creature.

Tiger-Man and I went early to bathe in the cold, clear water that looked like amber as it rushed over the dark floor of the stream. Whilst we were splashing in the shallows a long line of women, dressed in blue and carrying water-pots on their heads, came down the sandy path on their lawful occasions. Seen from the front it was an entertaining line, for it began with a dragoon of a woman, straight as a ramrod, and tapered away through small fat women to a tiny child at the tail who carried a minute pot with the pride of all the ages in her gait. They moved with a sidelong, squirming motion from the hips, their bodies absolutely rigid, necks taut, eyes staring straight ahead, while they placed their bare feet unerringly on the sloping ground.

"There is no need to be so modest about yourself," said Tiger-Man. "They are perfectly natural here."

I emerged from a deep pool whither I had plunged in my nakedness, and studied the women as they filled their pots. It was true. They neither gazed at us, nor avoided us, nor grinned as a European might have done. To them we were just animated boulders, of no consequence.

On the way back we encountered Bee-Mason. There was a wild gleam in his eye, and he glanced repeatedly into the bushes as though they were full of English speaking Indians.

"You know the Jesuits," he said. "Always burying treasure."

"Have you found a clue?" we asked.

"Yes," said Bee-Mason, "I have. You know how they used to mark a *cache*. Get a natural object in line with an artificial one and follow up the trail."

"Well?"

"Have you noticed anything about that cross in the square? I thought not. Well, the cross piece is pointing to the extreme end of that line of hills and it's not facing towards any of the cardinal points of the compass. What is the meaning of that?"

We could not tell him.

"I will tell you," he continued. "Either towards the hills, or backwards into the forest, there is a place where treasure is hidden. Any Jesuit revisiting Santo Corazón would see at once that the cross was all wrong and would know the reason. It might be worth while staying for a day or two. It would make a fine newspaper story."

And he went away to bathe. Filled with the gold lust, Tiger-Man and I strolled with studied deliberation into the center of the square. Slowly we approached the cross; guiltily we inspected it; and then the dead village awoke to the sound of our laughter. True enough the cross-bar pointed to the line of hills, but it hung loose and flabby in the breeze, like a damaged tooth. The upright was perfectly orientated and marked quite clearly with the date 1874.

In the future whenever Bee-Mason talked of shining tiger's eyes, I talked of buried treasure.

I was awakened at twelve o'clock that night by a noise that convinced me that I had disagreed with my dinner. A loud, dull screaming interspersed with the shriek of a weird instrument caused me to turn in my hammock and shut my ears. In a minute Bee-Mason was up, and with a hissing intake of breath stood beside me.

"Get up," he said. "You will never see this again."

So I stumbled out into the freezing bitterness that sometimes occurs in this climate at night, and blinked furiously at what I saw. The vast, open square was flooded with moonlight, and the crucifix cast long, unearthly shadows across the weed-clad surface. A small uncertain figure was tramping backwards and forwards with slow emphasis, rattling a refrain on a kettledrum.

From the church nearby came the sound of an untuned violin scratching and scraping its way through a tune that was no tune but all the strings played simultaneously at a slow pace. A terrible vocal sound accompanied it. Lofty, screeching, unutterly dreary it rose and fell like a damned soul that cried out for succor, more from habit than from any conviction.

"I like this," said Bee-Mason, "it is quaint."

The sounds grew. The drummer warmed to his work. The tap became a roll, the roll became a tattoo, until the *crescendo* of ever-rising noises worried at the nerves and reminded us of the Philippine Islanders who drive their enemies mad with continuous drumming. Suddenly the bells rang out, stirring the echoes and driving the bats in thousands from the roof, so that the air was alive with flitting forms. Increasing, dying, carillon and single, cracked and whole, it swelled and ebbed till the night vibrated, and the shadows called for peace.

I joined Bee-Mason at the open door of the church, where a simple but tremendous scene met our eyes. The building was ablaze with light from hundreds of tallow candles that flickered and danced in the cold night wind. On the earthen floor knelt three women facing the altar, and it was from their throats that the weird sounds came. They kept rude time with the violin that was being played with a wild ferocity from the musicians' gallery, and seemed to have forgotten their Christian history in a wild throw-back to their barbarous ancestors. Now and again they ceased and spat vehemently, but not despitefully. Indeed, it entered my mind that they were spitting with reverence. Such a thought was strange to me, and I drew near.

The back view of these women was straight and slim, of superb carriage, and Bee-Mason whispered that they were young widows who had just lost their husbands. From the noise they were making it sounded a likely explanation, but there was just a thought too much deliberation about it and too little frenzy. Suddenly they rose and the entire babel ceased. The violin died away, the bells hummed to a standstill and the drummer walked away. The women rose, and Bee-Mason and I gasped. They were old and lined, a thousand years or forty, it did not matter. They might have been either from their appearance. With an erect carriage that awed us they swept by, and the *cacique* clattered down the stairs from the gallery, hugging his violin.

At three o'clock that morning we mounted and rode away.

CHAPTER XV

THAT day we joined the noble company of travelers and suffered our baptism of thirst. It is an experience common to all wanderers, a touchstone of almost masonic significance by which those who return may conjure up the memory of their adventures; but it is undeniably crude at the time.

For fifteen solid hours we passed neither stream nor water-hole, and in so doing took the first bitter step towards the perfection of self-reliance. The northern road from Santo Corazón is, I believe, well served with water, but we were traveling due west into a district little known and less exploited. Before we started the *cacique* told us that we should come to a small farm, the last wild outpost of civilization, a league or two along the jungle path; which is an explanation but certainly no excuse for the fact that we allowed the unromantic hour of our departure to interfere with the filling of our water gourds. Tiger-Man, of course, student of the woods, made no such foolish mistake, for he had relied on himself too long to neglect his usual precautions at the casual word of an Indian. He urged us to follow his example, but finding us obdurate did not press the matter, preferring that hardship should teach its own lesson.

One thing only we had forgotten, and that was vital. In this part of the world, time, money, distance, and, indeed, all the little accuracies on which civilized people rely as a matter of course mean nothing whatever. Up in La Paz a league is officially described as five kilometres, or three miles; in Brazil it is one kilometre more; but throughout the east of Bolivia it is a personal equation depending entirely on individual feeling. Signposts are unknown, the land has never been surveyed, and so the judgment of distance is mainly a matter of guesswork. For instance, if a native has covered ten leagues in the company of a friend he will forget the tedium in pleasant conversation, and on being questioned will stoutly deny that he has traveled more than three. Similarly, if he has been bored by his own society he will remember the grim sameness of the forest, the lack of water, and the silence, and will grossly over-estimate his journey. As a rule, we observed, Indians travel amicably and in pairs.

We started out in darkness and bitter cold. Tiger-Man led the way as his custom was, and Bee-Mason, keeping a stern eye on the tiny brown mule that bore his camera, rode at his heels, while Urrio and I brought up the rear. It was an eerie procession tapering away into obscurity, for nobody talked, and the only indication of movement in the fore part of the column was a series of significant noises in the midst of a deep silence. Far in front, the dinner-bell clanked with weary monotony, as though the horse disapproved of our hours of travel. *Bouraccas* bumped against dim tree-trunks, tin plates rattled and hopped, hoofs struck loudly against stones and roots, stirrup irons rattled at the touch of spurs, and at regular intervals Cosmé's *chicotte* whistled and cracked till a bullock leaped at the sting of the descent.

Dawn appeared suddenly. One moment everything was dark, the next the world was clear, much in the way of a train emerging from a tunnel. Trees lost their air of black concentration and took on individual forms. Birds shook their feathers and went noisily about their business. Nature was awake.

By nine o'clock the sun was already high and the forest hummed with a hint of fiery majesty in store. At ten the atmosphere was definitely hot, horse-flies buzzed along the path and fastened their stings into the necks of our mounts which quivered under the visitation. At half past eleven there was still no water, and Tiger-Man decreed a halt, for the animals were tired after eight hours of march, and a stream seemed as far away as ever. At midday the sun is right over head, blazing, pitiless, seemingly immovable, and even in the thickest wood there is no shade cast; so we slung a canvas awning across a pole, and lay sweating beneath it on the ground.

"A long two leagues," said Urrio, wiping his face.

"I suppose we're on the right road," said Tiger-Man. "The *cacique* was positive, and we are heading about west by the sun, so we ought to reach the farm by night."

He unshipped his water bottle from the saddle and passed it over to Urrio who waved it away.

"Thanks, Tiger-Man," he said, "but I don't think I will. Later, perhaps."

He ran a furtive tongue along his lips and smiled, his attitude saying quite plainly:

"If I don't take your advice I can't take your water."

Tiger-Man nodded gravely and turned to Bee-Mason and me, but neither of us was bold enough to go behind Urrio's back.

A queer, amused look came into Tiger-Man's eyes, and he replaced the cork silently and without drinking. It was a silly little comedy, born of a too civilized feeling of security on our part and a really distinguished courtesy on Tiger-Man's. Nevertheless it taught us a lesson and made us feel more of a band.

That afternoon lives with me yet. Thirst, I have found, is easy enough to bear provided that one knows the whereabouts of the next drink. This is precisely what we did not know, for we were by no means sure that the *cacique* had directed us aright. For all we knew we might be days wandering about in the forest with only Tiger-Man's water bottle between us and extinction. Each one of us was aware that the comedy at midday was a pretty enough affair, but we were none of us certain how long we could go on refusing drinks.

The first thing that we felt was not the direct beat of the sun's rays but the uncomfortable warmth of the saddle. It made us stir uneasily, rise in the stirrups, settle our trousers, and wish for a parasol. The reins were hot to the touch, the barrels of our guns left a blister on careless flesh, and our feet ached with the heat that the iron sent through our boots. A heavy haze hung low between the trees, an almost tangible essence of white fire which struck the ground and was reflected into the air. An old horse suddenly took it into its head to roll, and was promptly whipped to its feet. A vast and terrible silence, as though the earth were about to bear a child in flame, fell across the afternoon.

The next four hours, moving as slowly as the tired horses, passed in a kind of drowsy stupor, for nature is more merciful than the minor prophets, and drugs the minds of those who suffer. At a bare two and a half miles an hour the procession crawled down the curling jungle track, and we regretted that we were not in the Amazon where the trees are thick overhead and grant a covering from the heat.

Sitting half asleep on my mule I pondered appropriately enough those characters of history who had been noted for their forced abstinence from drink. Columbus, given twenty-four hours' grace by an angry crew, discovering San Salvador by the skin of his teeth; Jonah, pessimistic and doubtful, squatting under a tree in the desert; the Conquistadores and holy fathers, seeking gold and converts in the sort of forest that we were coming to know, Green Hell at her most irritating; and Philip Sidney at Zutphen—there my vision became blurred and I confused his figure with that of Tiger-Man, erect, bearded, astride a white horse in the manner of a crusading knight leading his army through the wastes of Asia Minor—for I could almost hear Tiger-Man's deep lazy voice on a stricken field in the Netherlands:

"Let the poor blighter have it. This is not my first thirst."

Gradually the glare departed from the woods, the insect orchestra broke out, and just as the sun sank we heard a joyous hail from the front.

"Water!"

A stream, deep-set in the earth, dark and cool by reason of its high banks, sang and burbled over stones. With guttural, sobbing noises, the animals sucked in great draughts, and their bellies heaved at the effort. Then it was that I saw the reason for that highly illuminating bible story when Gideon took his soldiers for a route march through the burden and heat of a day, so that he might test their fitness when they came to a river. Tiger-Man was on his knees, but his face was not buried in the current. He scooped two handfuls from the stream and stood upright, watching the animals. This time we took his advice, even though it was unspoken, and did not drink too deeply. We were beginning to learn.

A few minutes later we came to Pacifiqui, a small, fertile farmstead where the evening breeze rustled the tall spears of sugar-cane, and the drooping plumes of slender palm-trees. The owner, a Brazilian from Cuyabá, received us cordially and sent us in the dour light of the last half-hour of day to his bathing pool in charge of his son. This tiny animal, aged five, was frankly exultant at escaping from his brother aged two, and flirted outrageously with all of us. He swam like a tadpole in the deep water, shrieked his delight when we splashed him, and with incredible strength threw boulders as big as his body in our direction. When we returned after dark his small wet legs were clasped firmly round my neck and he was whipping my back in an ecstasy of horsemanship.

That evening, when our stomachs had been filled, and the frantic heat of the day was no more than a mirage in our minds, the Brazilian asked a favor of us.

"There is a tiger in the neighborhood," he said. "One of my servants shot it in the head when he was walking from Santo Corazón yesterday. Unfortunately, it did not die. Here, Domingo!"

His yell arrested a shadow that was passing along the edge of the forest, and an Indian came blinking into the candle-light. He was a skinny little man, bare footed and ragged in harmony with his type. Also he was a liar.

"Yes, *patrón*," he said, swelling visibly, "certainly I saw a tiger. A great big brute that lay no more than

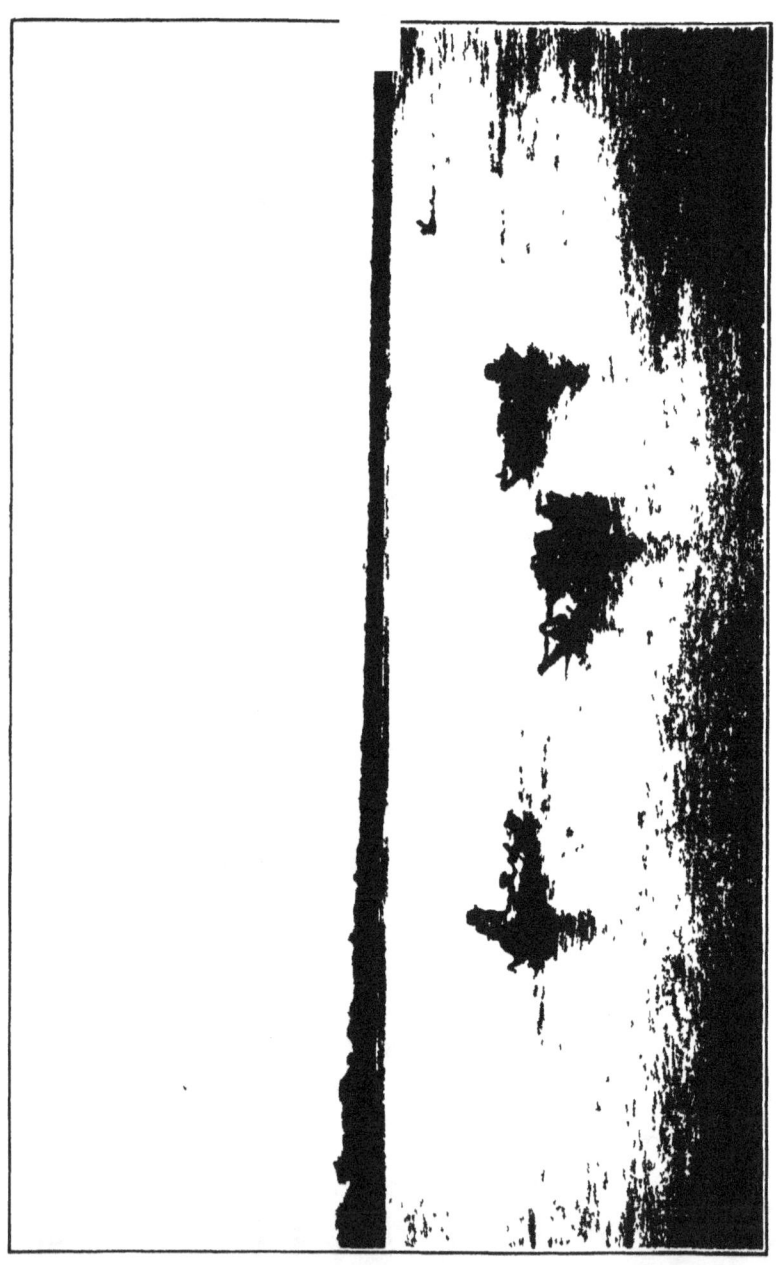

CROSSING A RIVER

three paces from me. My little dogs attacked it and I fired my shot gun into its head."

"Then it died?" said Tiger-Man solemnly.

"Unfortunately, no," replied the Indian glibly. "The tigers in these parts have thick heads. It ran away."

"Yes?" said Tiger-Man.

"It went into the forest whither the dogs and I followed it. I shot thrice more, wounding it in the shoulder, the head and the tail, but it killed three of the dogs and escaped."

Here was a fact that might be verified. Tiger-Man glanced at the Brazilian who nodded.

"Three dogs didn't return," he said.

Tiger-Man made up his mind at once.

"The man is obviously a liar in the small points of the story," he said in English. "No tiger could stand a shot-gun cartridge in the head at three paces; probably he meant thirty. But if three dogs were killed we shall find the tiger quite near, and he will be in a filthy temper."

"What are my chances of a picture?" asked Bee-Mason.

"Practically none. You would have to run through thick forest with a camera and tripod in your hand. One cannot wait for a wounded tiger; it isn't fair on the dogs."

"How far is it from here?" he asked the Indian.

"One league, señor, and a short one at that."

So it was arranged that we should borrow three dogs and set out at dawn, for hunting must be done in the early hours before the sun has baked the scent out of the dew. Tiburcio, the leader of our servants, was summoned and told to bring the horses at six o'clock. He looked sulky and cross, scowling out of his pock-marked face and mumbling something about a rigorous day. Urrio dealt with him and we went to bed.

I awoke early while it was still dark, and seeing an unwonted light, peered over the edge of my hammock. Tiger-Man, fully dressed, was sitting on a fallen tree-trunk, a native candle burning near by, and as he bent forward shadows flickered across his bearded face. His rifle was laid across his knee, an oily rag in his hand, and he fingered his weapon with the gentle touch of a lover. A spot of oil in the breach block, another on the safety catch, yet another on the bayonet groove. He wiped and polished until the barrel shone. Suddenly he drew his bayonet, snapped it into place, cocked the rifle, took steady aim and clicked the trigger. This he did several times until, satisfied with his experiments, he laid it down and turned in my direction.

"My life depends on my gun," he said. "I treat it as carefully as I would a wife."

"How did you know I was awake?" I asked. "You gave no sign."

"Three minutes ago I heard you turn over with a

sigh. The deep sound of your breathing stopped and did not continue. As I had no reason to suppose you dead, I concluded that you were watching me."

He rose from his log and strode over to where the servants were sleeping. He shook the leader awake, leaving the rest to their dreams, and sent him through the cane fields for the horses. This annoyed the ill-favored gentleman exceedingly, and by nine o'clock he had not returned. Cosmé of the great *chicotte* was despatched to find him, and while Tiger-Man paced the clearing in an ecstasy of professional indignation, we lingered over our breakfast.

"It is no use," said Tiger-Man, almost weeping with rage. "The scent will be gone. We must start now, and on foot, or not at all."

Urrio picked up his rifle.

"Very well. The horses shall follow us."

So the Indian was summoned, and, beaming all over, he appeared with the tattered remnant of his terriers, a flea-bitten white bitch and two brown dogs which bounced about in the dust and yelped appreciation of our rifles. The Indian set off with easy grace at a round six miles an hour, his shoeless feet making absolutely no sound on the forest path. Tiger-Man kept five paces behind him, his Stetson stiff and erect, his arms swinging, with Urrio at his heels while I brought up the rear. Once Tiger-Man turned.

"Please keep your distance," he said. "If a tiger

charges you won't have room to swing your rifle."

Thus we learned the meaning of Indian file.

Our guide had told us that the scene of action lay a bare league ahead, but once again we discovered the charming modesty of the Bolivian measurements. An hour passed and we were still striding hotly through jungle so thick that we could not see ten paces in any direction. The sun rose higher and higher up the blue arc of the sky, and the heat released the musty odor of the forest. Tiger-Man spoke to the Indian.

"We have walked two leagues already. Did you lie to us?"

A broad grin spread slowly across the yellow Mongolian features.

"Naturally," he said. "White men are lazy, so I thought it better. We have come exactly half way."

Tiger-Man laughed. "I like a keen hunter. Lead on."

It was now terribly hot, not with the steaming greenhouse heat of the Amazon, but fierce, intensive quivering, and when occasionally we left the wood and crossed a clearing, white.

At this hour the forest is hushed, the birds have finished their morning drink and are dozing in the branches where the insects are drowsing beneath the leaves. Consequently the smallest sound is as audible as a pair of nailed boots in a cathedral. As might have been expected, Urrio and I came off worst. We

CROSSING A RAPID

trod on dead branches and tripped over rope weed in a manner that quite drowned the silence of our companions.

At the end of another hour the Indian halted and pointed across a clearing to a block of jungle.

"This is where it happened," he said.

Tiger-Man immediately took charge. An air of intense, isolating concentration fell over him, and he whistled to the dogs. Moving as silently as the beast whose life he sought, he entered the shadows and trod delicately between the trees, making low crooning noises the while. His right arm jerked rapidly towards the center of the wood, after the manner of a keeper urging a spaniel to take the line of a wounded partridge. The terriers knew their job. Ranging swiftly through the undergrowth they passed from our sight, and we seated ourselves on a fallen tree-trunk to await results.

Hereabouts Green Hell was at her most magnificent. Purple orchids studded the vast tapestry of green, poking their parasitic heads through the rotting forks of trees; lianas hung in slender loops and festoons; underbush cluttered up the ground in luxuriant profusion. Mystery and gloom lurked in every corner of the crowded wood, and the atmosphere was such that one half expected a snake to slither out of every bush. And over all hung a brooding, watchful silence, a thousand times more terrible than the silence of a crouching tiger.

Suddenly from far away to the right came a shrill, excited yapping. Even before the message born of the sound could reach my brain Tiger-Man was off his log and ten yards away, running like a deer. Shouts of encouragement issued from his throat, the forest awoke with a start and the echoes clamored and rumbled through the trees. I had now got into my stride and was running easily a few paces behind the leaders, while Urrio, who was wearing heavy riding boots, crashed along in the rear. It is no easy matter to race through jungle, and it was soon apparent that we were in for a really stern run if we were to save the terriers from being mauled by the wounded tiger. Broken branches rose out of the bushes at our feet, lianas looped themselves about our bodies and refused to be snapped, that most adhesive of thorns, the Queen of Cats, leaned down from the shrubs and dug its claws into our shirts, so that we were in ever present danger of losing touch with one another. By dint of running at cross-country racing speed I just managed to keep Tiger-Man's brown shirt in view, but Urrio, hampered by his boots, was forced to run by sound alone.

Presently the barking ceased, and Tiger-Man stopped in his tracks. His face was seamed with anxiety, for it was a pride of his never to lose a dog. Once more his extraordinary insight into the minds of animals was shown.

"I always yell when I am hunting," he said. "It

gives the little fellows courage and tells them they are not forgotten."

His speech was bitten short at that moment, for quite near a frenzied barking broke out. We jumped into our stride at once and were soon within the sphere of action as was evident from a new and nerve-shaking sound. It tore through the mask of shrubbery, enveloping us all in the naked savagery of its note. A low, angry, musical rumbling growl echoed on all sides, and by reason of its volume was difficult to place. Tiger-Man, however, headed half right and snapped down the safety catch as he ran. In a couple of minutes we were so near that the noise threatened to overwhelm us, and I knew that at last we were in the presence of the lord of the South American woods, His Majesty the Jaguar.

Suddenly Tiger-Man fixed his bayonet and dropped on one knee.

"Can you shoot?" he called over his shoulder.

Now I have the misfortune to wear spectacles, and they were wet and fogged from my run.

"Give me ten seconds," I begged, "I am blind with sweat."

"Sorry," he answered, bending to his sights. "I can't wait. He is charging."

So I drew my pistol, for the place where I stood was too thick to swing a rifle, and poked about in the bushes, hoping to see the beast while he was still alive. Almost crying with anger at my helplessness I wiped my blurred glasses and stared at the spot whence came the sounds. I knew I could not be more than a few paces away, yet I could see nothing but a canopy of dappled gold and green. Then a shot rang out and I ran forward to find the dogs tearing at the flanks of an old female, stone dead, with a bullet through its brain.

"I was looking straight at that tiger," I said, "but I could not see it. Why?"

Tiger-Man smiled.

"In this bush, with the sun shining on his coat, he looks like any other spots. You cannot see him until you get used to him."

Then I remembered, years ago, stalking chamois in Austria. The mountain side was quite bare of any cover and yet, even with powerful field-glasses, I had been unable to pick out the small brown beasts at the first attempt. Soon Urrio joined us and we removed our shirts and wrung them out for they were soaking.

We tied the tiger to a pole with its feet looped together, and walked back two miles to the path. There was no sign of the horses, so, weary but triumphant, we set out for home; it was two leagues before we came upon the smirking Tiburcio riding gently through the forest. We removed his grin at once by forcing him to give up his mount to the Indian and compelling him to walk while a social inferior rode.

Never again did he allow his temper to interfere with his duty.

Thus, after a twenty mile walk and a two mile run, we returned in the early afternoon to Pacifiqui where the Brazilian celebrated the event by broaching his oldest and most potent bottle of spirits.

CHAPTER XVI

Our departure for the unknown corresponded with that of an Indian who died at dawn that day. It was an unfortunate affair, for we met his funeral in the forest at a spot where we could not avoid it, and the grim suggestiveness of the ritual shook our men to the depths of their half-awakened souls.

The first sign of anything unusual was a dull, high-pitched screaming that rushed at us from the greenery ahead. It arose out of the silence in eerie waves, ebbing and flowing with terrible passionless monotony in a cadence of two weary notes. Even at a distance it was sadder and more divorced from hope than any sound I have ever heard. It was as though a sinner had returned to earth with positive tidings that the next life was one long agonizing pain.

Suddenly the dinner-bell, proud emblem of our eldest horse, ceased altogether, and as that awful voice drew nearer it broke into a wild clatter, that was promptly followed by the hollow boom of *bouraccas* crashing against tree-trunks. Obviously the horse's nerve had failed. In an instant all the ears of all the mules stood up in rampant sympathy, and a ripple of terror swept quivering along the line of pack animals that stretched out of sight down the curling track. Tails switched, manes bristled, nostrils blew wide with fright, and it was evident that the slightest incident would send the whole caravan in one mad gallop through the jungle. Urrio rapped out an order, and Cosmé and Adolfo, themselves trembling, leaped to the ground and roped each nervous animal to a tree. In this half-hearted manner we witnessed a procession which, for sheer, stark significance, would have been hard to equal, especially to travelers with their backs to the haunts of men.

First, came three Indians, small, yellow, sad-eyed, each bearing an enormous candle whose naked flames stood upright in the stillness and gleamed dark and unnatural against the splendid background of green foliage. They were followed at a short distance by two haggard and wrinkled old women dressed in ankle-long blue garments, wide and girdleless after the fashion of night-dresses. Coarse black hair tumbled over their shoulders in unbound disarray, and they twined their bony fingers in the ends. They walked with an erect dignity born of generations of water carriers, slow and solemn, eyes hollow and expressionless, hard and unfathomable, like snakes. But for all the sinister repose of their demeanor it was their voices that caused the mules to strain at the ropes, and the men to cross themselves in hurried fear. Harsh, untrained, immeasurably scratchy and dreary, they prayed for the dead man's soul in tones that showed quite plainly that they cared for nothing beyond the fees.

"Professional wailers," said Urrio. "We heard them practising at Santo Corazón."

Whereupon, with a shuffle of naked feet, the principal actor made his bow. A silent, stiff figure, covered with a white cloth, he lay in a rough-hewn, open coffin, borne on the shoulders of six of his companions; and the tip of his nose was pressed against the shroud, giving a rough outline to his face. Occasionally one of the bearers trod on a thorn and, when the body rolled with an odd sound against the boards, a certain volume of anxiety broke from a number of women who walked immediately behind. These women, like the wailers, seemed to be more concerned with the ritualistic aspect of the matter than with any human sorrow. They neither wept nor beat their breasts, and the peculiar glitter of unshed tears was absent from their eyes. Their very annoyance at the rolling body appeared to be a mixture of family pride in the proper conduct of a funeral and the desire to avoid unnecessary delay. Not one of them showed any regret for the dead man.

That grief for the departed was no more than skin deep we saw when we passed his house. There, before the low doorway, were a number of buxom maidens disporting themselves in Botticellian attitudes, drinking *chicha* and singing, while a small boy

"TIGER-MAN" AT FOOT OF THE ANDES

worked a cane press in a corner of the clearing. This primitive machine stood between palm-trees, and consisted of two polished wooden rollers, upright and cogged at the ends, which crushed the cane stalks to pulp and squeezed the juice into a trough by the circular motion of a couple of bullocks yoked to a beam. The boy was enjoying himself intensely, swinging his raw-hide whip about his head and crashing it with loud yells of derision against the patient flanks of his charges. A very old man, quite toothless, sampled the liquor as it dripped from the wheels.

"It's all rather horrible," said Urrio, soothing his mule which had not recovered from the whiff of the corpse.

It was more than that. It was an extremely interesting study of the results of Christian interference, for it represented a cross between barbarism and Christianity with the spirit fled from each. Gone was the grief of breast-tearing that goes with savagery; gone, too, the calm majesty of sorrow with which a gentler faith consigns the dead to sleep. In this terrible procession I could see the stagnant soul of Chiquitos reaching back into the ages, far beyond the Jesuits to the forgotten voices of strange deities whose power had faded through neglect, and whose rites had degenerated into mere senseless babble.

A league further on we encamped, for night was

at hand and we had reached the end of a *cul-de-sac*. The path ceased abruptly and a wall of virgin forest rose sheer out of the ground. Exploration lay ready to our touch. Secretly, I believe, we were all a little awed now that we had come to the point. As we lay smoking in our hammocks after supper there was not quite so much conversation as usual. We just stared into the golden heart of the fire and gave ourselves up to meditation.

Green Hell, ominous and menacing, loomed above our heads, blocking a large slice of the star-studded sky. A vast silence that was no silence at all, but a holding of breath, warned us against the undertaking. The memory of the funeral returned to us, not as a terror so much as a solemn example of what might happen, and I reflected that we should be spared the honor of professional wailers. For if we died it would be from thirst and hunger, not singly but together. I glanced at the men. They were sitting in a little clump, uneasy and superstitious, looking over their shoulders from time to time as though some spirit of the forest mocked them.

"I feel rather like a new boy on the first day of term," said Urrio suddenly.

"It's a great life," said Bee-Mason, determined that none should read him. "Eat when you're hungry, drink when you're thirsty and sleep when you're tired."

This argument in a country where water is scarce

and game scanty was so open to criticism that we said nothing. Tiger-Man, with the facility of men who live alone, divined our thoughts and spoke lazily from the depths of his hammock.

"I have explored most of Matto Grosso to the north of Cuyabá," he said, "and there is generally a stream every two or three leagues. But once I came to a place like this and spent a fortnight breaking through the belt."

"How did you get water?" I asked, for Urrio and Bee-Mason were too proud to voice the question that touched us so closely.

"Waited till evening and followed the birds," said Tiger-Man cheerfully. "If darkness fell too soon I camped till morning and followed them then."

He cleared his throat and coughed. "There are one or two rules that help a thirsty man. Never take more than a sip at a time from your water bottle, and don't drink that. Rinse your mouth and spit. Never ride through the heat of the day. It is easier to be thirsty under a tree, and it saves the animals. Try to keep your thoughts on something cool, and above all never eat if you cannot see a drink."

Bee-Mason lit a cigarette from a flaming branch.

"How long can one do without water?"

"I once passed four days," said Tiger-Man quietly, "but I didn't like it."

We were up by four next day, shivering with the bitterness of the hour before dawn. The embers of the fire were still aglow, and we fed them heartily, fanning them into flame with our broad-brimmed hats; but it was an eerie business even after the yellow tongues shot up and chased away the shadows. A brooding grimness hung over Green Hell, as though she felt the cold as much as we and grudged us the heat. Massive, gloomy, incredibly overwhelming and near, she placed her formidable bulk in our path; a living barrier between us and San Juan, 150 miles to the west. The men felt her presence keenly. They grumbled in undertones and kicked surreptitiously at the mules, with one eye on the trees. Soon, however, the discomfort departed, and the air was full of little reassuring sounds. Mules stamped and snorted, leather fittings creaked as the cinches pulled tight and the straps took the strain of the *bourracas*. Spurs clinked against branches, and sparks sputtered out of the fire, and all the time we warmed ourselves and felt better. In under two hours the cargo was aloft, and we saddled the riding mules to the accompaniment of rattling bridles and the hollow plop of bits as they settled into the mouth, comfortably, behind the teeth. Gaily we mounted.

In every tale of tropical adventure the hero is certain sooner or later to "cut his way through forest." It is a perfect phrase, full-flavored and romantic, suggesting in five brief words a picture of indomitable men whirling polished axes in a dim green light, while gigantic trees topple off their roots like corn before the

RESERVOIR IN PATIÑO TIN MINES

reaper. As a confirmed reader of such tales I had promised myself a glamorous time spitting on my hands and laying lustily about me whilst the bright chips flew; but after the manner of anticipation it was different.

There are, I believe, mahogany forests inland from Pernambuco where the trees grow so close together that a laden mule may not pass between. If so, I do not advise a muleteer to journey therein, for a mile a day would be exceedingly quick traveling. In more reasonable country the problem is quite otherwise, because a tree-trunk is the last thing to be struck. The barrier lies not in solid timber but in the network of parasitic growths that link the trees in a confused trailing mass, adhesive and irritating. It is not unlike cutting one's way through a strong elastic spider's web, whose strands will bear an almost unlimited strain, but yield quickly enough to a knife.

At first we tried riding straight through without cutting, but we soon changed our minds. Immensely powerful rope-weed, looped and springy, leaned from a great height and folded round the *bourracas*. The mules, feeling the check, pressed forward, but the weed held, with the result that the baggage strained against the cinches, reared up and became unbalanced, so that the trunks dragged along the ground. After this had happened once or twice we altered our procedure, the men were left behind with the animals, while Urrio, Tiger-Man, Bee-Mason and I rode in advance like the

Four Horsemen of the Apocalypse, wielding our *machetes* and moving forward in a solid line. In this way we managed to make good time, though our arms became so weary that we had to change hands every half-hour.

At intervals in the forest came patches of more open country, low bush, where for a while we could sheathe our *machetes*. We entered these suddenly as a rule, for the sharp, blue line of the horizon lay surprisingly far down the tree trunks, a phenomenon which caused us to expect a clearing for several miles before it came. Towards evening these clearings were an immense boon because the wind blew lightly through them, and we were able to sleep away from the musty, inclosing smell of the jungle, but in the daytime they were not by any means welcome, because they meant a return to the piercing white heat that blazed down from a heaven gray with haze in a manner quite unknown under the green foliage; and thirst became a really vital problem.

In a thoroughly chastened spirit we paid heed to Tiger-Man's suggestion, and imposed on ourselves a rigid water-discipline. No longer did we drink gaily whenever we felt the need, but after one sad look turned our thoughts into soothing channels and passed our tongues along dry lips. At noon we halted and lay under a strip of canvas without speaking, for even a word is a waste of saliva, and we had none to spare. The cook made as if to light a fire and stew some rice, but Urrio, after a quick glance at Tiger-Man, shook his head decisively. There was just enough water for one boiling for eight men, and we had not found the evening's supply. At night, under the influence of the breeze, we should be able to eat something without much water, but at midday it would be madness. So we lay quietly on the ground and listened to the busy voice of Green Hell.

When the heat had nearly passed, we arose stiffly and set about the business of the afternoon. The animals stood about in groups, knees sagging, heads down, tails switching with spasmodic energy. Tiger-Man approached and scanned them one by one. Five of the cargo mules had sore backs, old wounds that were rising again in great lumps, and which, when rubbed against the packs, broke and suppurated. It was serious as well as distressing, for we had no spare animals and San Juan and safety lay 150 miles ahead, steering roughly by compass. In a great measure it was out of our control, because directly the saddles were removed, the poor beasts lay on their backs in an ecstasy of irritation, and even bit at each other's sores in order to ease the pain. We did what we could by retaining the straw saddle-cloths until the sweat had dried, but the one sure alleviation was salt and water, a cure we had practised twice daily in the land of streams, but which was beyond our powers now. It was pitiful to see them. Now and again a mule, driven beyond reason, would drop down on the march and roll on top of the *bourracas* in an effort to scratch away the pain.

That afternoon Tiger-Man decided to ride ahead in search of water and took me with him, for I wished to savor every aspect of our varied life. We abandoned our *machetes* and cut long sticks, because a horseman can parry the rope-weed, turning it aside as a fencer parries a rapier. By degrees the noise of the mule train dropped behind, and we rode straight into the sun's eye, alone and silent.

Never shall I forget the appearance of Green Hell on that occasion. She wore a symphony in green, beginning with a dark hem in the undergrowth, and passing from every variety of shade as it rose towards the pale green of the tree tops. Bright purple orchids hung from the armpits of great trees, blue butterflies fluttered across our vision, and lizards peeped at us curiously and without fear. There was a certain irritating atmosphere, described by Urrio on the river as "looking lived in," which made itself severely felt. Everything seemed familiar and friendly, as though one might see smoke from a cooking fire at any minute. I had the impression that no harm could come to us under the all-powerful protection of the leaves; and it took an immense effort of imagination to realize that a whole army might die and its bones whiten for years with nobody much the wiser. Hundreds of miles of jungle, rolling past countless horizons, league upon wooded league, each twenty yards promising to be the last, the spirit of Green Hell, merciless and indomitable, beckons the wanderer forward with a will-o'-the-wispy, tantalizing smile, hovering among the branches. I can quite imagine a traveler who was new to the game striding confidently onward, his palate tickled, and his fears lulled by the beauty of the place, while time passed like a cloud. It is all so green and luxuriant that it would never strike him that water might be hard to find, and then, growing thirsty, he would press a little faster, determined to bathe and rest; but the hours would pass and the sun would sink, and in the watches of the night a ghastly uncertainty would arise in his mind. Next day, he would settle down to business, his chin well out, his legs moving swiftly between the trees—and still the woods would mock him. Days would go by and his mouth would be a blistered hell, and his mind inflamed with a desire for water far beyond any desire for women. In the end he would lose his head, forget to steer by the sun, stagger in a great circle and fall hopeless and mad on the second round of his own tracks.

As we rode along I studied Tiger-Man's face, and thanked our beginner's luck for having secured him. He did not appear to be in the least perturbed, no shadow of mistrust showed in his bright blue eyes as they ranged the forest for signs of water. There was an almost jaunty air about him, buccaneering, yet watchful, that seemed to laugh in the face of trouble. His mode of life during the last fourteen years had made him immeasurably superior to our town-bred sophistication. He seemed to be part of the forest, his skin and beard and clothes merged into the background as naturally as if he had been a tiger. His very being was alert with the quiet strength of a wild beast. He turned in the saddle, his feet loose below the stirrups, his hat thrust back from his forehead.

"This must seem very strange to you," he said gently.

Later in the expedition I should have admitted frankly that I was not enjoying myself but, at that moment I was forcing my imagination to behave itself, and I did not dare to consider the possibility of the failure to find water. I knew that in his eyes I was still unproved and, my pride rising on its hind legs, I told him it was just what I expected, that I rather liked it, and that anyway it was better than going to an office in London. Gravely, and without the suspicion of a twinkle, he agreed. For Tiger-Man was perhaps the greatest gentleman I have ever met.

At half past five, when the sun appeared to be almost level with our eyes, we were still without any trace of water. Birds were scarce, and those that we saw were vultures sweeping the sky in moody, somber circles. No tracks of tiger or tapir were visible in the hard-baked ground, and it really looked as though we should have to go thirsty to bed. A slight furrow appeared between Tiger-Man's brows, and he spoke shortly.

"We can last some days longer than the animals," he said. "If they go we shall have the choice of walking forward or back."

I thought of the odds of five to one offered against us in Gaiba, and found no pleasure in it. Suddenly with a loud sweeping of wings and a deafening, hoarse cackle, four huge macaws passed overhead, casting a thick shadow as they went. Simultaneously, Tiger-Man's mule threw back its head and sent a throaty whistle echoing through the trees. It was a pathetic sound, mid-way between the contralto of a horse and the soprano of a donkey, but it made Tiger-Man slip his feet into his stirrups and grin.

"Water," he called joyfully and lifted his hat.

With that one word the benediction of nature descended on our bare heads, and for the moment we forgot our thirst. The animals needed no urging, they broke into a tired run that made us duck in the saddle and wield our sticks so as to parry the lianas and the light green claws of her Majesty the Queen of Cats. The scurry lasted for a quarter of an hour, and then we came to an open glade. Half way across was a red gash running diagonally, the top of which was shot with the dry roots of shrubs. It appeared to shelve deeply into a long green bed which ran the length of the clearing

"A stream," said Tiger-Man, dismounting.

Slipping our bridles through our arms we walked wearily across the glade, a lust for water burning in our hearts. Often we looked at each other and laughed in a perfectly idiotic manner which showed how deeply we were set on just this ending to the day. Quickly we approached the edge and looked over, and a low cry, quickly checked, broke from our throats. As far as the eye could reach the bottom of the water-course was dry, pebbly and bare.

Tiger-Man recovered himself at once. Indeed, I am still not sure whether it was not I who made all the noise in the beginning. He turned his mule and watched it intently. The beast, after one quick look at the bed, moved its head from side to side in an endeavor to scent the water. Almost without hesitation it jerked at the bridle, and tried to run away up stream. Tiger-Man eyed me.

"There is water up there," he said, "probably in a shady hole under the bank where the sun has been unable to reach. Pitch your hammock and unsaddle your animal, make a large fire, and keep your rifle loaded. I am going back."

"But your thirst?" I protested.

He touched his water bottle.

"They may be an hour behind us; remember they had to cut their way. I have a torch, but I don't want to get lost. The fire should guide us. If it does not I shall fire my rifle three times quickly, and you must answer. When the fire is well ablaze you can look about for water, but don't let the mule paddle until we have drawn our supply. See you later."

His tall, broad-shouldered figure vanished into the shadows, and while I set about my task I could hear his voice raised in song receding into the distance. So I pitched my hammock and tethered my mule and placed three dried tree-trunks in a heap, and, the flames ascending, walked quickly up the watercourse.

Half a mile from camp I came suddenly round a corner on to a most curious scene. A small round pool, winking like a Rabelaisian wit in the light of the setting sun, lay under an over-hanging piece of bank. Round it on three sides were the giant macaws which had passed us earlier in the evening. Royal blue and yellow, brilliant and grotesque, their tails spread out behind them like jeweled trains, they squatted on their little gray legs, and thrust their heavy beaks deep into the water. One by one they raised their heads so that the water might trickle down their throats, and made chuckling noises of supreme contentment. I crouched behind a boulder and watched them, unwilling to disturb their drink. A month back I should have sent them flying without a qualm, but thirst had sharpened my sympathies, and some of Tiger-Man's consideration for his fellow sharers of the jungle entered into me. In a few minutes they were satisfied and fluttered up into a tree where their tails could hang down in comfort, and sat close together crooning. I waved my hat at them and they jabbered back, not at all frightened, but inquisitive.

When I returned the rest of the party had arrived. We gave the cook ten minutes start with a bucket, and then loosed the mules. With a clatter of hooves and a perfect tempest of whistles they swept up the water-course and in due time were shepherded back, by which time a meal was ready and we sat down lazily like animals, supremely and blissfully happy under the glory of a cool, clear night.

Next morning when it was still dark I heard a noise. It came from the corner where the mules were tethered, and it was a most un-mulelike noise, metal against a tree, I gathered that it was Tiger-Man. Suddenly a light flashed and a white beam swept in a semicircle until it encountered the surprised face of the bell-horse. From there it passed to the mules, rested a moment on the back of each and snapped off, leaving the scene the darker for its loss. A rather somber grunt followed.

"What's the matter?" asked Urrio's voice from an adjoining hammock.

"Boils," said Tiger-Man abruptly. "Those blessed animals have rolled in the night and undone the work of the salt and water."

"What had we better do?"

"We must rest here to-day or they'll never come through to San Juan. They are raw already and another ten hours' travel will tear the flesh off in chunks."

"H'm," said Urrio.

Tiger-Man climbed back into his hammock, and a silence, heavy as the darkness fell over the camp. A match scraped along a box and Urrio lighted a cigarette.

"I will go on," said Tiger-Man quietly. "It would save trouble in the matter of finding water. We should blaze the trail, of course."

Urrio turned to me.

"Would you like to go too? You led the way out of Gaiba. It seems rather in your line."

So it was settled.

It was impossible to travel before it was light, so we turned over and slept till the dawn. There followed a day that in all ways was the counterpart of the one before—drought, thirst, blinding white heat in the clearings—except that no macaws thundered over us in the evening, and neither of our mules whinnied at the smell of water. Night found us with our bottles and a problem.

"Drink lightly," said Tiger-Man. "To-morrow our need will be double."

We lay for an hour and studied the matter from all angles. Finally Tiger-Man summed it up.

"If we don't find water to-morrow we must sacrifice some of the animals and baggage or else go back."

The forest was terribly still, not with the watchful quietude that I had noticed on the road from Gaiba, but with the silence that falls upon a house that has long been uninhabited. A big cat crouching in the shadows is as still as any living thing may be, but this was different. The atmosphere was different. The whole expanse of jungle was empty of life, one could feel it without being told. No bats, no birds, no insects, no animals, just a horrible lack of life which made the district into a kind of green vacuum, airless and stifling. Our mules sensed it for they would not be quiet. They moved restlessly within the circle allowed by their ropes and refused to sleep. Neither could we, and we yarned far into the night on matters as far removed from thirst as possible.

From the first moment that I met Tiger-Man I felt a great desire to know more about him. His shrewd simplicity of bearing, his quiet manliness and strength attracted me as I had rarely been attracted. But there was a certain deep reserve that forbade questions until a degree of intimacy had been reached. During the long hours of that night while the fire leaped and flickered that reserve was in some way lifted and I no longer feared to trespass on the more private portions of his life. Indeed, he seemed to welcome a friendship that was all the more potent for not being forced in its early stages.

Fourteen years ago he was earning good money in the machine room of a Buenos Aires newspaper, but he fell in love with his best friend's wife, and left the city. His pain was so great that he retired to the forests of Southern Brazil and worked as a woodcutter in the hope that it would tire him out and give him rest. For six months he toiled among Indians and Negroes, whose toughness of outlook gave him a fresh hold on life. So far there was nothing singular in his story. It has happened a thousand times before and so long as women have eyes it will happen again. But with Tiger-Man it had a different finish. At the end of the half year the wound had calloused, and although the scar was still a little tender to the touch it was no longer agony. Moreover, he began to look about him with changed eyes. The jungle seemed to be a good place to live in. The silence appealed to him and the bright clean nights. So he gave up the idea of returning to Buenos Aires, not entirely for the woman's sake, though he had not forgotten her, but for his own.

For three years he wandered about with a mule and a few tools, for he was a skilled mechanic, mending machines in return for food, and learning the law of the jungle. He had all the philosophy and calm courage of the Russian, and was perfectly content with food for himself and his animal, and a few good books to stimulate his intellect. Tolstoy, Gogol, Pushkin, Schopenhauer, Nietzsche, Freud, he knew most of their works by heart and applied them to his own life. Grimly he worked north through the cattle lands of Matto Grosso, absorbing the rough justice of the country, content never to use his strength unless he were provoked. At the end of the third year he came to the edge of the Paraguay River and killed his first tiger, having waited an hour beneath the tree where it rested while a boy ran for his camera. Then coolly, after a photograph at three yards' range, he shot it, and the selling of the skin opened up a pleasant means of earning a living.

"See here," he said. "I've one thing to be proud of and that's that no man is my boss. I can earn my keep from here to São Paulo, and when I have my film of a tiger's life I shall make money. My life is my own."

At times there was an undercurrent of sadness about him, for he was close on forty and he no longer saw the world through rose-colored glasses. Then he would leave his hammock and pace among the shadows alone with his thoughts. Nevertheless there was never a man who judged his fellows with less hostility or venom, and he never gossiped. Even when he knew a man to be rotten he tried to excuse him.

"I blame no man for being bad," he used to say in

his grave sweet voice. "No one is responsible for his parents or his upbringing. If he is bad it is just his nature. Naturally if he is dangerous the community must put him away, but for God's sake don't call it justice."

"Then justice has no meaning to you?" I asked.

"Is it just to kill a tiger that robs you of your cattle? His stomach is made for fresh meat and he only follows his nature. Some men are like tigers. I don't blame them, but I don't let them bite me. Is a sheep more righteous than a lion because its teeth are made for grass?"

He turned to me, and suddenly his tones grew bitter as an east wind.

"Here is a story for you. It may interest you for it happens to be true. My brother used to live in Cuyabá with his wife and his little boy. Somehow he managed to annoy a German who hired a bravo to shoot him in the back. It took him a long time to die and the child soon followed because there was not enough money to buy food. My sister-in-law took to the streets and is now a common harlot in the diamond diggings to the east. Pretty, isn't it? Yet I do not blame the German. It was his nature. But at the same time when I have finished my film I am going to pay a visit to Matto Grosso. I shall find that man and I shall take him aside and I shall shoot him in the stomach. That should give him a good thirty hours to remember my brother. Justice? Not a bit. Revenge."

That was the only time that I ever heard Tiger-Man speak bitterly of any one, and the change from his usual charming self caused a hush to fall between us. Moreover, I would not be that German in the hour that he meets Tiger-Man for anything in this world. I do not envy him that last moment before the bullet leaves the gun, when he shall see a pair of warm, pleasant eyes turn quickly to cold marble.

It is curious how obsessed one can become with a subject. For us, during the next three weeks, water became almost a mania. We thought in terms of liquid, wondered with a fierce intensity whether it would not be possible to squeeze a few drops from the leaves; whether, if the worst came to the worst, the blood of our animals would relieve the pangs, or whether the salt-sweet flavor would send us mad. We imagined ourselves up to our necks in a cold stream; dining in a hotel so magnificent that the waiter would sneer at us if we asked for water; and turning the taps of a bath full on for the simple joy of seeing so much fluid in the same place.

As luck would have it we had scarcely been traveling an hour next day when Tiger-Man's sharp eyes spied a couple of large tortoises, black and crimson in squares, laboring along under the leaves. His face cleared at once.

"We are all right," he said. "These beasts never go far from water."

We pressed forward with joy, the tortoises in our

NATIVES IN TARIJA, WEARING THEIR CARNIVAL GARMENTS

saddle bags, and in a few minutes the nostrils of our mules began to quiver. We dropped the reins promptly and allowed the thirsty animals to lead us where they would, and in a very short space we were dipping our wrists in a deep muddy pool the color of chalk. In England it would have aged a sanitary inspector, but we splashed and grinned like a couple of school children.

"Now," said Tiger-Man, when we had drunk our fill, "one of us should go back to the last camp. We don't want them to feel as we did at the end of a long day."

"If I went," I said, "you could cook those tortoises and have a cheery meal ready when we arrive. I am not enough of a cook."

We both felt it a gross discourtesy to the tortoises which had indicated the presence of water, but there was nothing for it. We had no other food and our companions would have faced a terribly long day by the time they reached us. It was the first time that either of us had killed a tortoise, though we had both discouraged the Indians from splitting them alive down the seams with an ax. So we laid them on their backs in the sun, and when their heads appeared severed them with a stroke of the bayonet. The meat is good, if a little salt in flavor and the heart and liver are enormous in proportion to the animal.

Late that night, aided by Tiger-Man's torch and a great fire, I guided Urrio and Bee-Mason into camp. We bathed the backs of the animals with salt and water, but even in the kindly light of the fire it was obvious they could not stand another day. The wounds were raw and broken and the poor beasts shivered when we passed our hands along their spines.

Next morning at eight o'clock sharp the first sweat-bee came out of the forest. It was accompanied by several hundred thousand of its relatives, and they worked steadily till the stroke of seven, when they departed. This they did for three days with such devastating punctuality that we were literally able to set our watches by them. It was the same yellow and brown insect that I had found in Harris's camp, but a thousand times multiplied. It has no sting, it builds its nest like a wasp, and it makes a species of honey, which, so far as we observed, has no relation whatever to flowers, being a mixture of sweat and filth. It was not that they hurt us. They did not, but they irritated us past bearing by becoming entangled in our eyes and noses and hair, swooping upon our food, following it into our mouths, blocking the nozzle of Bee-Mason's lens, and filling the air till it was literally speckled. What they lived on as a rule I do not know. They cannot have seen a soul for close on four hundred years, game was scarce, and the amount of nourishment to be gained from a tortoise would seem to be limited.

There is no reason to prolong a description of the exploring part of our trip. After a while even the hardship became monotonous. For three whole weeks we never knew from one day to another whether we should lie down waterless to sleep, the animals became more and more weedy and travel stained, our food showed signs of giving out, because we had not counted on so much stoppage, and we were forced to limit ourselves to one meal of rice a day. As a consequence we became thin and hard, and the few birds that crossed our path died. One does not miss when one is hungry. Indeed, there came a time when the bodies of three macaws were greeted with a ravenous smacking of lips.

Then one evening we came straight out of the jungle into a clearing where a long-deserted shed drooped and pined in a corner. It was rickety and the roof had collapsed, but we almost embraced the worm-eaten pillars in our joy. At one end there was a nest of humming birds. The gaudy little creatures showed no fear, but continued to buzz their wings at a speed which defied sight, hovering like helicopters, and dipping their long bills into the horn-shaped flowers. The covered mud runways of termite ants straggled along the beams and down into the ground where their nest was, for these ants hate the light and will repair any damage to their passages with incredible rapidity.

We were within a day's ride of San Juan, and the prospect elated us, for our animals were nearly dead and we longed for the sight of running water. After dinner, as we lay smoking in our hammocks, we reviewed our period of exploration.

"We have accomplished less than most expeditions," said Urrio bitterly. "A few tortoises and mud-holes. What else?"

"Argentina was like this once," I answered. "As you know I can divine water, and there is plenty below the surface all the way along."

"In fifty years," said Tiger-Man, "this may well be populated."

Indeed, many worse places in the world are fully peopled. The nights are fine and cool, the soil prolific, and the insect pest may be eliminated through clearing. Argentina has scarcely a stream to her name. She is a land of windmill pumps which draw supplies from a layer of water forty feet deep. In half a century it is quite likely that Bolivia will be as prosperous.

During the night Urrio became bitterly cold. Several times he wandered over to the fire rather than wake us and ask for another blanket. It was a courtesy that cost him dear for he was badly bitten by the smallest of all ticks, known to Brazilians as *garapate du châo*, a tiny white insect that becomes pink as the blood enters its transparent body. The bite is so irritating that nobody can resist a scratch and it gave rise to a series of frightful sores which worried him for several weeks on end. At lunch-time that day we rode into San Juan from a quarter that surpised the natives.

WATERFALL NEAR TARIJA

CHAPTER XVII

SAN JUAN was a little more dead than Santo Corazón, a little more dusty and decayed. The church had four pillars and a palm roof, but the whitewash had fallen away, exposing the mean poverty of mud; and a family of vampire bats hung head downwards from the rafters. In one corner of the vast weed-grown square was a belfry, high, like a scaffold, and approached by a rickety ladder. On a beam were five great bells, bronze memories of a splendid past, suspended by the tough bark of rope weed. Every evening the *cacique* labored up to the platform and sent the deep notes booming across Green Hell. Whereupon a few glum women used to follow him into the shadows of the holy building and for a few minutes shrieked untuneful praise.

In the days of the Jesuits San Juan was a prosperous settlement several thousands strong, but now a bare four dozen spiritless people moving furtively about like maggots in a corpse. It is a pitiful sight, a living example of the danger and impertinence of tampering with the religion of a country. As missionaries the Jesuits were superb, probably the most powerful and enlightened that ever lived, but they were not prophets, and their expulsion left the Indians in the case of the man who drove out a devil without filling his place. I wish with all my heart that some prominent member of the Mission World could have been with us on our trip. He would have read in Señor René-Moreno's work the courage and resource and amazing self-denial of the Jesuits; he would have seen with his own eyes the utter death in life to which their departure subjected the Indians of Chiquitos. For there, as nowhere else in the world, is the whole grim comedy played out. A few bronze bells and a mumbled mixture of Christianity and savagery, both imperfectly understood, and a ghastly lethargy a thousand times more destructive to the soul than the worst form of barbarism—that is the result of conversion.

It is perhaps in the matter of marriage that the condition of Chiquitos is best illustrated. As a general rule, the more civilized the country the greater the precautions against unfaithfulness and immorality, both for the sake of the children and for the stability of property. But in a wild state these are not necessary. A savage faced with the misconduct of his women neither rails against God nor considers that she has transgressed the divine law. To him it is purely a personal matter, a flouting of his authority, an insult to himself, so he hits her over the head with quiet efficiency and passes to the next. For it is only in questions beyond his power, such as the regularity of rains or the fertility of his crop that he admits the presence of a vast controlling agency, potent to hurt or to favor.

Consequently, when a missionary with one eye on the white man's sins, introduces matrimony into a savage tribe, one of two things may happen. The natives may decide that it is a waste of time or an ill-judged impertinence, and eat the gentleman, or if he has taken the trouble to cure their diseases and improve the yield of their maize, they may submit to the ceremony, under the impression that it is a kind of ju-ju calculated to help them in life. The inner meaning simply does not occur to them.

They talked very freely with Urrio, partly in broken Spanish, but more frequently in their own tongue of Guarani and Quechua which he understood. They spoke of natural matters in a natural way without any prudery at all. And if a woman had lived with a man bearing him children she said so, and she neither lowered her eyes nor blushed with shame. She did, however, distinguish between *amigado,* or a state of nature, and that blessed condition achieved by the *cacique* mumbling a few words in Latin over her uncomprehending head; but without heat or emphasis. It was just a fact, of no importance. When they bathed in the stream they slipped off their one-piece garment and played like kittens, their wet, brown skins gleaming in the sunlight, but they did not consider our approach of sufficient moment either to cease their game or to scramble into their dresses. They just smiled amiably and went on playing.

The first evening of our arrival Tiger-Man and I went for a walk past the lemon-trees planted by the Jesuits. We had just cleared the outskirts of the village when we heard a child's scream. Once it rose on the still air, and once again, and then it stopped, abruptly, with a little gurgle. We thought that a tiger had sought its prey, and broke into a run, our pistols drawn and cocked, but as we rounded a large tree we came upon a sight which halted us in our tracks. A girl of about twelve years of age was lying on her back upon the ground, held flat by a stout woman in a blue frock. Another woman knelt at her head and had just inserted a thick stick into her mouth. The child wriggled and coughed, but her strength was no match for that of her captors and she lay still, her dark frightened eyes bearing witness to her protest. From the fold of her dress the second woman drew a file of the kind sold by traveling Turks and held it over the girl's face. At the sight all her struggles broke out again, but died down quickly as her tormentor thrust a heavy hand against her chest. I thought that a murder was about to take place before our eyes, and was not at all reassured by the bright smile with which we were greeted. But Tiger-Man held my arm. He explained that it was a tribal custom to file the teeth of the women into sharp edges, like cat's teeth, and that the gruesome sight we had blundered into was only a very natural protest on the part of the child. I then noticed that the teeth of the women were pointed and filed away. They were black and decayed from exposure of the nerves and the consumption of molasses. I knew now how it was done. I turned away quickly for there was a wild terror in the child's face that was not pleasant to watch.

The inhabitants in San Juan soon exhibited their character. There were chickens and calves and maize and sugar-cane in plenty, yet they professed a bland ignorance of our needs. In full view of this plethora of food Urrio asked to be allowed to buy some, but it was the old story of money in a wild place, and not even our beads tempted them. Driven back on our resources we tried the gramophone. The natives were frankly pleased, but not enough to trade us food. Urrio questioned them.

"Have you calves?"

"No."

"Chickens?"

"No."

"Cakes, eggs or maize?"

"No."

"Mandiocre, molasses, cheese or sugar-cane?"

"No."

"Then what do you eat? Air?"

"Yes."

That finished Urrio and he turned hopelessly to Tiger-Man, who drew his rifle and pointed to a calf that plucked the weeds in the square.

"You said there were no animals in the town, old woman?"

"That is so," mumbled a withered hag fluttering her eyes from him to the calf and back.

"Then it doesn't matter if my gun barks at what appears to be a calf?"

With a shriek and a swirl of skirts she bounded from her haunches and drove the beast out of danger. Later in the day we shot it for we were well-nigh starving, and respect for property dies quickly in the waste portions of the world. Nevertheless, inhospitable though it was, we intended to spend a week in San Juan so as to give our animals time to recover. But a walk after supper changed our plans. It was brilliant moonlight, and Tiger-Man and I strode over to the horse lines with a bucket of salt and water for their backs. Suddenly, as we drew near something rose from Bee-Mason's horse with a swirl of leathery wings, and a large black shape flung away across the moon.

"Good God," said Tiger-Man. "Vampires."

We inspected the damage by the light of Tiger-Man's torch, and we were appalled to see a thick sluggish stream of blood flowing down the white flanks of the horse. It was in a bad way to begin with, but now its bones stood out so that one could rattle a stick across its ribs, and its eyes were so tired that all expression had vanished from them. We staunched the blood with salt, but the beast was too far gone even to resent the sting. Next morning it was nearly dead. Obviously the vampires had returned in force, for it was not the only sufferer. Four of the mules had dried runnels of blood plastered over their bodies, but Bee-Mason's animal almost made us cry. Its haunches had fallen in, it dragged its feet as if it were numb, and a pair of dull eyes looked out from the bottom of what appeared to be deep wells. Clearly it was dying, and we hastened its end with a merciful shot.

We were now in a rather serious position. It was impossible to replace the dead horse, for the villagers did not possess such a thing. The backs of the remainder were raw and bleeding, but we did not dare stay for fear of another casualty. And fifty miles lay between us and the main Puerto Saurez–Santa Cruz road at San José. Now fifty miles in a motor-car means something over an hour and a half, but with maimed animals in Bolivia it means a little more than four days; and Tiger-Man, who is no mean judge, was openly pessimistic as to the chances of the animals lasting the distance. From the natives we learned that vampires abounded all the way, which meant four days of hot travel and four nights of blood letting. Could we do it? Obviously not if we tarried, so we set out at once.

Over those four days I prefer to draw a veil. Even at this distance a haze of red-hot air seems to rise from the ground and cover our automatic movements with a dream-like miasma. For the most part we walked so as to change the packs on to the riding animals, but one day we started before it was light and rode on in the hope of making the next waterhole before the heat became unbearable. Somehow or other we wandered from the path and found ourselves in a waste of low bush which stretched away to the horizon, and which all looked the same. For hours we wandered steering roughly westwards and becoming more and more doubtful of our ability to find water, when we happened on a scene which did nothing to raise our spirits.

Tied to a tree by thick cord was the skeleton of a donkey, the halter hard and taut with the heat, standing rigid over the skull. The bones were white and unbroken, though scratched by the beaks of vultures. Nearby was the body of a man long since picked bare, with little tatters of dark cloth lying among the wreckage. He lay in an attitude of despair, with one arm doubled under his head as though he wished to die with his back to the sun which had killed him. By his side were two large packs, open for the world to see, filled with pitiful gimcrack ornaments and cheap jewelry. Silently we drew near.

"A Turk," said Tiger-Man briefly. "A poor, wandering huckster of a Turk who died from lack of water."

We could picture the burning agony of his last few hours, the frenzied search for a drink through that damnable low scrub, every tree of which looked familiar. Then, the hot fury ended, nerves mercifully be-

PANORAMIC VIEW OF THE ANDES

numbed, he hitched his donkey to a tree, buried his face in his arm, and died. Then came the vultures, black and naked as to the neck.

The irony of the matter was borne in on us a little later. Though off the track he was only an hour away from a farm-house. Having no picks ourselves, we asked the farmer to bury him.

Three days afterwards, when the sun was sinking in the heavens, we came straight out of the forest into San José, the old Jesuit capital of Chiquitos, where a magnificent cathedral, red and castellated, glowed like a furnace on one side of the great square.

CHAPTER XVIII

IF ever San José de Chiquitos becomes fashionable—which God forbid—the palm-trees in the great square will shake at the sound of Americans bidding for the cathedral. I have seen my share of historical buildings in the way that they should be seen, silently, on days when the cheerful chatter of tourists does not goad the echoes to rebuke. I have wandered, quite alone, when dusk was falling, through the grim Medici fortress of the Bargello. I have lingered with an ancient monk in the room of that Carthusian monastery where an outraged Pope was imprisoned by Napoleon. I have spent a winter in a pre-conquest Austrian castle among yellow parchment books where the ancestors of my host stared down from time-darkened canvases. Above all I have savored the electrical antiquity that surrounds the bronze guardians of Maximilian II's tomb in the Silver Chapel at Innsbruck. But I have never felt such a blaze of pure light beating upon time as on that first day in San José.

The place drips history. It is the original Santa Cruz de la Sierra, the haven which Nuflo de Chavez created after his terrible journey through the forest.

GREEN HELL

To it, in 1694, came the Jesuit Arce, and here the spiritual conquest of Chiquitos began. The cathedral was built in 1748 when Jesuit rule was at its height, when the Indians were already in thrall, and the province bade fair to be the nucleus of a vast agricultural state, spreading southwards to Paraguay and northwards to the Amazon. The cathedral itself is a dream crystallized in stone, an everlasting memorial to the Jesuit power in South America. Every stone is an achievement, every bell a just source of pride. And it may well be that the very magnificence of their building laid the foundation of that suspicion which was to end in their expulsion.

On that first morning in San José I took a seat in the nave and surrendered myself to the luxury of historical imagination. I saw the black-coated fathers, keen-faced and vigilant, directing a stream of sweating natives from the quarries two leagues away. On their lips were cheerful words of encouragement, phrased in the language of the scriptures, and in their eyes a quiet triumph as the walls mounted stone by stone. Their genius was such that to the Indians it was not a matter of compulsion, but a labor of love, a thank-offering to the new God who had cured their ills and improved the maize crops. Indeed, there was a fierceness in their devotion not unlike that of the Incas, for where these warlike tribesmen loved they did it whole-heartedly with a passion for service. And the walls grew. A turret at each corner, and a belfry between the southern turret and the main façade, with covered cloisters to fill the spaces and give shade to the fathers under the blazing sun. At the top of the battlements above the great west door a six-pointed star and a gigantic I.H.S. equalized the Moorish influence of the structure, and proclaimed it for Christianity.

Meanwhile the bells were approaching, hung on rude bullock-wagons, lurching and pitching up the forest track from Laguna Cacerés, where Puerto Saurez now stands, the nearest point to the Paraguay River and Asuncion. Shining and lustrous, straight from a Spanish foundry, they swung from the cart beams, while the great clappers, bound in rough cotton, boomed muffled and ghostly on the lonely road. And the Indians who had received the precious cargo from the river vessel sat round them at night when the oxen grazed in the forest and the bells were still. Finally the last scene when, with cords made from twisted ropeweed they lugged them up the tower of the belfry, and hung them on a *quebracho* beam that they might send send their hollow cry across the jungle that all the world might know that Father Miguel was about to perform a Vespers.

In those days the Indians had life and their wives bore them male children, and they were able to sink their individualities in a happy sea of religion. They had an ideal and lived up to it. The cathedral stood for a sign that they had worked personally to the glory of God. Even now, low though the candle burns in the socket, they are not irreclaimable. A strong force of Jesuits at work in the east as the Franciscans are in the west would send the flame soaring once more, and Chiquitos would have peace.

After a while I bestirred myself and explored the lofty, beam-supported building that was so rich in past life. A series of round, white-washed pillars bounded the main aisle on either hand. At the foot of each were small, rough-hewn, bodiless cherubim, wings outspread over grave, old faces, the red and blue coloring faded with time. They were made from *quebracho* wood, and the insects of the country had eaten round holes in the back, though the faces were perfect. Near the altar, on the left-hand side, sat St. Peter, a smooth-faced, black-bearded, noncommittal old man, a bunch of wooden keys dangling from a stiff wrist. He was dressed in fine brocade, purple and scarlet and white, and a long skirt fell straight to his ankles, while on his head was a cotton cap like a chef's. Two curious winged figures, obviously of native workmanship, faced one another across the aisle. They were of opposite sexes, and seemed oddly in keeping with the legend of the Amazons, for a man clad in knickerbockers and an opera cloak held a silver fish in his hand, and his consort, a fiery, war-like wench with a blood-thirsty expression, waved a sword at him. In the vestry were images on wheels like gigantic nursery toys, designed to be dragged through the streets on feast-days. A large tableau of the flight into Egypt, pathetically crude, showed the Virgin on a solemn wooden donkey and St. Joseph standing resignedly by. Other and lesser saints languished in corners.

I was at once struck by the dearth of silver vessels in the cathedral, and on inquiry plunged straight into that wonderful old legend that goes so far to prove that faith may remove mountains, hard physical mountains with trees on them. It is an amazing legend, so subtly savage and ironical, yet withal so romantic, that it might have been invented by a Calvinist on his honeymoon; and it concerns buried treasure. Moreover, with a wild, unconscious gaiety worthy of Rabelais it links the Pirates with the Jesuits in a cheerful conspiracy to benefit posterity. I have nothing to say of piratical treasure. It has happened before and will happen again, that thieves fall out and conceal the booty; but to rank the Jesuits in the same category reveals an ignorance of history that is as profound as it is optimistic. The Society of Jesus was an army, a highly-trained, rigidly-disciplined army of brilliant men. The newest-joined private had served a seven years' apprenticeship to learning, and was on the high-road to becoming a shrewd man of the world. When the fathers were recalled from South America they undoubtedly hid their treasures, but they were nevertheless responsible to their superior officers for a full inventory and a map of the place of hiding. They were not promiscuous philanthropists, and the thought of allowing their sacred vessels to fall into alien hands would have filled them with a blazing heat of horror not far removed from fanaticism.

A bare sixty years passed between the expulsion of the Jesuits and the end of the Spanish rule. During that time it is utterly inconceivable that they should have lost the documents relating to so much latent wealth. If, as company promoters and gullible adventurers would have us believe, the Bolivian hills are stiff with treasure, the Jesuits are *ipso facto* proved to be incompetent nincompoops. Yet I venture to think that each new treasure-hunt will fail in turn, and that the faith which in sober reality has removed mountains will find little therein beyond empty caves. Personally, I prefer to believe that somewhere about 1840 an inconspicuous little band of devotees crossed from Spain to South America in a specially chartered vessel, combed out the hiding places and returned whence they had come.

However that may be, there was a man in San José who disagreed with me.

"Somewhere quite close," he said, his eyes aflame with greed, "the Jesuits buried their treasure. Their expulsion was so sudden that they had no time to go far."

In this I knew he erred, because the Governor of Santa Cruz had been unable to keep the secret from the

Archbishop, but I was drinking his *chicha* and held my peace.

"It is a dangerous job, looking for it," he continued. "At the first sign the Indians rise and massacre those who seek."

This was obviously a perversion of a perfectly true story that the Quechua Indians discourage searchers after the Inca treasure.

"If only I could divine for water," said our avaricious friend, "I might be able to do something."

Urrio chose his moment and winked at me.

"Here's your man," he said. "His rod does the most amazing things."

"Can you divine metals?"

The question came like a bullet.

I told him I had never tried.

"The Government would be most grateful if you could restore the plate to the cathedral."

With an effort he controlled his feelings and waited for me to speak. The tip of his tongue peeped from between his lips and crept backwards and forwards stealthily, while in his eyes was a look which, in connection with sacred matters, was not pleasant to see. Now that morning I had carried out my practice of walking about the country-side with a forked twig so as to divine the water system of the place, and I fancied I could give the gentleman something to think about.

"The moon is up by nine," I said. "Come with me then and I will show you."

There was no mistaking the lust in his face as he said good-by.

There was no cinema in San José, and our little company was badly in need of entertainment, so I told them to join me after dinner for a bit of fun. We buckled on our revolvers and contrived to look incredibly fierce and mysterious, and when the treasure-hunter, unable to contain himself, arrived three quarters of an hour early, we talked of irritatingly mundane matters till the moon was high in the sky. Then, in the manner of stage conspirators, we stole across the square. As an actor Urrio was perfect, getting exactly the right emphasis into his rôle of urbane villain, and Bee-Mason over-acted just enough to be noticeable; but I thought Tiger-Man was going to wreck the whole show. At intervals he made a sharp whistling sound between his teeth, halted us in our tracks, whispered that he knew we were being watched and ostentatiously drew his revolver. The moon was quite brilliant enough for the sweat to be visible on the treasure-hunter's face.

Then began a scene so farcical that the laughter hammered at my ribs in a wild desire to get out. A solemn little procession formed up in the shadow of the cathedral and in deadly silence began to move southwards along the wall. The night was of that almost painful stillness when a foot kicking against a stone sounds like a thunder-storm, and a good many feet were surreptitiously kicked against stones so as to heighten the tension in the mind of our fat friend. He walked quite close to me with little shuffling paces and an anxious expression as he kept his eyes on the point of the slender forked stick which I held in my hand. For a while nothing happened, and then just opposite the great west door the twig snapped up in my face. A shrill squawk of excitement, sternly suppressed by Tiger-Man, broke from his throat, and, brushing aside the stick, he shook me warmly by the hand. Urrio's face was a model of diplomatic congratulation, but Bee-Mason and Tiger-Man had to turn away lest they should disgrace themselves.

"Wait a minute," I said. "It may be water, you know."

His face fell a yard, and when I conclusively proved that in fact a strong stream flowed all the way down under the main aisle and out across the square, he nearly wept. Gloomy and restless we started again and skirted the walls till we came to the middle of the east face where the water flowed in from the forest under the altar. Once again the twig snapped up, once again the little man bubbled over with joy, once again I damped his ardor. When we had made the full circuit I turned to him.

"I am afraid I have been no use to the Government, señor."

He seized my arm.

"Try just once through the forest."

I looked at his bloated form and his greedy little face, and made up my mind.

"Very well, follow me."

For twenty minutes I led him through the forest and alternately roused and damped his feelings, until we came to a huge tree whose roots stretched far and wide in a great bony circle. There was water, plenty of it, at about eight meters depth, and the rod was dancing about like a wild thing.

"There is something here," I said, "probably water. But I have had no experience of metals, and I don't know how they react. Still if you think it worth while we might come back to-morrow and do a bit of digging —for the Government."

His eyes narrowed at that, and with ill-concealed impatience he bundled us back to our lodgings. We gave him an hour's grace, and then stealthily we crept through the wood, while the moon made fantastic, streaky patterns among the leaves. In a few minutes an orgy of sound enveloped us, drowning our footsteps in a tearing and crashing of boughs. Still more stealthily we approached, groping and ducking through the undergrowth until we saw him. He was buried to the depth of his fat little knees, the long blade of his pick rose and fell in a polished arc of light, and from time to time he seized a shovel and sent a cloud of rubble rattling over his shoulder. We watched him from the shadows with real pleasure. He was glistening. It was enough.

It was in San José that we first came into contact with a magnificent body of men, the Bolivian Air Force. Theirs is perhaps the hardest and most trying task of any Air Force in the world. Their base is on the bitter, barren plateau of the Andes above La Paz—a veritable condor's nest, for they land at roughly the height of Mont Blanc. A few hours flight to the east and they are over Green Hell, a beautiful, rich, mountainous carpet of death whence there is no escape should the engine fail. Between Puerto Saurez and Santa Cruz stretched five hundred miles of forest and, in all these terrible leagues there are only two landing grounds. In terms of English scenery this means that whenever an airman starts his course in the east of Bolivia he is forced to fly the distance between London and York without the possibility of landing alive if his engine fails him. In addition to the grave dangers of death each man has to face the peculiarities of the climate. Few countries have quite the Bolivian range within so short a space. At ten o'clock one morning a man leaves La Paz perhaps in a snow-storm, at any rate in a rarefied atmosphere, where the minimum exertion brings the maximum loss of breath. By noon he is in Santa Cruz with the thermometer anywhere between 90 and 105 in the shade, in a land of palm-trees and oranges and mosquitoes. By seven o'clock that night he may arrive in Corumbá where the limestone makes the night foul with its sticky breath.

The first Bolivian pilot who came our way was a certain Captain Jordan, and he passed over San José at a great height. Suddenly, as we watched the dying silver speck speeding into the distance it appeared to fall, and a minute later tore back on its course. Even at that range there was a distinct break in the rhythmical noise of the engine. As it came nearer every Indian in the place stopped being idle and ran rapidly along the forest path to the aërodrome. A few minutes later we rescued Jordan from the friendly, gaudily-dressed crowd of loafers, and bore him off for a gramophone record and a drink.

His story was one of the most pathetic I have ever heard. Long distance flights were very much in fashion in South America, and Bolivia was easily leading the way. Major Santalla had just flown from La Paz to Buenos Aires, and Jordan, as the second best pilot in the Air Force, was asked to take his machine from La Paz to Rio de Janeiro, a pioneer flight of an importance little short of flying the Atlantic, since it might open up a passenger service that would bring the Atlantic Ocean ten days nearer to the Andes. Jordan had passed the most dangerous portion of his flight. He had landed in Puerto Saurez with the Bolivian part of Green Hell behind him, when the Brazilian Ambassador put his foot down flat. He wanted no blood shed of the United States in Brazil. Jordan, remembering the reputation of Matto Grosso, felt murderous. Why should not he shed his own blood if he wished to? However, he was not a civilian and he had to obey.

He dangled his legs over the edge of my hammock, and though he said little we understood his bitterness and the blasphemous impotence to which a little red tape may reduce a man of spirit.

We cheered him as best we could until, three days later, Santalla came to look for him. Santalla was accompanied by Major Le Maître, the famous French ace who, in 1925, flew with Pelletier d'Oissy from Paris to Dakar, and who is now in charge of the Bolivian Air Force. With them came an all-steel Junker monoplane of the one-engine type, a beautiful shining machine well-suited to that kind of work. Bolivia is in a curious state of development. Between the forests of the east and the plateaux of the west there are no motor roads. From Cochabamba to Santa Cruz there is a mule track of fearsome steepness which rises and falls thousands of feet at a time in a series of mountainous waves, and which takes ten days of hard labor to pass. It may, on the other hand, be flown in a couple of hours. Between the two there is nothing.

For the Junker machine there is nothing but praise. It is a German, run by German pilots, and the Bolivian Government is very deeply interested in its development. Indeed, they have the controlling shares and in time of war may call on six large bombers of faultless design to supplement the other army machines. No other state in South America can say as much.

Two days later Jordan smashed his machine to pieces on returning to the landing ground from a trial flight. The under-carriage caught in the last line of trees and was torn bodily away. Jordan and his mechanic, however, climbed down the trees to safety.

Never, since the days of the rubber boom when San José was alive, had such excitement been felt. Three aëroplanes, two ranged neatly under the forest wall, the other hanging in shreds from the branches, tickled the bored fancy of the inhabitants. Nor did our expedition detract from the shimmering glamour that hung over the place. Every day the landing-ground was packed. A gaily be-shawled, silent, ecstatic throng surged out of the woods and surrounded the machines. Inquisitive women and open-mouthed, vacuous boys submerged Bee-Mason when he wished to film the aviators and led to a wordy warfare which had to be settled by the local policeman. When we returned to our lodgings we were besieged by a crowd of idlers only too pleased to find something with which they could while away the time.

I did not envy the life of the Chiquitano Indian. He is perpetually engaged in the bloodiest of all battles, the war with the years. Sometimes he manages to kill an hour or two, but the vast majority of hours kill him, turn him from the bright-faced baby into a lolling, useless man, a burden to himself and a nonentity to his women, a bored lover, an uninterested father, an old, bleary-eyed, sodden skeleton, nodding away the weeks in an endless welter of idleness. His women are more to be envied, for they have the burden of keeping him, and they grow sleek with good living and the procreation of children. Their backs are straight and their skins clear, and they wear their highly-colored garments with the air of those who earn them.

May the Jesuits come back to Chiquitos and once again sing Mass in the cathedral of San José!

It was perhaps natural that, having emerged from the forest on to the main Puerto Saurez–Santa Cruz road, we should think that our troubles were ended. In actual fact nothing could have been further from the truth, for, during the next three weeks, we suffered infinitely more and peered closer into the eyes of death than we did in all the unmapped leagues of Nuflo de Chavez's course. A few days before we started from San José a man came to us with a warning.

"The Indians are out, señores. Last night they raided a farmstead two leagues from here and beat a man and his wife and child to death. You should take care. They are in large enough numbers to invade San José itself."

Tiger-Man is used to the Indian of the river, the Guarayos, Chamacocos, Caduveos, and Bororos, and was inclined to take the matter lightly.

"They were hungry, poor devils, and found food easy to hand. You yourself would kill if you were as wild as they and as famished. What they want is a missionary."

"One missionary would not feed hundreds," said the man with a wry smile. "How are your animals?"

"Pretty well played out," said Urrio. "Those vampires have nearly killed them, but I daresay we shall manage to make Santa Cruz."

Our friend jumped up.

"You must do nothing of the sort, señores. Pardon my heat, but it would be sheer madness. Two hundred miles lie between you and your goal, and a nastier stretch of road I have never seen. Even the Amazon is more friendly. Gentlemen, there is a little bug, so small that you can scarcely see him, so numerous that he obscures the sun, so poisonous that his bite is like fire. Unless you have mosquito nets without any holes whatsoever you will not sleep when he is at hand. Neither will your animals. I implore you to send two of your men back to Gaiba with the worst of the horses, keep enough mules for yourselves, and send the rest by ox-wagon."

Urrio turned to Tiger-Man, who fingered his beard before answering.

"If I come to a new place," he said with that simplicity and shrewd clearness of thought which marked him, "and a little child tells me of snakes in a certain wood, I look carefully before seating myself."

"Right," said Urrio. "I agree. Tiburcio and Cosmé shall return; Suarez and Adolfo shall come with us. I will look for an ox-wagon this evening."

Bee-Mason rose abruptly.

"We must photograph the cathedral," said he.

Now it was a point of honor with Tiger-Man that he should never take a picture of a cloudless sky. He was an artist in photography with an artist's clear sight and restless seeking after the most effective angle for a study, and he hated sham. He was perfectly aware of those ingenious mounts which stamp clouds on to a print, but he considered them neither artistic nor honest, and he vastly preferred to wait a week, a fortnight, a month for a good rich, creamy bank of white clouds, riding like galleons with sails full-bellied to the wind against a background of pale blue sky. Like all artists he had his tribulations, especially in the matter of churches, for the tropics are not helpful in this matter. As a general rule clouds spring up at three o'clock in the afternoon when the sun is not far enough to the west to throw a good light on to the main entrance, for here as elsewhere the buildings are perfectly orientated. Just about this time, however, the clouds took to arriving in the morning, and the sun shining directly into the eye of the lens irritated Bee-Mason beyond bearing.

"It's those damned Jesuits," he stormed. "No imagination whatever. Why can't they face their churches the other way? It's very little further to Jerusalem across the Pacific."

CHAPTER XIX

It is an open question whether a powerful, progressive state is justified in stripping savages of their lands for the sake of an outlet for its own enterprise. On the whole, I suppose that it is. T'gers have mauled cattle since they first grew teeth, and minorities are only sacred when three or four powers desire them. It is a law of nature affirmed and sealed by the hand of Green Hell herself.

When Boadicea reigned in the east of England her tribesmen had much the same outlook on life as the Indians of South America at the time of the Conquistadores; always excepting the Incas of Peru. They had mud and wattle dwellings which they regarded as home, and were perfectly content to live on their bows and arrows without any great hankering after the intellectual life of a race of brutal men in Italy. Their fat, brown babies rolled in the dust before the huts and ran howling for comfort when they sat on a thorn. Their gods were natural and familiar, and when the lightning occasionally flashed his displeasure or the moon hid her face, they bowed their heads and remembered their sins. When they killed a notorious boar they feasted and danced and got drunk like any other healthy savages; and were supremely happy.

Into this woodland scene came the Romans who were not particularly cruel or vicious but were just human and lustful after the rigors of a long campaign. They were bored with marching through jungle and wanted some fun, so they raped the women and finished the drink and stole the hides off the warriors' backs as souvenirs for their wives in Italy. After their playful custom they killed the chief of the tribe and whipped his wife and daughters, and, in general, caused so much resentment that the business of educating their new subjects was put back a good two centuries. One outrage alone was spared, that last impertinence. They did not force those simple souls to worship either Mars or Venus or Jupiter. Possibly they were too wise, knowing the limitation of savage humor.

It was, perhaps, unfortunate that the Conquistadores should have conquered first of all the Incas of Peru. A clear conscience is necessary in matters of rapine, and the end is held to justify the means when, by sword and stake, a people is saved from barbarism for the clear water of learning to be poured down its throat. In the light of history it was not the Incas who needed saving but the Spaniards. The old Peruvian Government was as near perfect as makes no matter in a wicked world, and the great Inca rulers held sway over a vast nation where adultery was unknown and where private property was never kept under lock and bar because most

WATERFALL NEAR TARIJA

men were honest. Hundreds of thousands of Indians worked happily in the fields, old age was respected, idleness was punished by prison. And since the smell of earth is more pleasant than the dank stench of a dungeon, the land became rich in corn. Gold and silver were quarried in the hills round Cuzco, not for the glory of the Incas themselves, but that the Temple of the Sun might be worthy of the great health-giving god who gave his rays so freely to his people.

It must be admitted that the Spaniards, travel-stained and feverish, their eyes bleared by the lust for gold, cut a sorry figure beside the courteous and dignified presence of the Inca. Morally there was no comparison, as is seen in the pathetic written confession of a common soldier on his death-bed, who deplored the lust and terrorism of himself and his companions in the face of such a model civilization. The Church, too, was wonderfully unwise in its dealings with the natives. Its champions, in the fanaticism of their conduct, laid the foundation of the massacres of priests which continued until 1882. There was no tact in their approach, no humanity, and less than no imagination. So convinced were they that their own religion was right that it never occurred to them that the Incas might have views of their own. They came, bearing the message of a God of Peace, with a sword in one hand and a faggot in the other, and held the peaceful man by the throat that he might acknowledge the supreme charity of their Saviour. Now, this was asking rather much of the Inca, who, although civilized himself, was not as civilized as that. His brain failed to grasp the niceties of religious argument. Muttering the Bolivian word for hypocrites he retired into a corner, and with a shrug of his royal shoulders settled down to meditation. Shrieking that the infidel had blasphemed against God the priests demanded vengeance. Even the military might have seen the irony of the position if there had not been a strategic side to the matter. So long as the Inca lived he was a possible rallying point of the tribesmen, so, with a heavy heart, the leaders of the army decreed that he should die. He took the sentence unmoved. It had happened before and it would happen again. Leaders must expect such treatment. Enough. Get on with the business. But the priests, burning with zeal, irritated his last hours by asking him to become a Christian. A little wearily, but with his usual courtesy, he inquired how it would help him. He was told that the Christian God was a good, kind God, who would see to it that he was strangled and so be spared the tortures of the stake. Indians are not much given to laughter, but it may be supposed that Atahualpa concealed a smile as, with more prudence than conviction, he suffered himself to be baptized.

The news of his death swept like a flame through corn from one end of South America to another. Other tribes, less civilized and courteous, old enemies of his, made an end of the gentle religion which covered the deeds of the sword in a black cloud of hypocrisy. They made a note of the signs by which such men might be known. Black-coated men with a gold cross on their bosoms and a string of beads round their waists, thin-faced men with eyes of fire and a bald patch on their heads. And they remembered.

Those who remembered the best and the longest were the Chiriguanos, a fine, war-like race who lived in the foothills of the Andes, and smiled nastily whenever Christianity was mentioned. In this they were unfair, justifiably so it is true, for the fathers who followed the Conquistadores, men who arrived fifty years after Pizarro's death, had the welfare of the natives at heart and tried to found missions in their territory. After the gold-lust, conversion. But in many cases it was too late. Atahualpa's death was a warning, a message of distrust, and the missions between Tarija and Santa Cruz de la Sierra were periodically swept free of priests.

Dominican, Augustine, Franciscan, even Jesuit, penetrated into their fastnesses and returned discouraged. Savage men in full war paint laughed contemptuously in their reverend faces and pointed derisively to the vast bulwark of the Andes where Atahualpa died. One of the Jesuit fathers, after an expedition in which he had barely escaped with his life, was forced to admit: "Humanly speaking there is no hope whatever of the conversion of the Chiriguanos, *Manus Domini non est abbreviata;* but they will sooner allow themselves to be cut in pieces than become Christian, so great is the horror they have for this name." If the Jesuits failed, none could succeed, and the Chiriguanos were left to themselves. It was only in Mojos and Chiquitos, in the district from Santo Corazón northwards to the Amazon that the Jesuits were successful. Here the horror of the tragedy was blurred and indistinct, and the fathers were able by their devotion to convince the natives that they meant them well. Here, indeed, was the teaching of Christ personified, purged from the influence of gold and the lusts of a conquering army.

Eastward from the Chiriguanos, along the river Pilcomayo, in the terrible swamps and thickets of the Chaco, lived the Tobas. They were even more savage and untamed than their neighbors, and Christianity has barely touched them to this day. D'Orbigny describes them as being: "robust with large legs, broad shoulders, full chests, and body not slender. Their features resemble those of the Charruas, a broad but not full face, a projecting forehead, the nose is broadened by wide nostrils and in old age they have pronounced cheekbones, the mouth is large and the teeth splendid. They have small ears and eyes, the latter sometimes *bridés* at the external corners. The hair, when not plucked out, is like that of all the American aborigines. Altogether their features are most serious, and accord perfectly with the taciturnity of the man." Tiger-Man gave it as his considered opinion that he would rather go down the Amazon alone than take an expedition through the southern Toba region of the Chaco. In the 1890's a French expedition set out from the west of Bolivia and tried to force its way to the Paraguay River. One evening they came to a Toba village and, deceived by the false charm of their hosts, they joined a feast and kept no watch. During the night they were all killed, with the exception of a young boy who escaped and brought the news to Tarija. The very next year the identical thing happened. A Bolivian colonel took some men into Toba territory, and he too was deceived. One man alone escaped. And the Tobas to this day remain the most lawless tribe in all that fearful region.

Personally, my sympathies are all with the Indian in his fight against extinction. When the hardships of a conquest are not softened by a very sane and sympathetic Government the savage dies. Traders cheat him, hunters frighten his game, farmers force him to work, and, by making him live in civilized surroundings, spoil his splendid physique. White men introduce him to wasting diseases which he never knew, his daughters bear a despised mixed race with the vices of both, and, his hunting stopped, he has no need for a clear eye, and so he soaks himself in spirits till his flesh wastes away. He may be seen all over South America, flabby, sodden, blear-eyed, his children skinny and diseased, himself lost in a civilization that he does not understand, and which helps him not at all. Sooner or later he will pass, his magnificent savagery will die, and South America from Cape Horn to Maracaibo will know him no more. It has happened in Canada; it has happened in the United States. Argentina has almost thrown off what she calls the native yoke. Only the forests of the Chaco, vast and unburnable because of the hard wood, have prevented the Tobas and the Chiriguano from wasting unto death.

And now the movemets of Bolivian troops on the Pilcomayo have sent large numbers of these Tobas to prey on the main caravan route between Puerto Saurez and Santa Cruz. We met them ourselves, and I do not envy the authorities their task of uprooting the evil.

CHAPTER XX

WE had ridden scarcely a league from San José when the heavens began to mutter and a huge cloud rose out of the north. It reared up, menacing and majestic, with the black and purple coloring of a bruise, and it stooped over Green Hell as an overhanging cliff stoops over the sea. All nature knew what was coming. Lizards, dry and automatic as hinged toys, scuttled across the path. Parrots chattered like mad things, telling their children of the fury they were too young to know.

Suddenly it came, a soft, rushing sigh, advancing swiftly out of the heaviness of the cloud. The trees heard it and passed it on, bowing their branches with time-serving humility. The parrots heard it and screamed off down-wind, hardy and optimistic, like boys trying to race a train. As it drew nearer, the softness vanished, and a metallic note, steep and shrill and ominous, whistled through the forest. It was as though a great wall of sound, inevitable as a tidal wave, were bearing down on us. In another moment we were overwhelmed, gasping, and, as our shirts bellied with the force of the wind, the lightning broke and a jagged monstrosity of flame split the cloud to pieces. Almost simultaneously a crashing gong of thunder blackened the air.

It was my first experience of a tropical storm, and I was wet through before I recovered from the savage beauty of the sky. As I struggled with my rain coat I had the humiliation of seeing Tiger-Man dimly through the solid veil of rain, high and dry in the saddle. At the first quick sigh of wind he had slipped from his mule and, no longer so impressionable to such scenes, had preferred to witness the grandeur in comfort. As for me, I confess that I lose my sense of realities when anything exciting happens, and my mind becomes drugged with new experience—a fact which nearly cost me my life in the later stages of the expedition. I become so exalted with describing the event to myself, with picking the exact phrase, that consciousness of danger only arrives when it is too late.

I had often read of the reverence paid by natives to the majesty of the elements, but the justice of such a worship had never occurred to me. Now, amid the artillery of nature, I found myself in the center of a vital fact, the supreme difficulty that must face every missionary, noise. For how can a savage man grasp the idea that there may be something vastly more powerful, vastly more beneficent than the bewildering bombardment of a storm? What courage, what persistence, above all what imagination must a missionary use to convince a creature little higher than an animal of the power of a still, small voice? Quiet strength means nothing to an Indian. A tiger roars over his meal as soon as the stalk is finished. A tree broken by the wind is not silent in its fall. The wind itself sobs and moans and howls as it lashes through the jungle, and it is only when the virtue is gone out of it that it is silent. Yet the Jesuits in Chiquitos overcame the obstacle. They succeeded in explaining that the volleying uproar of the thunder was as nothing compared with the concentrated power of a foreigner who died nailed to a tree, and his mother who watched the cruelty in silence. Nevertheless generations must have passed before the Indians lost their doubts, and November with its mutterings must have been a trying month for the missionaries who could never have known when their latest converts would rush into the forest and throw themselves on the ground in an ecstasy of noise worship.

Green Hell has a quick temper, but her moods are soon over. In half an hour the storm had passed and the sun was busy soaking moisture from the puddles. The ox-cart, a large wooden affair with eight-foot wheels, creaked and groaned over the uneven ground. The rawhide roofing, stretched tight over a framework in the shape of a half-loop, smoked as the water evaporated. So did the eight sturdy oxen which lumbered along to the tune of whip and native blasphemy. All that day we rumbled westwards, alternately soaked and baked, and at ten o'clock in the moonlight came on to the first of the Government rest-houses called *fortins*, where a retired soldier kept guard. There is a regular chain of these huts spaced at eight-league intervals from the Paraguay river to Santa Cruz, and the duties are so terrible that a large bribe of land is needed to keep them occupied. At first sight the duties look easy enough, only a year's residence and a walk to the next *fortin* if a traveler should desire armed company, but a year on this route would drive most men out of their minds. For the whole caravan track to the interior is plagued and made abominable by a tiny fly, surnamed *ihenni*. It is black and prolific, and its bite is like fire. There is not a single moment from day's end to day's end when it is not present in vast, hovering, blood-sucking clouds. At night it takes no rest, and if a man can manage to sit tight for three consecutive minutes he must have a hide like an elephant. Not long ago a German and an American started to walk from Puerto Saurez to Santa Cruz, and they died on the way—from lack of sleep.

Into this first hell of unrest we rode all unsuspecting at ten o'clock of a moonlit night after eighteen hours of preparation and travel. We were ready enough for sleep and we slung our hammocks to the poles of an open shed. In ten minutes our skins were burning and our minds inflamed, for the nets which were good enough for the mosquitoes of the Paraguay were laughably inadequate here; the *ihenni* sailed through with wings spread. Before long Urrio, Bee-Mason and I met near the cattle corral where a bunch of long-horned, sleepy bullocks grunted through the bars at us as we passed. None of us spoke, but we walked into the forest in the urgent hope of finding somewhere to rest. Soon we found it, and in our excitement ran back to the hut for our hammocks.

In the meantime, however, the insects had spied out the land and were waiting for us. Weary and disheartened we plunged down a steep slope to a tiny stream and took it in turn to lie buried in the water rushes, but the pain of dressing was too much for us and we desisted. Back at the hut we discussed the matter with the guardian. He told us grimly that no one had ever become accustomed to the scourge and that the only way to sleep was to possess a net of thick, holeless material like Tiger-Man's or his own. At this we settled down to the inevitable and walked about the clearing while the moon sank behind the black wall of forest and the real darkness began.

"Cheer up," said Urrio, after an hour or two of this, "we shall get our second wind."

Suddenly, as he spoke, a torch flashed near the hut and Tiger-Man's voice came across to us.

"I have had my sleep," he called. "Take it in turns to lie in my hammock."

This was a matter of pride. We were all three on our first tropical expedition and had not proved ourselves. So we shouted back that we were perfectly happy, and went on tramping, Tiger-Man, gaunt and sleepy, joined us and pressed the matter, but we were obstinate, and with a queer little laugh he went back to sleep. In the morning, being unaccustomed to *ihenni*, we expected a release, but, if anything, their marauding instincts increased with the light. We breakfasted as we walked, bleary-eyed and fretful, swallowing our coffee as we brushed them wretchedly away. Under the influence of a little whisky the guardian told us of a tree called *palo santo,* holy wood, whose smoke discouraged the insects. He added that the nearest specimen was sixty miles away. Then and there we resolved to push on, leaving the bullock carts and our luggage to follow as they might. So we started, swaying a little in the saddle through weariness, our eyes fixed on a succession of definite objects by the wayside so as to retain our balance.

All that day we rode, and as league followed blazing league a queer thing happened. Nature gave us back our strength, toughened and made elastic in the shape of a second wind. No longer were we worn out and irritable, forcing ourselves to silence lest words should betray our weakness. A new world, brilliant and care-free, opened its gates to us and we sang and joked, infusing some of our new-found energy into our tired mules. Subconsciously, of course, we realized that we were one degree nearer to the animals, that the first soft skin of civilization had thickened, and that a second and a grosser had been added, that we had sunk from our previous high plane of suffering. The thought did not disturb us. We were traveling through the kingdom of animals and it seemed only right that we should learn to feel as they did. Our pulses quickened and suddenly we found that life was supremely worth while.

Late that night we came to the second *fortin.* It was surrounded by marshes, and the chattering of bull-frogs rose on the still air. The cold, naked light of a full moon blazed down on a white open square surrounded by native huts, and an old wooden bridge led away into the shadows of the forest. The *fortin* was built on an island among the swamps, and was approached by little more than a causeway. On either hand the stagnant water reeked with the pungent odor of moldering vegetation, and an atmosphere of almost theatrical unreality brooded over it.

We had scarcely dismounted before the *ihenni* were upon us, biting and worrying our tormented skins and sending us into transports of irritation. We knew instantly that another night of walking lay ahead, but we treated the matter lightly, for our animal resilience was still upon us. After a while Bee-Mason and I lost Urrio and ran him to earth in one of the huts. His legs were bare, and by the light of a tallow candle we saw that his skin was covered with sores. His face was pinched with pain, but, as we entered the low door, he looked up and smiled. Then he uncorked a bottle and poured some peroxide of hydrogen into the wounds. The festered flesh bubbled and cleared, and instantly the places were covered with *ihenni*.

"When on earth did you get those?" we asked.

"That night before San Juan, when the ticks bit me," he answered grimly, and I saw the sweat stand out on his forehead. I fetched a towel and flapped vigorously while he dressed his legs. Into each hole he put a dollop of zinc ointment and covered it with gauze. When he had done his relief was audible. But he was clearly tired out.

"A few hours sleep for you," we said and stretched him on a kind of bamboo sofa. In a moment he was asleep and I signed to Bee-Mason to leave us. At the end of an hour he returned and took over the business of the towel while I went for a walk. How exactly like Urrio, I reflected, to conceal his troubles, suffering agonies in silence lest he should give extra work to his friends. As a companion he was unique.

When I got outside the moon was low in the sky and a curious watchful silence covered the world. The bull-frogs were asleep, the insect orchestra had gone home, only an occasional splash from the marshes told of our animals at feed. Suddenly, a hollow boom, loud as a drum, broke into my thoughts. It came from the wooden bridge, and as I turned I saw a mule walking slowly with halting footsteps towards me. It seemed to be in trouble, for its ears were flat and it moved with a restless, tortured action, as though it wished to be soothed. I went up to it and discovered that it was my own mount, and that its belly was black with mosquitoes. From time to time it kicked itself and whickered, rubbing its nose against my trousers and looking up into my face with an expression of appeal in its dark eyes. Soon I was surrounded by mules which poked and looked appealing. Then it was that I realized that they were hungry, that they had been unable to feed on account of the insects in the swamp. I led them to the food trunks and restored their energy with bread.

By five o'clock next morning Bee-Mason and I had

not slept a wink for fifty-five hours, and were considerably less tired than we had been at the end of twenty-four. All that day we rode through the burning heat of the forest under a brilliant sky, and towards evening we began to rise. A thick wedge of rock towered above the plain, and the path became stony. Up we went, walking for the most part so as to ease our animals, and gradually we came upon a marvelous view. Mile upon mile of tree-tops stretched to where the horizon teemed in a heat mist. Not a breath of air stirred the branches, not a twig moved in the heavy languor, just a great green sea of trees. There was something rather terrible in the sight, and for the first time we realized to the full the indomitable courage of the aviators. Two hundred miles over that frightful, unyielding ocean, staking their lives on a series of explosions in a cylinder.

By the time we reached the summit the sun was sinking in a furnace of gold straight ahead of us. It illumined the trees, bathing them in a fierce light which turned to purple in the afterglow, and in ten minutes we were in darkness. We were still three leagues from our objective, and if ever nine miles seemed a long way it did then. We advanced at a crawl, over rough sloping ground, forcing ourselves to trust in our animals though we well knew they were worn out. We talked little, especially Urrio, whose legs were causing him the most acute agony, though he never complained. Once, when he kicked his shin against a stone, he cried out in pain, but he changed it to a cough and carried on.

Those three hours of darkness before the moon rose were the longest I ever spent. We were like beings enfolded in a cloak, blind and almost suffocated by the pressure of the blackness. Our strength oozed away uselessly in the manner of swimmers battling with a strong current. Suddenly one of the mules raised his head and whinnied, the call was taken up and a great volume of sound thundered down the hill. Our spirits lightened immediately for we knew that something was near, possibly the farm that we were seeking. We strained our ears for a dog's bark, but we only heard the click-clock of unshod hooves striking against stones. A man rose at us out of the night and called a cheerful *"Buenas noches, señores,"* and was gone, leaving us more silent than before.

After an interminable time a silver radiance edged the black outline of the trees, and the moon shot up like a catapulted stone. The scene before us right down in the valley caused us to draw together and speculate. A huge bastion of gray rock reared up out of the forest. A single turret, rounded and embrasured, stood out from the main mass, and a luxuriance of creepers clutched and twined amongst the fissures. One could almost imagine a blaze of ghostly lights shining through the gaps in the dilapidated structure.

"A castle," I said, amazed and awed by the sight.

"A Jesuit monastery," said Bee-Mason.

"With bow-slits and battlements," said Urrio.

Tiger-Man, more skeptical and keener-sighted, sniffed.

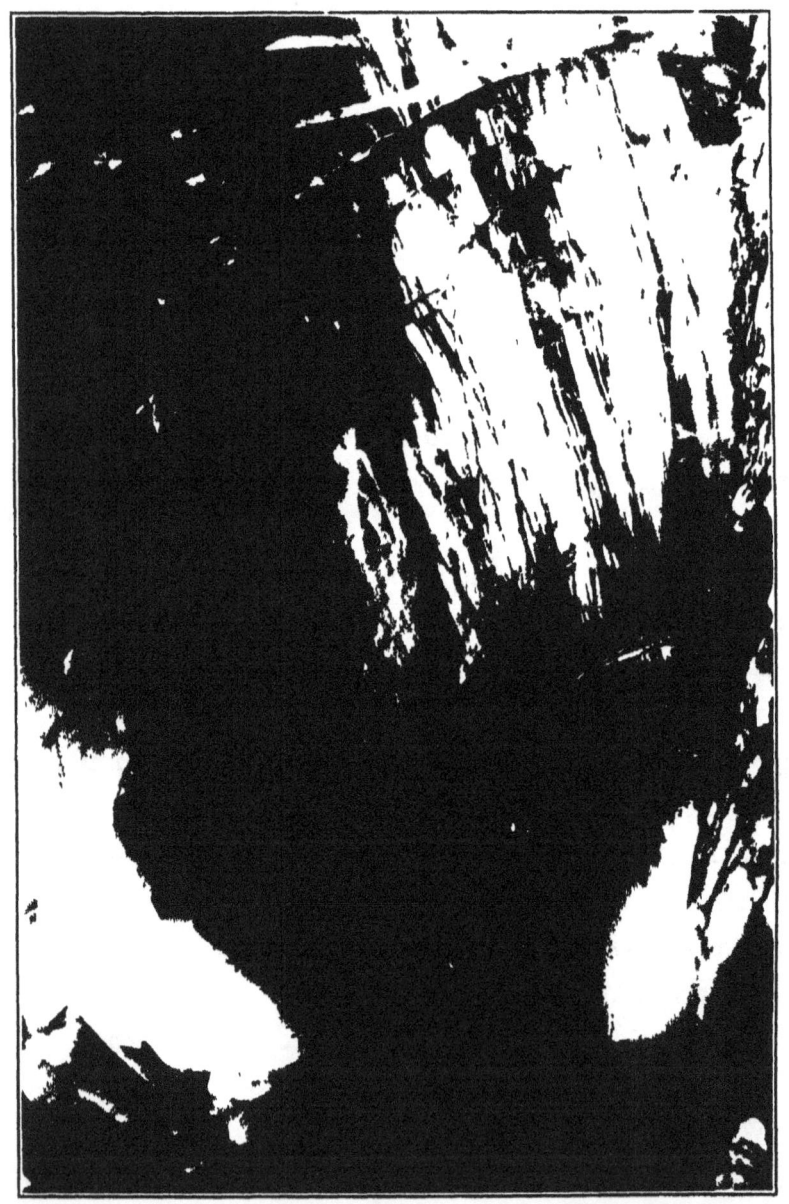

CAVE IN THE BOLIVIAN ANDES

"It's nothing but a natural formation of rock."

"Rubbish," said we, rather tartly in one breath, "it's too beautiful."

"Now, now," said Tiger-Man soothingly, "don't go casting stones at Nature. She has more imagination than any Jesuit."

And so it proved.

When, an hour later, we arrived at the farm we found the owner petulant and sleepy, entrenched behind the white mask of a mosquito net. He neither welcomed nor repelled us, but made us realize, by a weary creaking of his bed and a burst of yawning, that he wished to be left alone. Clouds of *ihenni* swooped ravenously around us, and we shuffled and scratched and moved aimlessly round the clearing while Urrio parleyed with the voice. No, we heard, there was no *palo santo*, neither was there any room where we might sleep; yes, some one might fetch a log or two in the morning. Meanwhile—that hopeful, devastating yawn.

Urrio, diplomat of genius, retired gracefully and was promptly seized by Tiger-Man and cooped up in a mosquito net. When he protested he was told that he would need his energy and diplomacy on the morrow, for our food supply was low and the ox-wagon two days behind. With a humorous twist of his mouth he obeyed, and was soon breathing peacefully and in comfort. Bee-Mason, Tiger-Man and I saw the dawn into the sky.

With the first streaks of light the farm was astir. Women of all shapes and angles, buxom servants, thin relatives of the farmer, little yellow children with serious expressions flitted across the scene and set about the master's breakfast. Eggs were gathered from errant fowls which cackled foolishly at their efforts in the forest. Maize was pounded in a wooden mortar with implements shaped like baseball bats. Hunks of meat were sliced from the blankets of *charqui* which hung from a tall scaffolding, and two small girls milked a herd of cows. Presently a smooth white cloth was laid on a trestle table, tin plates rattled on the board and a kettle was suspended over a fire. We watched hungrily from the distance speculating on the number of places for the meal. Our hearts sank when we saw that three lots of spoons and forks were alone forthcoming. When the preparations had ended the patriarch arose. Throwing aside his mosquito net with the pomp of a potentate, he emerged into the cool breezes in a dirty old pair of pajamas and a pair of bedroom slippers. His eyes were bleary, his face flabby and pendulous covered with a week's growth of beard. Steel-rimmed glasses stuck half way down a bulbous nose glanced in our direction. Then he began to munch. The sight was too much for us and we inquired the way to the bathing-pool.

Bee-Mason and I had now passed seventy-five hours without sleep, and we had reached the stage when we felt we could go on undefinitely. I think our chief emotion was one of uncleanness, a sort of clammy wakefulness that comes to a man who awakes in front of a fire at three o'clock in the morning. Wherefore we went off to the drinking pool, the only water near, and took it in turns to sluice each other out of a bucket.

On the way back Tiger-Man, who was walking ahead, stopped suddenly and held up his hand. Curious, we approached, and beheld one of the weirdest battles that it is possible to conceive. In the middle of an open space was a tarantula, covered with reddish hairs, horrible and obscene to look upon. It was crouched in an attitude of fear, and from time to time it shuffled forward, halted, and then ran backwards, obviously trying to escape from something that we could not see. All at once it subsided on to its haunches and threw its two front legs into the air. There was a loud buzz, and a huge wasp, purple-bodied and glossy, with orange wings, swept to the attack. Easily avoiding the spasmodic jump of the spider, it stuck its tail into the gross envelop of the body and zoomed out of reach. Fifteen times did this gallant aviator puncture the tank, and with each stab the brute became weaker. Finally it lay over on its back and expired, its legs kicking feebly in the air. Then the wasp with a triumphant hum flew away, presumably to call other wasps to the feast. Bee-Mason made a personal matter of it, saying that it made up for his fright in Corumbá.

When we returned to the farm Urrio was in full blast. He has a delightful laugh, full and rich and friendly, so deep that it is almost a chuckle, and he was using it with tremendous effect. Under his soothing influence the farmer had thrown off his aversion to visitors and was lying back in his chair, his fat sides heaving, the tears rolling down his furry cheeks. In an instant he had changed his character. No longer were his eyes small and black and distant; no longer were his spectacles used to repel invaders. He was rolling about and aching with merriment. Gaily he called us.

"Our friend the Minister has been telling me a story about a girl who—" And he clasped his stomach in ecstasy as he repeated the episode. Nor did Urrio think it necessary to point out the difference between a Minister and a Consul-General. Pedantry is not one of his vices.

"You have no idea how pleasant it is to talk with a man of culture," continued the farmer. "As a grandfather I have many duties—"

Tiger-Man and I leaped to Urrio's assistance.

"A grandfather!" we cried. "Señor, it is not possible. You are too young."

In this low-down manner we got our breakfast. Yet it is only fair to add that during the four days that we rested at his house we came to value him for himself. He was always cheerful, always the courteous host, and for hospitality he stood out like an oasis amid a race of inhospitable men. Long may he live.

After our meal some logs of *palo santo* arrived, and we crouched in the smoke which smelt of incense, and so escaped the *ihenni*. As the day advanced great masses of black cloud banked up on the horizon and our host sighed, with pleasure, saying that the rain would thwart the insects. Before long the thunder cracked and the lightning played about the forest and, with a rush of wind, the heavens opened. As if by magic, all the children in the place tore off their clothes and dashed out into the storm. Their arms flew up to heaven and they shouted joyfully, welcoming the water that splashed off their bare skins. A shadow passed across the face of our host.

"Poor kiddies," he said. "At the end of the dry season the rain is their only bath."

He found us a deserted, closed-in barn, for which may his soul escape a thousand years in purgatory. At last Bee-Mason and I were able to sleep. For ninety hours we had not closed our eyes, and as we slung our hammocks in that stuffy, windowless room, we sighed in utter thankfulness, and slept the clock round twice.

After four days of comfort and good meals we said good-by regretfully. A large crowd came to see us off, and after a volley of farewell our host came close to Urrio. Suddenly his voice was grave.

"God go with you, señor," he said. "Remember the Indians, and keep watch at night."

CHAPTER XXI

At our first halt we overtook the Republican mail for the province of Santa Cruz. It lay on a pile of saddlery in a weather-stained canvas bag, and the romance of travel exalted the chipped seals. The postman was an Indian, short and yellow and wiry, with a crop of cat's whiskers on his chin. His cheek bones were high, and his eyes ran away at the corners to such a marked degree that it seemed as though in distant centuries South America had been a suburb of China. He was a courageous little man, cheerful and fatalistic, with an almost animal delight in the sensations of the moment. As he lounged against his saddle, his stomach full and satisfied, he had clearly forgotten the heat of the day and had given no thought to the dangers of the morrow. A maize-leaf cigarette, tucked neatly in at the ends, hung between his lips, and a haze of smoke encompassed his face. A living image of Buddha enjoying incense. After dinner I went across to him and he arose with the courtesy of a Hidalgo to offer me his seat. We sat down together, and my Spanish being adequate by now, I asked him discreetly of his profession.

"The postman's life isn't what it was, señor," he said sadly. "Years ago I could go to sleep at Puerto Saurez and wake up in time to deliver the Brazilian mail at Santa Cruz, my mule was so intelligent; but now those sons of Satan, the Toba Indians, have left the Chaco to prey upon this road."

"Have they ever attacked you?" I asked.

"Once they made fun of me," he admitted; "of me, the Republican postman! It happened ten leagues from here in a round, bare patch of land with a water-hole in one corner. As I rode along, half dozing in the saddle, for it was hot, my mule nearly rubbed me off against a wigwam of green poles, which had certainly not been there on my last journey. The place intrigued me, and I dismounted, hoping to find a reason for so strange an erection, and, suddenly, I was surrounded. One moment the clearing was empty, the next I was in the center of a circle of grinning savages. *Dios mio, señor*, how I sweated! Scores of naked men with matted hair to their shoulders, nude women with slim figures and pigtails, crowded out of the forest and jabbered at me. They waved their rough weapons and dug me in the ribs, punched my behind and squawked with laughter when I jumped. I made sure I was bound for the cook-pot. Luckily, however, they were in a good temper and contented themselves with tearing up the letters and scattering the paper as monkeys do. Then they pushed me on to my mule and sent me away at a gallop."

"Are they always as peaceful as that?" I asked pointedly.

He sat up with a jerk.

"Did you never hear what happened to that muleteer from Cochabamba?"

"No."

"Well, they killed his mules and stole his merchandise, left him dead in the road, and took his wife and daughters into the forest. A punitive expedition? Señor, it is impossible. The forest extends for hundreds of miles, and no man can see ten yards in front of him. These Indians grease their bodies and slip between the trees where clothes would tear. Their skins are as tough as a tiger's hide, and their feet are inured to the thorns. An army would get lost in an attempt to round up three hundred Tobas."

"Aren't you afraid?"

"Sometimes, señor, when my belly is empty; but you see I never shoot at them. The pay is good, and my wife and children have large mouths. Besides, the beggars know me. Time and again I see them grinning from the shadow of the forest, but I never hurry and they never disturb me. Of course, there is always the chance that I shall meet them on a bad day."

"And then?"

The postman smiled.

"I think they would be sorry—afterwards."

"They may be angry to-morrow. Won't you ride with us?"

"I thank you from the bottom of my heart," said the little man softly, "but you have to keep in touch with your ox-wagon, and people grow impatient for their letters."

He was gone before dawn, and I never saw him again.

At the next camping ground, a sandy clearing in the midst of jungle, we found two caravans. One was commanded by a sporting old lady, weather-beaten to the color of a Malaga figure, who, with her two sons, was piloting a mule train to Cochabamba. In addition, she had an eight-bullock ox-cart filled to the roof with woolen goods from Manchester. Her elder son was seventeen, grave and responsible beyond his years on account of his father's death, and the younger was a jolly little urchin, an excellent rider, aged nine. The second caravan was also owned by a family from Cochabamba, birthplace of the most famous muleteers in South America. By dint of using the stars as a ceiling for themselves and their families, they reduce their expenses to a minimum and defy competition. The wife of this man had just given birth to a boy by the wayside, and the party was encamped for a day or two to give the mother strength. Urrio, with his usual kindliness, congratulated the couple on their adventure, and we all drank to the sleepy newcomer by the light of the camp-fire. The woman, her breasts protruding from slits in her dress, fed the child and looked at the ring of friendly faces with a contented grin. Her husband, sucking the whisky off his gigantic black mustaches, bent and patted her shoulder with rough approval.

Long before dawn next day I heard the crackling of flames and a hundred sounds that told of mules being loaded. Over the edge of my hammock I watched the old lady helping her sons in the work of preparation. In Cochabamba they take no chances with the backs of their animals, and layer upon layer of straw pads were piled on to each. Instead of *bourracas*, which are quite needlessly heavy, they place their belongings in tough hide nets. By six o'clock, the last bullock had been yoked and the caravan lurched away into the morning mist. I stood in my pajamas and saw it out of sight, noting particularly the cheerful child swinging his whip and yelping at the oxen. Before evening he was dead.

We arose at our ease, for we meant our own wagon to overtake us. But at eleven o'clock there was still no sign of it, and we decided to push on to the next *fortin*. We were heartily sick of the gray water in the mud-holes and wanted a bath, so we asked the remaining muleteer to hasten our baggage, and at noon set out on an eight-league trek. These details are trivial enough in themselves, but they had an important bearing on the events of the afternoon.

We had lunched before starting, a fact which, combined with the midday heat, caused us to move drowsily. The sun beat down on the narrow road, a shimmering haze hung between the trees, and a heavy, languorous smell of vegetation drugged our senses. Through this mental mist came the noise of horse-flies buzzing about the necks of our mounts, and the lazy, half-hearted chatter of a colony of parrots. Gradually gaps appeared in our formation, for the reaction from the days of sleeplessness was setting in, and before long, half a mile separated Tiger-Man from myself. I was terribly thirsty, my water gourds were blistering in the heat, and the liquid inside was clammy and fetid. I had just fixed my thoughts on a good polar scene with icebergs and bears, when my eye caught the glint of yellow in the solid wall of forest. Curious, I drew near, and perceived a bright, pear-shaped fruit stuck on the edge of a cactus leaf. Drawing my mule underneath I stood upright in the stirrups and poked with my machete; but it was too high, and I had to throw the knife before the fruit would fall. It turned out to be unbelievably refreshing, of a light gray flesh studded with black pips. Instantly I awoke. I pressed forward with my eyes ranging the jungle for more of this luxury, and before long my pockets were full. I had just pictured to myself the joy on my companions' faces when I should produce the fruit at dinner, when suddenly, from far ahead, came the shrill blast of a whistle. Once, twice, three times it blew, and I set my spurs into my mule's tough flanks and galloped up the road. It was a signal that had never been used before, but long ago in Gaiba we had arranged that three blasts meant danger. After a sharp burst at top speed, I came upon a grave little party standing in the middle of the road. Tiger-Man looked up.

"I saw three naked Indians just now," he said. "We should keep together."

He pointed to some footprints on the sandy surface, and I saw that they were flat, without trace of an instep. Sobered, with a certain premonition of danger, we formed into line and rode slowly on, our servants wedged in the middle, for we did not know whether they would stand firm in the event of an attack.

From then on Tiger-Man was our leader. He stepped quite naturally and tacitly into a post that was his by virtue of fourteen years' experience in Matto Grosso, and it never occurred to us to question his command. Gone was the easy, charming philosopher of the campfire, gone too, the laughter from his eyes. He sat erect, composed, intently alert and alive, his phenomenal hearing stretched to the uttermost. His hat was cocked at an aggressive angle and there was an atmosphere of terrific mental power in the set of his body. Without moving he managed to convey the impression that he was absolute master of whatever might occur. Wherefore it was with a rising thrill that I saw him laying his rifle across the saddle-bow and snap down the safety catch. Suddenly a curious feeling came over me. I was riding last in the line, and it seemed as if something were burning a hole in the back of my shirt. I scratched it absently with a twig, but the sensation persisted, and I turned in the saddle. There, not fifty yards behind, were a number of savages, stark naked, stalking us. They ran from tree to tree, furtively peering round trunks and retiring into the underbush; and it was the concentrated gaze of their eyes that had caused me to look round. I had a glimpse of fierce, dark faces with tangled hair to their shoulders, and then abruptly they vanished.

"Hey, Tiger-Man," I called. "Got any missionaries?"

"Rifle loaded?" he asked, ignoring the sally.

"Yes."

"Pistol cocked and easy to draw?"

"Yes."

"Well, be ready. Don't do anything unless they attack. They may be just curious, but don't hesitate if they try to surround us."

Half an hour passed. From time to time we turned, conscious that the numbers of our pursuers were increasing, but they were nervous and kept to the shadow of the trees. In spite of their reputation we refrained from shooting, chiefly because of the acid fairness of Tiger-Man's brain. During that afternoon it would have been easy to kill half a dozen, but as he pointed out, they had done us no harm and the stories of their cruelty were purely second-hand.

Presently, round a sharp bend in the road we came upon the place mentioned by the postman. It was large and bare and circular, and the yellow sand had been beaten flat by hundreds of naked feet. In the furthest corner was a tall wigwam of green poles, empty and unstained by smoke, joined together at the top by a leather thong. And the outlet to Santa Cruz was blocked by a low hedge of thorns. With a cry of surprise Adolfo began to dismount.

"Stay where you are," I said sharply and repeated the postman's tale to Tiger-Man.

He looked at the wigwam reflectively. "It is not a dwelling," he said, "and I don't think it is a scaffolding for meat. Probably they put it there to arouse interest and make people get off to examine it."

He drew his pistol.

"These thorns," he added, "are quite new. You can see the wheel marks of that old lady's wagon, and they don't pierce the hedge. I hope they have not attacked her."

Once again I experienced that uncomfortable feeling in the back of my neck. It seemed as though hundreds of eyes were observing us, saving us up, as it were, for a great occasion. I turned quickly and cantered my mule across the clearing, and round the corner so as to get a clear view of the road. Thirty yards away a frightened figure, slim and glistening as if it had been oiled, ran madly towards the trees. A single plait of coarse black hair flapped against its buttocks, and it gave voice to a little cry. There was a certain wild grace in the freedom of the movements and the rippling muscles of the back, and a certain virginity in the litheness of the poise. So must have Atalanta looked round, and I regretted I had no mirror to drop. I had scarcely a second in which to admire it, and then, like an arrow, quite silently it sped into the forest. Further down the road a gleam of sunlight caught my eyes. It was reflected apparently from the back of a huge red and black tortoise which trundled across the open space. In an instant a dark, nude shape broke cover, scooped the animal under its arm and sprang back. I had a sight of long hair, matted and shaking, and straightway the scene was as empty as before. I blinked and returned to my companions.

"I have just seen a native woman," I told them, "running like a deer."

"What did you expect her to do?" asked Bee-Mason rudely. "Kiss you?"

"Give her time," said Urrio, grinning. "They are often coy at first."

We jumped our mules through the thorn hedge and followed the wheel tracks of the ox-wagon. For a full hour we rode, uneventfully, listening to the silence and gazing at the tangled mass of underbush that lined the blazing canyon of trees. The postman had been right. Overwhelmingly right. No army could hope to exterminate a tribe whose confines were Green Hell herself, hundreds of miles of pathless jungle, dry as a bone and cluttered up with vegetation. Even a squadron of aëroplanes would be useless, for in that country the range of a bomb would be limited to a few yards. So did we muse in the flaming heat of that December afternoon.

Suddenly Tiger-Man reined in his mule and leaned forward in the saddle. His attitude was alert and aggressive with more than a threat of danger, and we shaded our eyes with our hands. The road was quite straight, mile upon mile of yellow ribbon stretching to the skyline, and a quarter of a mile away a strange blot was evident on the left-hand side. We approached with caution, and as we drew near something detached itself from the ground and flapped up into a tree. Another followed and yet a third, the air resounded with the leathery beat of wings, until the branches were covered with the black and white forms of vultures. They sat in glum silence, angry but impotent, deprived of a meal that we could not see. We dug our spurs into our mounts and cantered up to the scene of carnage. Then it was that we encountered a sight that changed us from ordinary human beings into furious and revengeful men.

Two of the old lady's bullocks lay heaped together in a ditch, and the manner of their passing raised a lump in our throats depriving us of speech. At first we thought that one of them was alive so peaceful was its expression, so natural the poise of its black head; but a second glance convinced us that it was as lifeless as its mate. They had not been dead an hour, the bodies were still warm, and the vultures had not been able to secure more than a hasty peck. As we sat our mules and looked down at the wreckage, a vast pity filled us, and there came into our hearts the same reverent heaviness that accompanies the death of a friend, for these animals had suffered the agonies of hell, and their patient faces cried aloud for vengeance. Their backs were a sea of blood, clotted and sticky where the hides had been wrenched from the living flesh. Great flaps of skin hung backwards from the wounds, and the horns had been splintered and smashed by terrific blows from wooden clubs. Spears had been thrust into the intestines which lay looped about the

VILLAGE OF LAGUNILLAS IN THE HEART OF THE OIL DISTRICT

hooves, and a number of broken bows stuck out from the haunches of the smaller beast. Tiger-Man turned in the saddle, and his eyes were hard as stone.

"That settles it," he snapped. "We shoot at sight. If they attack us our fate will be the same; but it will last longer."

He dismounted quickly and poked about on the ground, reading us the story as it was written in the sand.

"See here," he pointed to a score of naked footprints, "the devils sprang out from the trees and unyoked the first pair of oxen. They were so busy mincing them that they forgot the others, and that sporting old lady whipped her team into a gallop. I hope she was not caught."

"Can we help her?" asked Urrio.

"No. It is an hour since this happened, and they are either safe or dead. Nothing else is possible in this kind of warfare."

He placed his foot in the stirrup and swung himself up.

"I won't blink matters," he said. "From now on our lives are in danger. A hundred Indians could lie within three yards of the road and we should be none the wiser till they charged. We must go back to our last camp and wait for our wagon."

He wheeled abruptly and set back up the trail. Bee-Mason followed him, and so, tail to head, we rode, with scarcely twenty yards between front and rear. Before we had covered fifty paces, a hollow bump sounded behind us. We turned and saw the vultures dropping one by one, gradually, from the branches. We quickened our march. Outwardly it was a sober little party that trotted back on its own hoof marks. Each one of us had his mask on, unwilling to show feeling, and it was only when I looked round and caught the flame in Urrio's eyes that I realized I was not alone in my excitement. He saw at once that I had surprised his thoughts, and his face grew bright.

"What price an office now?" he gloated. "How do you feel?"

"I'd give £20 to see an Indian over my sights. Those bullocks haunt me."

"The same here," he said. "I should have preferred the body of a man."

We soon perceived that our keenest enemy was not the savages but the sun, which had long since passed its height, and was slowly slipping down the sky. We reckoned we were twelve miles from safety, and a bare two hours of daylight lay between us and the horrors of a night attack. Now this meant an average of two leagues an hour, or double our normal speed, and although it would have been simple enough to have flogged the animals we were anxious to avoid any semblance of flight. For we knew that the smallest trace of fear would bring the Indians upon us like wasps round a honey jar. It was a situation which called for an extremely nice judgment of pace.

"Hullo," said Tiger-Man after a while. "They have been tracking us."

There, in the loose sand were eight pairs of naked footprints pointing to Santa Cruz. We could distinctly see the place where natives had halted, caught wind of our return and faced about; and we guessed that they were now in front of us; some way ahead. From time to time we looked over our shoulders and saw a number of black heads peering from behind trees, but they were too wily to give us a clear shot. In this way we came back to the wigwam, and if anything seemed sinister and forbidding in the light of our discovery that curious erection did.

Once again the corner of the road provided an encounter. We were scarcely round it before Tiger-Man's rifle was at his shoulder and the echoes were roaring through Green Hell. I didn't see the preliminaries, but when I looked a dark body was lying in the fairway 150 yards distant. It was swaying from side to side, holding its leg, whining. Suddenly the whole roadway was alive with men. They picked their comrade off the ground, and before Tiger-Man could re-load were safe in the forest. For sheer speed of movement I have never seen anything like it.

We now realized from a number of significant signs that we were caught in a movable trap. In front the footprints continued unbroken; behind we caught glimpses of our foes and from either side came a succession of noises which aroused in me feelings more acute than anything I have obtained by reading Rider Haggard at night. I am well used to the danger-signals of the country-side. When I was a boy I spent my holidays alone in the woods, and it was my particular pleasure to piece together the chronicle of the thickets from the voices of birds and animals. It was not long before I came to know when a jay was reproving his wife and when he was abusing a fox; when a rabbit was caught in a snare and when by a stoat; and one evening, having heard something peculiar in the roosting note of a cock pheasant, I had the supreme satisfaction of finding my doubts proved in the presence of a poacher. Wherefore it was not difficult for me to translate the movements of our enemies. An atmosphere of perturbation and unrest overhung the forest like a cloud—such an atmosphere as occurs in an English wood when a fox is at large. A parrot screamed out of the trees on our right, high and wide, shrieking obscenities. A small brown deer broke cover on the left, entered the underbush on the other side, and, finding that occupied as well, fled for its life down the yellow pathway. Twigs cracked, voices murmured in low, guttural accents, and all the while the sounds kept pace with us. Once a jungle cock gave its clear musical bugle call, but it was just a thought too harsh, and I knew that it came from a human throat. A great company of vultures swept hopefully above our heads.

It is a curious sensation, not by any means unpleasant, being inclosed in a hostile land. Civilized trappings fall unwept and forgotten. Fierce little shivers pass through one's body, and there is a wild exaltation of spirit which asks for nothing better than a good stern fight. In such a case comradeship is tangible, the living essence which binds one to one's fellows and makes one swear by all one's gods that there shall be no betrayal. Fear is impossible for the whole scene is so packed with interest that there is no time to be afraid. Once or twice at least in a man's lifetime it is well that he should find himself in a position where no amount of rate-paying will produce a policeman. I began to reckon up our chances.

South of the main stream of the Amazon, savages do not use poison on their weapons. Why this is I do not know, but it may be taken for a fact. The Tobas were armed with bows and arrows four times barbed and fatal to withdraw from a body wound, but the thickness of the forest made it unlikely that they would shoot before we saw them. In addition they carried heavy wooden clubs, deadly enough at short range, but only useful after our guns had ceased to fire. Of steel they had none. Each of us had a pistol with seven shots in the magazine, and our servants had a double-barrelled shotgun apiece. Altogether, counting our rifles, I fancied that we could kill thirty-five of them before being reduced to boots and fists. All of which stood on the credit side of our balance. I am bound to say the debit columns were well filled. As time went by, the Indians ceased to whisper, and a rising clamor encompassed us like a wall. I judged by the racket that there were close on two hundred men on each side of the road, and I thanked my stars that we were not in an open place where they could take heart from the visible signs of their superiority. Their cries which echoed across our heads had lost the furtive note and ever gained in confidence as the afternoon wore on. Morally they were certain to attack us. They had never encountered a well-armed party of desperate men, and they had long since passed the stage when the mere sound of firing appalled them. The real question in our minds was whether they would have the courage to withstand that first devastating hail of lead. If they could weather that storm we were as good as eaten.

Meanwhile, the sun was sinking fast and we were still some way from camp. So we pricked our animals and broke into a trot. Now the savages were at least fifty yards from the road, and since the density of the forest prevented them from seeing any difference in our gait they must have heard it. At any rate they decided that we were running away. Instantly the cries of the leaders grew louder, and I realized that the spear-points, so to speak, of the parallel Indian files were turning towards the path. A simple calculation convinced me that they would converge upon the road within the next quarter of a mile. Tiger-Man thought likewise and spoke without turning.

"They are preparing an ambush," he said. "Fire for their stomachs when they charge."

His voice was cold and steady, without trace of feeling. A lesser man might have attempted a few words of encouragement, especially to the servants, but he showed from his manner that he trusted us absolutely. Indeed, I believe that at that moment we needed no encouragement. Our minds were inflamed by our memories of those tortured bullocks, and we desired nothing so much as the sight of black bodies kicking in the dust. At the same time, though I was not afraid, I could not trust myself to speak. I was trembling with excitement, and my voice would most certainly have quavered. We halted a hundred yards short of where the natives were massing and, for a second, the gravity lifted from Tiger-Man's face. He smiled cheerfully at me.

"You wanted adventure," he said. "What about it?"

The Indians knew at once what had happened. Their cries stopped short, and we could hear the stealthy movements of a large number of men moving through the forest. We could see nothing, though we peered anxiously about us in the hope of a long shot with a rifle before they closed. Leaves rustled and the soft smack of released branches came to our ears. Our servants fidgeted in the saddle, but made no attempt to run in spite of the fact that, being natives themselves, they feared their wild brethren a thousand times more than we did. Suddenly a terrific noise broke from the trees, scattering the echoes and causing our horses to rear. It rose like a thunder-clap all round us, steep and hoarse and angry, within ten paces. We looked at one another in amazement for this was no human speech but the language of the bullfrogs. An immense croaking, lifting and falling, grating in harsh cadences, sounded for all the world as though we had blundered into a pre-historic marsh in the mating season. Question and answer couched in frog terms rattled like musketry out of the silence and drowned the screams of a covey of parrots that rushed madly away. Perhaps it was a war-cry, perhaps it was intended to stampede the animals, perhaps it was just a method of instilling courage into their souls. Whatever its intention it saved our lives, for Tiger-Man, with a flash of genius, took advantage of it. He rose in his stirrups, his face bright with amusement and sent a single, stupendous cat-call crashing in answer. The effect was immediate. All sound ceased; and the hush that fell over the forest was more appalling than a battle hymn. I could feel the savages considering the matter; I knew, as though I saw them, that they were searching one another's eyes, peeping round tree-trunks to discover their neighbor's thoughts. During these breathless moments our lives hung in the balance and we knew it. Little objects became indelibly impressed on my mind. I noticed that Bee-Mason's jaw was set like a bull-dog's, that a horse-fly was sucking the neck of my mule, that Tiger-Man needed a barber.

I am no psychologist. I do not know why the savages acted as they did. It may be that Tiger-Man's greeting was so immeasurably louder than their own that they feared the approach of a new god. They may have felt dimly in their rude interiors that a further concert from them would be gross anti-climax. Possibly they needed time to adjust their impressions. At any rate they retreated. A tittering and chittering broke out, low and cowed and fearful, and the massed spear-head of their formation was dissipated. Soft little sounds filtered among the thickets and told us quite clearly that they had taken up their former positions. They still followed us, but without threats. We could hear the old, familiar movements indicative of parallel lines fifty yards from the road, but the electricity had gone out of the air and we were not slow to profit.

"A song," cried Tiger-Man. "The louder the better."

So, just as the sun dropped like a blazing ball behind the trees, we rode into camp. The muleteer from Cochabamba left his fire to stare at us for we were singing "Loch Lomond" with dry, harsh voices and pistols in our hands. As for the Toba Indians, they surrounded the clearing as we could feel in our bones, and sat down to watch for any slackening of our guard. Only they made no fuss about it, squatting at a respectful distance as silently as vultures.

When darkness fell we proclaimed martial law. Two by two, with drawn pistols, we ransacked the forest for brushwood and lighted an enormous fire at each corner of the clearing. As there was already a large blaze before the tent of our friend, the muleteer, we ensured that the savages would have to cross fifty yards of open ground which was almost as bright as Piccadilly. Urrio, though he was almost mad with the pain of his sick legs, hastened to cheer the frightened mother. "There is no danger, señora," he said gently. "We are well-armed and passably tough. Henceforward you are one of our party."

A pair of soft brown eyes, fearful yet fierce on account of the child, looked up at him gratefully.

"I am not afraid," she said, lying.

Urrio laughed.

"Of course not. What an education for the little one! Born practically in an armed camp! He will rise to be a general."

The father twirled his mustaches.

"He will become Minister for War," he boasted.

The future favorite of Mars awoke with a jerk, kicked, and was suddenly hungry. A peculiarly unwarlike mouth nuzzled along the front of a dress, found what it wanted and closed. Urrio returned to his hammock.

"Now," said Tiger-Man heartily, "we must prepare for the night. That muleteer will be terribly hurt if he is not given a watch, and so will our servants. Let them begin before we go to sleep."

"You haven't bathed your legs yet," I said slyly to Urrio.

He glared at me.

"If you're thinking of doing my turn for me, you'd better keep it to yourself."

"Rubbish!" said Tiger-Man. "We all share alike."

So it was arranged that the muleteer, Suarez and Adolfo should watch for an hour apiece between eight and eleven, and that Bee-Mason, Tiger-Man, myself and Urrio, in that order, should divide the rest of the night into two hour shifts. Urrio summoned the muleteer.

"My friend," he said gravely, "this camp is besieged. Will you bear your part?"

The man swelled like a bullfrog.

"Señor," he said with dignity, "my wife and my little son are in danger. I cannot fail."

We gave him my shot-gun and Tiger-Man's torch, and watched him swagger round the clearing in search of savages. He poked the bushes at each corner, hurled logs on to the fires, and, at intervals, strutted past his tent in the full glare of wifely admiration. Indeed, so proud did he become and so convinced of his value, that he had quite a tussle with Suarez when the hour came to an end. Presently Tiger-Man sat up and listened.

"Mules!" he said. "About twenty of them."

The night was very still, but although we strained our ears to the uttermost we could hear nothing. Then dimly and from a great distance, came a dull beating of hooves growing louder and more distinct until we could make out the rattle of bits. We sprang up and ran to the Santa Cruz road, where, not a hundred yards away, was a mule column moving fast. The cold radiance of a full moon streamed down on it and picked out a number of points of light which turned out to be the buttons on army tunics. An officer rode jauntily behind. Urrio hailed him.

"Seen any Indians?" he asked.

"I have seen and heard nothing else since mid-day," said the officer. "The devils shot a little boy."

Urrio started.

"Not the son of the female muleteer from Cochabamba?"

"Unfortunately, yes."

"The smaller one?"

"Got him in the temple with an arrow."

"Dead?"

The officer nodded.

"I am afraid I cannot stop to protect you," he continued. "I am under orders to take ammunition to Puerto Saurez. Those Paraguayans, you know."

Urrio looked at him meaningly. Neither spoke, but the officer winked. A salute, a handshake, and a swift order and the column had moved on.

"I should like to see a war," I said sleepily.

Urrio grinned.

At eleven o'clock Bee-Mason started his patrol and we went to bed. Scarcely had I snuggled into my blanket when Tiger-Man awoke me. For a moment I felt myself aggrieved, and then I noticed that the moon had sunk and the smell of dawn was in the air. I arose hurriedly.

"You devil," I said. "What's the time?"

Tiger-Man's beard opened and he laughed.

"Four o'clock," he said. "Bee-Mason called me half an hour late. I have done the same by you. Urrio's feet are in a bad state." He tumbled into his hammock.

Never shall I forget that watch. A deathly stillness had fallen over the world, and the cold ate through my shirt. I was hungry and tired and dirty, and for the first time in the trip I knew fear. It looked me in the face and yammered, urging me to run from the dancing shadows and the terror that lurked beyond the fires. It reminded me of the ghastly reputation of the hour before dawn, and whispered that I was an easy mark as I passed in the glare of the flames. A twanging bowstring, a shaft through the neck, and the camp would be at the mercy of the Tobas. My imagination leaped into the bushes filling them with stealthy forms.

Presently a thought struck me, blinding me with shame and pride. I was by far the youngest member of the party, yet my companions had entrusted their lives to me, simply and without a word. Our servants and the muleteer had grown to middle age in the woods, but Tiger-Man had not trusted *them*. He had insisted on our sitting awake till they had done. With me he slept. I wandered past their hammocks and murmured their names, but no one answered. I was good enough for them. Then and there a great thankfulness took possession of me and my fears were stamped into the ground. Only the memory remained, a living hostage against the presumption of judging a coward.

Fired by my responsibility I set myself to thwart the savages. I recalled a host of adventure stories in which sentinels were outwitted, and remembered that in nearly every case it was the regularity of their beat that had been responsible. The enemy had waited until the sentry had passed, knowing where he would be at a stated time. I resolved that they should have a harder task with me. I started from the great fire in the center and walked to the Santa Cruz road. Nothing stirred. Just there the forest was thin, small trees and no undergrowth, like a newly-planted orchard. I bent down and flashed a pencil of torchlight under the branches. A rabbit blinked and tried to escape the brilliance; nothing else moved. Then I walked briskly round the clearing; then back to the fire; then to the Santa Cruz road again, keeping as little method as possible in my wanderings, and hoping that the Indians would fear the torch.

By and by I began to have the same feeling that I had experienced during the day. Somebody was watching me. I knew it, though the darkness was as silent as a cellar and my sight was limited to the clearing. It was not fear, that night-mare had been banished forever by the sight of my sleeping friends, it was sober reality. Soon I became aware that the ring of Indians was elastic, that they were afraid of my gun and torch, that they cleared off into the forest when I approached them. So I put more variety into my walks and flashed my light more frequently.

Suddenly a strange, high whistle sounded from the

Santa Cruz road. I hastened towards it and was nearly knocked over by a mule which broke from the trees on my left. It passed me in a canter, ears back, tail extended, and it had entered the forest on the other side of the central fire before I could collect my wits. It was one of our own animals. I recognized its white-stockinged feet, and I came to the not unnatural conclusion that it had been disturbed by the Tobas, and called Tiger-Man.

In a second he was out of his hammock with his rifle cocked and ready. I told him of the mule but omitted my impression of watching eyes, for my fears were too recent for me to wish my courage to be questioned. He sniffed at the sky.

"Dawn will be here in half an hour. I will help you till then." So together we saw the light into the heavens and felt the wind blow cool from the south. We placed a cook-pot on the fire, and when the camp awoke breakfast was ready. Urrio was furious and tackled me.

"My dear fellow," I said, "you must blame the Indians. Bee-Mason was so fascinated by the new experience that he forgot the time. Tiger-Man could scarcely take less, and that only left me two hours till dawn."

He looked at me suspiciously.

"You weren't trying to save my feet?"

"If I were you," I said, "I should take the first watch to-night and make sure."

By ten o'clock we began to be seriously alarmed for the safety of our ox-wagon. Even the most dilatory driver, so we thought, could have been up with us by now. Tiger-Man was not so sure.

"Leave an Indian alone," he said, "and he'll stay alone."

Wherefore he took Adolfo and rode back in search. When he had gone we settled down to a day of rest, but we had scarcely posted the first sentry when clouds of *ihenni* appeared. They swarmed out of the forest and hailed us joyously, glad of a little white meat. So we returned to the old familiar amusement of tramping away the hours under the heat and silence of a tropical day. Suarez provided the sole diversion. The silly creature had been expressly forbidden to leave the camp, but feeling himself secure, had escaped towards the water hole. He returned at full gallop, his water tins rattling against his knees, and good honest fear in his eyes, and a tale of Indians in the undergrowth. Urrio, whose legs were one long agony, cursed him for a fool, and asked me to escort the man with a pistol, whilst Bee-Mason and he guarded the clearing. Sure enough there were any number of footprints in the sand, and the filthy liquid which, in the absence of a stream, we drank greedily, had been rendered filthier than ever. The Indians had been wading in it, to judge by the spiral columns of mud which were slowly settling. Moodily we filled the tins.

Towards evening, as the *ihenni* showed no signs of departing, Urrio and I went for a walk. We passed through an open glade, and just as we were considering

RUINS OF AN OLD CEMETERY, NEAR POTOSÍ (NOTE THE CARVED STONE OF THE PORTICO AND THE DOOR)

a return to camp, encountered a most formidable smell. Thinking that perhaps the savages had killed a hostile traveler, we rounded a tree and found bathos in the shape of a rabbit. Yet not quite bathos, for it was covered with the blue and yellow and white of a flock of butterflies. Their slim legs were pressed into the fetid flesh, and their brilliant wings fluttered in ecstasy as their faces sunk into their prey.

"I thought they lived on flower-dew," I said.

A mischievous smile came into Urrio's eyes.

"I wonder whether the term 'Society Butterfly' was an accident."

I caught his meaning.

"A cynical entomologist—"

"Having visited a *cause célèbre*—"

"Got a lot of pleasure from his joke."

So did we.

Tiger-Man's return by moonlight coincided with a violent feeling of internal discontent. We had eaten nothing unusual, and our drink had been the mud-laden water to which the past ten weeks had accustomed us. Yet each one of us was ill. Our heads ached, our digestions groaned, and a series of hot shivers passed rampant through our bodies. Tiger-Man eyed us anxiously.

"It can't be malaria," he said. "There are no mosquitoes and *ihenni* are not carriers."

I told him of the disturbed water-hole and of my slowly growing fears.

"Of course," he said abruptly. "Those devils have

tampered with the supply. It is one of their habits; I wish I had told you."

He called the muleteer.

"How are you this evening, my friend? Feeling fit?"

"Certainly not, señor, nor my wife and child. We are all suffering from the same thing."

"Water?"

"Yes."

"What drug do they use in these parts? Think well. It may be of vital importance."

"I have heard tell that it is piñon, señor."

Tiger-Man sighed.

"Thank heaven for that. It is not poisonous, only purgative. They make croton oil from the berries."

Urrio sat up with interest.

"So? The case of the Prince Imperial and the Zulus all over again. They wait till you leave the saddle and then cut you off."

"My God, what swines," said Bee-Mason.

Then and there we made up our minds to a night of toil. We were exquisitely tired from the long tramp in the sand, and Tiger-Man had ridden close on forty miles, yet the nature of our malady made it imperative that we should patrol in pairs, and we apportioned the hours till dawn.

All through the dark watches we brooded on the foul methods of the savages, and by morning we were out for blood. The slow, sullen fury, which had burned within us from the moment we had clapped eyes on the tortured bullocks, burst into flame. We swore that if we could rid the caravan route of a few pests we should go out of our way to do so. Just after daylight Bee-Mason came to us, his face alight with anger, and suggested a bright idea. It was the fruit of an uncooked breakfast and forced abstinence from water, and he spoke with gusty eloquence.

"They attacked that poor old lady," he said. "Do you think they would go for us?"

"It doesn't matter if they do," said Tiger-Man idly, "we are well armed."

Bee-Mason swept his arm in a circle that embraced our men and the ox-cart.

"What about an ambush?" he said.

We perked up.

"How would it be if we sent our wagon on ahead apparently unattended and left Tiger-Man and the muleteer to come along behind? How would it be if my camera was hidden in the front with Urrio to cover it and Duguid to fire out of the back when we were surrounded? We could stay quite quiet until they unyoked the bullocks, and thus mow them down."

"It would be terribly hot under that leather roof," said Tiger-Man drily.

"It's worth it for a film like that."

"Very well," said Tiger-Man, "don't blame me if you are in a bad temper this evening."

Urrio was worn out by the pain in his feet, and assented limply. So Bee-Mason and I spent a hectic morning arranging three nests in the bowels of the ox-cart. We placed a barrier of mule trunks across the front and a couple of seats behind them in such a way as to be invisible from the road and yet clear enough for a camera and a rifle to command a view. Then we did the same with the rear. We were so wrought up with indignation that we noticed neither *ihenni* nor thirst, and by eleven o'clock we were ready.

Suddenly, the shrill sound of bickering came from the tent of the muleteer. In another instant that gentleman, purple with a fury he was too uneducated to express, panted across the clearing. His fingers were tight about the ear of an unfortunate child, a ragged, shoeless urchin, an apprentice who had hitherto kept in the background. The pair came to rest in front of Tiger-Man.

"This imp of Satan, Pedrito, won't obey me, señor," said the muleteer.

"No, indeed," groaned the boy, his thin yellow face peaked with tears. "I want to avenge Miguel, and this old—"

"Hush!" said Tiger-Man.

"How can I hush," cried the child, "when those devils go unpunished for the death of my friend?"

Tiger-Man turned to the Master.

"Was the boy who was killed a friend of this kid?"

"Yes, señor."

"Well, listen. I don't think there will be any more

THE PATIO OF THE MINT HOUSE IN POTOSÍ

danger to the ox-cart than there will be if he rides with us. Will you leave the matter to me?"

The muleteer nodded.

"Give heed, O little one," said Tiger-Man gravely. "Will you swear by Maria and the Blessed Saints to do as I tell you?"

"By the whole army of heaven, señor, if you will give me my wish."

"Good. Then you must ride at the head of the bullocks so as to give an air of innocence to the wagon. At the first sign of Indians you must leave your mule and dash inside. Remember, nobody may fire until you are safe. Will you promise?"

"By Maria and the Blessed Saints, señor, yes."

He caught Tiger-Man's hand and kissed it passionately; then, leaping into the saddle, he drummed the ribs of his mule with the swagger of a medieval mercenary. In a moment he was at the head of the oxen, his whip in the air, imperious and beckoning.

"Come on!" he cried. "Come on. It will be night before we kill the first savage."

I tried to laugh, but found myself closer to tears. Not every one is permitted to see Jim Hawkins in the flesh.

"Gutty little devil," said Bee-Mason, arranging his camera.

We had scarcely settled ourselves before Pedrito emitted a terrific cat-call and whistled his thong over the back of the bullocks. Traces creaked as the animals leaned into their collars. The wheels groaned stiffly and we were away, lurching towards Santa Cruz. Over the back of the wagon I beheld Tiger-Man's bearded face split in a satanic grin, and then a turn in the road hid from him my sight.

We talked little during that trek for we had our work cut out to keep our armory in its place. On the top of the mule trunk, behind which I crouched, were a rifle, a shot-gun and a pistol. Piles of cartridges suitable to each weapon lay side by side in neat boxes. For perhaps three minutes they kept their orderly habits, and then the motion of the cart overcame them. One by one they rolled into the scuppers, and it was only by the exercise of unusual agility that I was able to stay on at all.

There was an air of hope about the party, a bright, crusading glamour which canalized our senses and made us deaf to the hum of insects under the leather roof. Our eyes swept the road with the greediness of vultures, noting the passage of each butterfly and the flight of each gaudy parrot. Our minds flew back to the grim ride of two days past, and we watched the undergrowth in silence, our fingers itching for a shot. Nothing stirred. The heat flamed up from the yellow road, the trees shimmered in the haze, but we scarcely heeded, so strong was our desire to kill.

By and by the strain of gazing at a brilliant sheet of sand became too much for our eyesight. We blinked, and sought relief in the darker details of our moving cave. Through the open sides of the wagon we followed the movements of the great wheels, ponderously squeaking, loose, rising slowly and as slowly descending. We stretched our legs among the hide trunks and wriggled into more comfortable positions. Lightly we brushed the insects from our faces.

At the end of two hours we discovered with a shock that the atmosphere was thickening. The first fine edge of our enthusiasm had passed, and we knew that the glamour was over. Nothing remained but a desire to end our imprisonment one way or another.

"See any one behind?" asked Urrio.

"Not a soul."

"If they attack us at all it will be at the wigwam."

"Which is two hours ahead."

Those hours passed somehow. The afternoon sun blazed down on the stiff roof and bounced up from the road until we could scarcely breathe. Mosquitoes, *ihenni*, horse-flies, swarmed out of the forest and sucked themselves full on our sticky bodies. Almost in despair we waited for the wigwam clearing. At last it came, and we craned our necks to peer between the trees.

"It's no use," I said after a minute, "we shall have to stick here till dark."

"No Indians?" asked Urrio.

"The place is dead," I answered. "Can't you feel it yourself? It isn't possible for a large body of men to hide themselves. They can always be felt."

Urrio nodded.

The afternoon droned on. The cart became a slow hell. We lay with difficulty, staring at the roof and fretfully flapping at the insects. Even the bones of the butchered oxen failed to stir our interest. The evening faded into night. The bull-frogs awoke, and still we lay, half dead with irritation and cramp, but too proud to get out and walk. Tiger-Man had predicted failure. He should not see our shame.

After eight and a half hours the cart drew to a standstill under the shadow of a *fortin*. It was quite dark, but suddenly a torch gleamed and I had a glimpse of Tiger-Man. He rode up to the tail-board and peered in.

"Happy drive?" he asked.

"I have three weapons," I said, hoarse with thirst, "any one of which may explode."

I heard a chuckle in the darkness and the sound of retreating hooves. Stiff, parched, almost crazy with fatigue, we scrambled to the ground. Urrio turned to Pedrito.

"Well, my friend. They did not attack."

Against the light of the fire, the child drew himself erect.

"Are you surprised, señor? I was riding ahead!"

We blessed him and ate.

CHAPTER XXII

THERE are ten Rio Grandes between Texas and Patagonia, but none to match the quick, black stream near Santa Cruz. It is the dirtiest river I ever saw, fast and shallow, opaque with the loam it has scraped from the banks in its scurry towards the Amazon. Never more than eight feet deep, never less than half a mile in width, it calls for a peculiar type of ferry, manned in a peculiar way.

One morning, some ten days after the Indian episode, we stood on the edge and looked out over the flats. On the other side, a massed battalion of trees, half hidden by a glassy haze, paddled its roots in the water. In the distance a dozen natives, clad simply in straw hats, their bronze legs raising a scutter of dark foam, splashed towards us through the shallows. At their heels a swarm of craft, led like puppies on a string, slapped their bottoms against the waves. Presently they reached the main channel, where the stream ran swift and choppy, and, without hesitation, plunged in, the cords held tight between their teeth. Then, after a long, diagonal swim, their bobbing heads drew clear of the flood, and their charges were beached. With a shout of pure exhilaration, these river men waved their arms and raced for our patronage, rumbustiously, like American taxi-drivers.

"*Pelota!*" they cried. "*Pelota, señores!*"

Suddenly Tiger-Man laughed, a clear, jolly sound which doubled the grins on the swarthy faces.

"For a full-blooded liar," he said, "give me a traveling missionary."

He marched off to the landing place and gazed at the queer boats that lay high on the mud. In shape they resembled closely the vast water-lilies of the Amazon. Square, water-tight, clumsy as a tub, they were made from a couple of dried bullock skins laid on top of each other, and pinched round the edges until there was a hollow in the center for a man to sit cross-legged. Tiger-Man rumbled with amusement.

"Pelotas," he chuckled. "I have read of them before. A German missionary, describing his passage of the Rio Grande for publication at home, swore he was sewn up in a ball of hide and rolled across. What a novelist!"

"How?" I asked.

"*Pelota* means ball; it is also the name for this type of craft. Our religious friend knew that leather tubs were used, and guessed that they were shaped like a ball. Naughty old man."

Meanwhile memory had been stirring in my brain. Dimly I remembered having heard of the practice before, but it is only now that I am able to give Tiger-Man the history of *pelotas*. In 1657 an anonymous gentleman left London for Buenos Aires and Peru on a mission for the Directors of the notorious South Sea Company, four years before the bubble burst. He rode, this intrepid creature, from the River Plate to Potosí, and his account, published by John Darby of Bartholomew Close, is a little gem. I will transcribe his remarks on *pelotas* verbatim.

"Let it be observed," he writes, "that the rivers Lucan and Salladillo, as well as all the rest in the Province of Buenos Aires, Paraguay and Tucuman, that fall into the River de la Plata are fordable on horseback; but, when the rains or any other accident swells them, a traveler must either swim over or else get upon a bundle in the nature of a Raft, which a Savage hawls over to the other side. I could not swim, and so was forced to make use of this expedient twice or thrice when I could not find a ford. The way was this; my Indian killed a wild bull, flayed the hide off and stuffed it with straw and ty'd it up in a great bundle with thongs of the same hide, upon which I placed myself and my baggage; he swam over, hawling me after him by a cord ty'd to the bundle, and then he re-passed and swam my horses and mules over to me."

While our personal baggage was being stowed into *pelotas*, I asked a native for a drink. I thought perhaps there was a spring near by, or a small stream that poured clean water into the river. I was surprised beyond words when the man scooped a hole in the mud, tumbled a bucketful of Rio Grande into it, and demanded, quite solemnly, an egg. This he broke, explaining that the white bound the dirt together and made it settle. In half an hour I was able, with a fair amount of comfort, to drink a cup of warm, brackish fluid. He told me sadly that his fellow villagers, who eked out a living by ferrying merchandise, never drank anything else, and admitted that all the women were afflicted by goiter.

The crossing was an adventure in itself, spiced novelty without danger. We started a few hundred yards up stream, and taking advantage of the current, steered a diagonal course through the waves. Each of us had an Indian in charge, and we soon found that the nicest sense of balance was required if the water were not to slop over the clumsy gunwales of the hides. As we sat within a few yards of one another, a hilarious flotilla separated by thousands of black bubbles, we marveled at the skill with which our pilots worked. They swam a little below the *pelotas*, a leather cord between their teeth, and humored the bouncing craft with their shoulders when they showed signs of drifting away. From time to time a native would swallow a mouthful of Rio Grande, and then the *pelotas* would rock at the ecstasy of spitting. When we came to a mud bank our guides ran knee-deep in ooze lest they should sink, and we lay back like kings against the leather, and slithered softly towards deeper water. Safe on the other side we considered each other ruefully, for our clothes had been trade-marked by the river, and we were wet through.

That night we camped within striking distance of Santa Cruz, and a storm came up with the darkness.

CLOSER VIEW OF POTOSÍ MOUNTAIN SHOWING HOW THE EARTH HAS BEEN REMOVED IN ORDER TO EXTRACT MINERALS

Through the wrack and wrath of a rain-swept dawn, two aëroplanes swept towards the east. Their wheels almost brushed the tree-tops, and as they roared over our bivouac we recognized Santalla's sage-green fighter, and the silver Junker monoplane, "Charcas." We leaped from our hammocks, one thought only in our minds. War! Nothing else could justify the hour, the speed, or the height at which they were traveling.

We saddled in haste, and soon, the storm clouds clearing, found ourselves free from Green Hell for the first time in three months. The relief was amazing, almost tangible. Gone was the stuffy, inclosed atmosphere of the forest, teeming with constriction and decay; gone the solid, inexorable walls which, for so long, had been our dwelling. In front, stretching into a background of thick-set, purple mountains, was a plain that was wide and undulating and treeless, and our hearts rejoiced as though we had just escaped from a cell. The landscape was covered with grass, a luxury forgotten by our animals, and we allowed them to fill themselves to the end of their desire. Heavy-eyed oxen raised slow heads at our approach. A bunch of mules danced across the turf and whinnied the latest story to our tired beasts. A flock of blue-gray pigeons circled around us.

Santa Cruz de la Sierra! Sacred Cross of the Mountain! Romantic name, and, seen for the first time by weary travelers, romantic place. We were riding into a poster with its absence of subtlety, its crude, accurate coloring, its freedom from unnecessary detail. Just a green plain, a block of upstanding mountains, and a sky that was full of stationary clouds, thick, white, glorious, shaped to suit the fancy of the beholder. St. George on a snowy war horse drove his spear into a snowy dragon. A ship set out to sea, sails bellied by the Trades, foam creaming at her stem. All the angels of heaven sang praises to the sun. Urrio drew near.

"Come down from the clouds," he said, "and help me architect a golf course. It's the first chance we've had since Corumbá."

So we plotted the full eighteen holes, and lingered sensuously over this cross bunker and that pond-guarded green. Neither Tiger-Man nor Bee-Mason played golf, so we had the course to ourselves, and reveled in our absence from the woods. Soon the jungle faded from our minds.

Towards evening we entered the suburbs of Santa Cruz, and found them desolate and deserted. Miles of straight, silent road, sandy and unpaved, lay four feet below the level of the houses, and I make no doubt were excellent water-courses in the wet season. Presently a low, angry hum of voices, varied by an occasional shout, came to our ears. We pricked our mules, and rode into the main square. There, under the windows of a yellow building, in the shadow of a vast cathedral, was a crowd five thousand strong. A man was leaning from the balcony, pouring a flood of burning words over the silent throng. At intervals a roar went up to him.

"*Viva Bolivia! Muera el Paraguay!*" accompanied by shrieks of valor and rage.

Since we had no wish to spend a night on the edge of the square, we set our mules at the crowd, pushing gently through, as mounted policemen do at a football match. Instantly the attention was drawn to us.

"What of the war, señores? You have been exploring round there" (our mission had been boomed in the Press). "Tell us."

We were surrounded, and halted by the pressure. "I know nothing of the war," said Urrio, "except the sight of Santalla's plane this morning. Tell me."

A tangle of words burst from all about us.

"Vanguardia, the *fortin* near Puerto Suarez, has fallen. Twenty-five Bolivian dead. The Paraguayans stole up in the night and murdered them. But we got our own back. Trust us. This morning we captured Galpon, and killed fifty of the bastards. God grant us a war to the death! Rivers of blood shall flow, and Paraguay shall bite the dust! *Viva Bolivia! Muera el Paraguay!*"

We moved on. Something touched my foot. I looked down, and saw a small boy with a box over his shoulders.

"*Lustra,* señor? Shoe-shine?"

I laughed, and the urchin polished my boots as I rode.

That night, in the cool *patio* of our hotel, we decided to offer our services to the Government in case of need. Englishmen enjoy this sort of thing, and even Tiger-

Man, who despised warfare as childish, offered to take me into the Chaco, saying that I should need a nurse. Outside in the *Plaza*, we could still hear the howls of a blood-mad populace, and the sounds came queerly after the silence of the jungle. Tiger-Man was very sarcastic.

"They want their rivers of blood," he said, "for they have never passed San José. To-morrow, if their wish is granted, they will rot in heaps from hunger and thirst and *ihenni*. Soldiers are fools."

Urrio felt sure that nothing would come of it, that the powder would flare and die down, and so it proved. Argentina and the United States who, between them, will cause all wars to cease in South America, threw their weight on the side of peace, and vested interests prevailed over hot blood.

* * * * * * *

Now that I have guided my narrative through the joys and uncertainties of exploration, and the still greater joys and uncertainties of a caravan route, I feel that some apology is due. The Indian affair and the abortive war scare were unsatisfactory, but that is one of the penalties of a chronicle. The writer is a slave, unable to twist events to his liking. The novelist that lies buried in all men writhed at the waste of such material. What a scene I could have created out of armed savages invading the camp at dawn, with oiled skins gleaming in the light of the fires! What pleasure I could have felt in the creation! And few could have called me liar. Only my companions now in England, a few Bolivians and Tiger-Man, who hated lies.

So, if I have raised hopes which have been dashed in the ending, I ask forgiveness. The expedition, small as it was, is too real in my mind for me to play pranks with the facts.

PART TWO

CHAPTER XXIII

SANTA CRUZ DE LA SIERRA is a feat in itself. On three sides it is hemmed in by Green Hell, and the fourth is a rising wedge of rock that mounts to Cochabamba. No railway engine has ever shrieked through its loneliness, though the roar of a weekly monoplane now mingles with the mule bells. Yet there is a mighty stone cathedral, a legacy from the Jesuits, and a multitude of yellow shops; while twenty-five thousand people take in each other's washing. This, in the middle of a forest with the Amazon no more than three days distant, is little short of amazing.

Santa Cruz is dead, but in the days of the rubber boom she was rich. Prosperous men swept down from the fever-ridden zones to the north and spent their short holidays in joyous freedom. Nobody looked too far ahead, the city danced and was glad, and all the while the black cloud of a rubber slump lowered on the horizon. It was inevitable, that slump, for the gum forests of South America were always difficult to work. The trees grew haphazard, many paces apart; and the cultivated estates of the Malay Peninsula soon supplanted them. In a few years prosperity will return. The land is bountiful, the fruit delicious, and millions of oranges rot yearly for lack of a market. Already a railway joins Buenos Aires to the Bolivian border, and an extension is only a matter of time. When that happens Santa Cruz will arise from the dead.

The war rumors quite spoiled our enjoyment of the place, for the atmosphere was brittle and fiery, terribly similar to that of 1914 translated into Spanish. We had arrived without a shilling in our pockets, and although I had a letter of credit, it was a month overdue, and the banks were using every loophole to avoid payment. Wherefore, Tiger-Man and I dressed ourselves to kill, with jingling spurs and broad-brimmed hats and a brace of heavy pistols at our hips. As we strode across the palm-lined square people drew away, and even the noisy shoe-blacks kept their distance. In this character of aggression we entered the bank and demanded the manager. I am bound to say he showed no signs of panic, but, on the other hand, he did not go too deeply into the question of dates. Our march back to the hotel was one triumphant swagger.

At the first hint of trouble, every mule of fighting age was bustled into the forest for fear of conscription. There were muleteers and to spare; we interviewed a bunch each day, but they were all smug and uncommunicative, and swore that their animals had strayed. Our own beasts were wearied almost to death and would take four months to recover, so in an evil moment we fell in with a builder of roads. He was a cheerful card, an American, supremely and rightfully proud of the track he had driven through the jungles to the south. Moreover, he had three cars at his command, and we were in a hurry. Slightly against our judgment, we believed his statement that we should be in Lagunillas, two hundred miles distant, in two and a half days.

Thus, on New Year's day, we set out amid the cheers of the populace. The local band, arrayed in purple and frayed cotton, assembled in the square and blew itself hoarse. Prominent officials gave us to understand that we were christening the road to the honor of the State, and for a few minutes the war was forgotten. They do these things very pleasantly in Latin countries.

Let me say at once that the road, as a road, was perfect. A broad band of red soil ran straight as a sword-slash through an ocean of Green Hell. The surface was smooth and bore little trace of the pock-marks left by extracted tree roots, and we were able to keep up a comfortable thirty-five miles an hour for the whole of one day. That night disaster came. As we lay in our hammocks, with the cars shining monstrous and ghostly through the fire, the road builder strode across to Urrio. Tiger-Man joined them.

"Shouldn't wonder if it rained," said the American, laconically.

"Sure to," replied Tiger-Man. "Clouds have been banking since lunch."

Urrio groaned.

"There are two deep rivers between here and Yacuiba. What shall we do?"

There was a full and concentrated silence. I believe that everybody present knew that we ought to return; yet no one had the courage to suggest it. The noise of that band was too vivid in our ears.

"It may be only a shower," said somebody.

And the rest of us leaped at the excuse. Of course it was no shower; subconsciously we knew that we were fools, that the rains were long overdue, and that we were in for a time of trial. Yet, obstinate as pigs, fearful of ridicule as a colony of monkeys, we deliberately preferred the hardship to the indignity of failure.

After supper the weather broke. Even as we ate, a great black pall crept up the northern sky. One by one the stars went out, snuffed by the climbing clouds. Soon we were inclosed as in a lightless room, and directly we left the red circle of the fire we held our arms protectively, as men do in dark places. A deadly silence, pregnant with all manner of possibilities, settled over the land. We talked instinctively in lowered voices; even the chattering of the natives was hushed.

Suddenly, out of a quiet that was almost a vacuum, a roaring, mighty wind swept past us, sighing, and swaying the trees. In a moment every man of us was under cover in the cars, with nerves keyed up for something really magnificent. Up to that evening I had always supposed that the storms of the theater were overdrawn, that the magnesium flares and beaten trays were as unlikely as the stories they bolstered. Never have I been more mistaken. The greatest electrician and the heftiest stage-hand that ever lived were mere wax vestas and penny drums beside reality.

The ball opened with a wavering flash of green light that filled the horizon and showed up each leaf and twig and bough in black relief. An emphatic, though distant, crash followed the illumination as surely as the roar of a cannon followed the flaming linstock. Then darkness, a thousand times deeper than before, fell across us. Gradually the storm approached. Each appearance of the lightning was yellower than the last; each volley of thunder succeeded it at shorter intervals, and then, just as the brilliance and the noise met in one huge, devastating consummation above our heads, the rain came.

Such rain! It tumbled out of heaven with all the frustrated energy of a season of dryness. It was so eager to reach the ground that it did not bother to resolve into drops, but poured in a continuous running stream that obscured the forest with a white veil, even when the lightning shone upon it. It made the hoods of the cars rumble like a roll of drums, and the harsh, metallic clang of empty petrol tins sounded through the night. At eight o'clock there was a gray film over the world, and the cars had sunk almost to their hubs. Miraculously, an army of eager bullfrogs had issued from the womb of the storm. The wet season was upon us with a vengeance.

It would be tedious to stress the hardships of that three weeks' journey. For me they were particularly arduous because my legs were festering with a multitude of those sores which had bothered Urrio in the *ihenni*-stricken forests near San José. I lost my strength and was reduced to such a skeleton that my companions restrained me with gentle force from the harder labors of the day. When we came to a marsh and had to unload it was they who carried the baggage and I who drove. Nothing could have exceeded their care of me, they were tender as women and very thoughtful. One morning Tiger-Man pushed his bearded face through the curtains of the car in which I was dressing my wounds. I was weary and faint and disheartened from tearing matted bandages from the sores. He smiled encouragement.

"I'm a terrible coward," I said, "about pain."

"It's a filthy job," he said, "stick it out."

He hovered around, coming back every five minutes to see how the peroxide of hydrogen was cleansing the matter and the zinc ointment filling the holes. Indeed, from that moment, intimate as we had been before Santa Cruz, we were more like brothers than acquaintances.

Day after day we pursued the old dismal round of driving cars through swamps, pushing, hauling, advancing a few heated yards, and then leaving the engines to cool. In this manner we sped forward at a rate of five miles for every twelve hours—less than our poor, wearied animals had made from Gaiba. It was irritating work, strenuous and boring, with no spice of danger to mitigate the toil. Now and again we passed broken-down, native villages, but for the most part it was just hard slogging through marshy forest.

Then, suddenly, we left Green Hell, and stepped out upon the muddy shores of the Rio Grande. The change was amazing, for the river had swollen to gigantic size, and was quite impassable. Directly opposite, across half a mile of black, tormented water, a great red cliff rose sheer into the sky. Along the top, a fringe of forest stood dangerously near the edge. Indeed, even as we watched, the treacherous soil gave way, and a huge tree slipped into space, waving its branches piteously, and rolling to its doom with a noise like muffled breakers. Within thirty seconds there was a cloud of dust and a floating body. Nothing more. This went on all day.

By and by we noticed a native village that lay back among the trees at the summit of a square headland. It was so far down stream that at first we paid little attention to it, but our interest was forced by the arrival of a number of stark naked Indians with logs over their shoulders. Quite placidly they announced that they were the Passers of the River, and would handle our cars in the event of the water decreasing.

Their leader, a fat, bearded little man with enough Spanish blood in him to breed hair on his face, squatted near the gramophone and refused to move until a record had been three times repeated. Then he murmured that if no more rain fell we should be able to pass in two days. He looked regretfully at the clear sky as he said this, for he loved music and would fain have increased the flood.

For the next two days we worked hard. These Rivermen had us in their power, and knew it. They were so far from a town that money meant little to them, and they preferred to take payment in kind. On the second morning, the entire male population had crossed the water on their logs—thick tree-roots of an incredible lightness on which they balanced themselves with tight knees, and swam with their arms, as one does on a rubber horse in a bathing-pool—and announced that they had come to hear a concert. Moreover, they showed every intention of going back to their village if they were not humored; so we took it in turns, and for nine solid hours on two successive days that gramophone sang and played and laughed among the trees. At intervals Tiger-Man, Urrio and I boxed for their edification. This was not so easy with festering legs, but it had to be done.

At last, on the evening of the third day, the leader proclaimed that one of the cars might cross. It was still dangerous, he said, but at any moment a cloud might burst and we should be trapped for a week. So he and his merry men towed two flat-bottomed barges lashed together across from the village, and we ran the heaviest car astride the gunwales on a couple of wide planks. This took some time, for the mud of the Rio Grande when almost dry is as tricky a surface as toffee in the sun. It is really a thick top dressing laid loosely on the banks, and it literally flaps like a pegged canvas in a wind when anything is so ill-advised as to step on it. However, half an hour before sunset we were ready, and I climbed to the driver's seat. In a moment there was a burst of protest from the natives. We were top-heavy enough, they clamored, without that. Would the gentleman be kind enough, to squat under the engine, level with the water? He could be of no possible use in any case, and the least he could do was to cease to be an active hindrance. Swearing, I obeyed.

That journey will remain with me till I die. Four stalwart Indians stood at each end of the raft, and plied vast, wooden "sweeps" in the manner of a cook stirring a Christmas pudding. Thirty-two smaller natives, of the same color as the river, crouched on their tree-roots and dragged the barge with thongs held tight between their teeth. A continuous chittering accompanied our sedate movements into the center of the stream.

Once there, all power was swept from us. The age-old Rio Grande, released from the leanness of the dry season, was enjoying itself. Large, coffee-tinted waves jostled us, hurled us to their friends, treated us in the most undignified and hurly-burly manner, and slopped pailfuls of themselves into our craft. We lurched and groaned and climbed and bumped in a giddy, nonsensical, drunken dance, while the natives screamed exhortations at each other. Twice my gunwale went under and righted itself, leaving me to sit in a mud bath.

It was immediately under the tall cliffs that the real

danger came. The water was intensely rough, choppy as the Channel, and far dirtier, and I hauled myself into a position whence I could dive into the wrack. Suddenly, drawn by some impulse, I looked up. There, miles above my head, so it seemed, a little puff of sand spurted from the side of the cliff. The natives noticed it too, and a loud wail broke from their throats.

"Jesucristo," they cried, "save us!"

Instantly the voice of the headman was raised above the waves.

"Let us be silent," he called, and the loyal answer shrilled back from the logs, "We are silent."

Then, with a ghastly, sliding motion, a tree broke away and came rocketing down the face. Crackling and rumbling in agony, it threw up its branches and dived. Now this might quite well have been the end of this chronicle, but the Rio Grande having placed us in peril got us out of it with marked address. Quickly and violently we were seized by a swirl of the current and carried a full twenty yards past the place where the tree crashed in ruin. For all that, the dust from the descent covered us like a sheet. It was an uncanny escape. Gradually the men on logs drew us clear of the water, and, wet and dirty and very thankful to be alive, we landed under the brow of the square headland.

That evening, when the villagers were cooking a chicken for my supper, I strolled on to the cliff and stared across to where Urrio's camp-fire shone vivid in the darkness. Soon the headman joined me.

"It was a near thing just now, señor. Those trees are the devil."

"By the way," I said, "why did you tell your people to be silent when you fought the waves?"

"The river spirits, señor, they do not like us to shout."

I went away thinking. His first call had been "Jesucristo."

While in this village I was treated to one of those rare glimpses of dignity which are sometimes found in native peoples. The whole population cannot have been more than ninety souls, men, women, and ragged children; everybody must have known all there was to know about the character of his neighbors. Yet no one could enter another's house without the most elaborate etiquette. As I sat in my hammock a woman came up to the hut. She was dressed in all her finery, from a handkerchief over her head to a shiny prehistoric black dress. She approached with circumspection, and asked with the manner of a grandee:

"The señora is at home? How lucky to find her this sunny morning! And her son? Is he still the manly fellow that I remember?"

My hostess arose from her haunches and bowed courteously.

"Will not the señora be seated? My son is indeed in good health, but"—glancing over her shoulder at the child—"it is a long time since he was whipped. Perhaps to-day, perhaps to-morrow. Who knows?"

A solitary Englishman dressing for dinner in the jungles of Penang could not have kept up appearances with a better grace. Another debt to the Jesuits.

One more incident stands out in my mind from the long, tedious welter of that disastrous motor trip. We had stopped for lunch in a tiny village not far from our destination, just where a huge, rain-born lake slopped over the street. Suddenly, from behind, came the sound of pipes and violins joyously played in the tripping measure of a dancing jig. We looked up, expecting a wedding, or at least a festival, and were frankly amazed at what we saw. A struggling, laughing procession, headed by a man on a horse, made its way towards us. As they drew level we perceived that the horseman was the *cacique*, and that he held in his arms a small, smooth coffin, open at the top. We stepped on to the running-board of the car and caught our breaths at the vision, for a little child was lying in the stillness of death. The crowd swirled past us, and splashed through the water at the headman's heels. Their instruments, painted in vivid yellows and reds, squeaked an accompaniment to this strange scene. On the other side they halted, not because they had reached the burial ground, but because an excessively stout woman was crossing the lake on the back of an excessively stout man. The whole company lined up and yelled their delighted approval, and then they moved away to the cemetery.

It was so different from the funeral we had seen in the forest, with its callous, griefless wailing that at first we could make nothing of it. And then it struck us how

POTOSÍ MOUNTAIN FROM WHENCE GREAT TREASURES HAVE BEEN EXTRACTED

supremely right they were to jest with death, even when it was represented by a minute brown body not two years old. Moreover, we fancied that the soul of the child, should it have chanced to witness the affair, would have rejoiced, even as its relatives, at the grotesque fording of the fat woman. There was something grave-defying in the conception.

Unfortunately the leading car tried to follow the procession, and the magneto fizzled out. We reached the end of our journey ignominiously hauled by bullocks.

CHAPTER XXIV

ONE evening in a hot courtyard near the center of the small, dead town of Lagunillas, Joselito, the muleteer spoke:

"Who knows, señores? Perhaps I catch them to-day, perhaps not for a week. No, señores, there are none in the corral. At least only three—and what are they among so many?"

Joselito was a half-caste, a true son of the lazy tropics, and his rich, dark skin glowed with the color of pure tobacco. Quite obviously he thought us mad. His black eyes said as much, and so did the gesture with which he flung his arm towards the sharply rising woods to the westward, where his animals sauntered at their ease.

"You see, señores, it is rough country; and the bullfrogs cry in the marshes. It is not the season for traveling."

It was indeed rough country, silent and rugged, more than a little frightening. There the flat carpet of Green Hell, sweeping across the terrible Gran Chaco from the Rio Paraguay, took the first step in the Andean staircase that ends on the bitter plateaux near La Paz. In the very sands of the town the plain ceased with a jerk, and we were suddenly aware of a great army of trees that climbed like ants into the sky-line, thousands of feet above.

During Joselito's speech Bee-Mason had been sitting very still, his face worried and strained. He knew no Spanish, but when the muleteer had ceased, with an expressive drop of his hands, he said bitterly:

"I shall look a proper fool when my film-boxes are opened and there is nothing to develop."

We knew what he meant. Sooner or later, even in temperate climates, an image fades from the celluloid, leaving it as blank as when it started. It vanishes just four times as quickly in the jungle.

We had left Gaiba in October, it was now late January, and although Bee-Mason had intentionally overexposed the film, we knew that time was vital if his work were not to be wasted. In a moment Urrio's mind was made up; he turned to Joselito.

"I want those three mules to-morrow. Señor Bee-Mason and I go south at dawn. See to it, my friend."

Joselito departed, grumbling. When he had gone, Urrio became apologetic.

"I am sorry," he said. "It means that the expedition, as a whole, is ended. We shall meet again in Tarija—but that is civilization."

Soon, by the light of yellow candles, a sad little party drank to the days that were gone. None of us spoke much, but in each of our minds was a series of vivid scenes recalling the humors and hardships through which together we had passed. Somberly we doused the lights and went to bed.

Directly Urrio and Bee-Mason had trotted away Tiger-Man and I tackled the muleteer. We drew a pathetic picture of our needs, and let slip a few dusky hints as to his future if he failed us. Accordingly, on the following afternoon, a bunch of flea-bitten, miserable animals assembled round our door. In the same hour the weather, which for a week had favored us, broke out afresh, and the poor brutes' backs were sodden before the packs were settled. Under a mantle of teeming, destructive rain we rode off towards the Parapití, the last river between us and our goal.

That night we lay in a bug-devoured camp, and scratched our way to sanity and the dawn. They were amazing, those bugs. They overflowed through sheer abundance from the roof, walked down our hammock ropes, hid themselves in the cracks of our boots, and caused us, to the great mystification of the farmer, to strip to the skin and cool our aching bodies in the storm. The women-folk, debarred by etiquette from open vision, peered through the slats of the kitchen; but bugs are a swift antidote to modesty.

For miles before we reached the Parapití a strange, low, muttering fell upon our ears. Snarlings and rumblings and big, hollow bumps mingled with the sigh of the rain and the rattle of shaken bridles. Wet, white, fleecy clouds raced over the Cordilleras, and lent point to the rising anger of the river. Even the road was a rushing stream that teased the fetlocks of our mules.

Suddenly, through a brake of scrub, we pushed on to a lofty headland, and the Parapití lay brawling at our feet. A swollen, sullen, coffee-colored waste of waters, it fought and tumbled its way towards the east. From where we sat we could see a slender thread of pathway venture to the brink and trail away among the trees. Sadly we realized that our companions, whom we had hoped to overtake, were as surely cut off from us as if they had been dead. In heavy silence we slipped down the red cliff path and camped by the shore.

For a whole, long, irritating week we squatted on our haunches, and watched the waves go by. Tall and dark, ridged in furrows like a potato field, they roared between us and the Yacuiba road. Enormous tree-trunks, with branches waving haphazard, scurried past us in impotent revolt. Boulders boomed along the bottom with a noise that could be heard for a league, and, all the while, a patient band of Indian baggage carriers stood on the farther bank and watched for the ebb.

Some nights later, when Tiger-Man and I were yarning beside the fire, Joselito detached himself from the shadows and approached us.

"I do not know if it is worthy of your attention, señores," he said calmly, "but the river seems to be rising."

Instantly Tiger-Man was on the brink. Stooping, he placed a twig on the waterline, and, in sixty seconds by his watch, a foot of black, creeping liquid had wandered up the bank. The time for action had come. For the half of a frenzied hour we fetched and carried, and sweated and slithered and swore, while half a ton of luggage was shifted to a tiny eminence a few hundreds yards away. Just as the last mule-trunk was dumped in safety the fire began to float. In another hour we were on an island.

All through that night the sounds of fury continued, magnified and made monstrous by the darkness. The water lapped against the flanks of our hillock, the flood bellowed like a herd of oxen, our animals whickered and whinnied in their fear, and over and above these usual noises, those terrible boulders rolling along the floor of the river gave an eerie point to an evening that was morbid enough as it was.

Next morning the Parapití which, in Guarayo, means "Waters of Death," subsided with a rush. A sudden cloud-burst in the mountains near Sucre had caused the disturbance, and the surplus having moved on, we came down from our island. Everywhere was an orgy of wreckage. A gigantic tree had been lifted without effort and was reposing soberly some quarter of a mile inland; a similar tree which had decorated a sandbank was nowhere to be found. On the red sides of the cliff a dull, dark line, two meters high, showed the extent of the rise. Still, the sun was ablaze in a cloudless sky, the waters were fast abating, and all was right with our world.

That afternoon, so mercurial is the nature of Bolivian rivers, Tiger-Man and I decided to try the temper of the stream. The breakers were still steep, but the potato furrows had gone out of them, and they were merely waved, like the hair of an Italian dandy.

Moreover, the Indians had crossed, and we had our pride. Accordingly, we moved over to where a depressed-looking group was lying on the sand, and asked for advice. It came—and quickly. A completely naked Indian of miserable physique sprang to his feet and waved his hands, the finger nails of which were bright orange with the cold. He informed us in a rapid mixture of Guarayo and Spanish that it was quite a simple matter. No one would come to harm, provided that one ran diagonally to the breakers. He added the seeming platitude that one should not linger by the way.

Presently, clad quite simply in a green scarf and a pair of dark spectacles, I touched the river with my toe. It was beyond doubt chilly, so much so that Tiger-Man and I raced each other across the sand-spit, the sooner to finish our ordeal. We were followed by a respectful cheer.

At first it was easy. We abandoned ourselves to the waters, and forged automatically through, despite the muddy compound that splashed into our mouths. It was about half way over that my curiosity betrayed me. I remembered suddenly that I was the chronicler of the expedition, and that it would be hardly fair to Urrio if the rivers lost their proper share of description. Struck by the logic of the thought I stopped and looked up stream to see how a Parapití wave appeared at close quarters. With characteristic bad manners it refused to wait, and my mental notes went rapidly eastwards along with me. A huge, black monster picked me up, hugged me to its bosom, tossed me to a companion, and I was able without difficulty to visualize the feelings of a rugger ball at the feet of an International pack.

"You fool," roared Tiger-Man, who had attained the bank.

I had a hurried vision of a frightened, bearded face, and then I was fighting for my life. For a while I really thought I should die, the shore was moving so fast. There were rocks ahead, and I seemed to have no power over anything at all. Even at that moment, however, certain vivid phrases anent disembowelling persisted in my mind. Nevertheless I managed to force myself out of the stream, and half a mile away I was hauled out ignominiously by a grinning Indian. Tiger-Man, who had arrived like a meteor, looked at me in pity.

"An author is a great responsibility," he said.

Henceforward that priceless companion took care that in the passage of the Parapití I went first.

Up to a few years ago a raging wilderness lay to the south and west of the Waters of Death. It lay to the east as well, of course, and so it does to this day, but it was in the slanting forests of the Andean foothills that the Chiriguano Indians, keening like ghosts, harried the Spaniards with flame and arrow to the memory of Atahualpa. A narrow, tree-girt road twisted along the valley as far as the Argentine border, but it was a bold man who faced it when every yard was a potential ambush.

To a nervous muleteer the silence must have been appalling.

In their rough and eager way the Chiriguanos were men of humor. Since the days when a mad, white race had dropped from the sky on to the Cordilleras, a black gown and a shaven pate had spelt danger. Captured tribesmen, dying in agony at the stake, had glowered bitterly at the unctuous, mumbled spells, and the clicking waistbands of dark beads with which they passed the remaining moments of their lives. Wherefore, although the natives loathed all foreigners with every muscle of their yellow bodies, they reserved a peculiar and sardonic hatred of the priests; and with the pure joy of Robin Hood castigating prelates, they indulged in a little fun before spitting them to a tree. They jumped out from the shadows like so many prancing fiends, and chased the reverend fathers for miles, until the comic aspect began to pall, and they made an end—eventually. And so the missionaries for the most part ceased to roam and kept behind the stone walls of the monasteries of Tarija and Macherití.

Religion having retired from the fray, it was left to commerce to open up the district. Somewhere about 1912 a rumor blazed throughout America that deep under the ridged *sierras* of Bolivia there was oil. Instantly the inferno of uncharted forest was invaded by a band of men who held their lives so lightly as to scorn the Chiriguanos. They were spare and slight, northerners for the most part, narrow of feature, tough and resilient as whalebone. Drawn from every nation of the world they gathered under the joint banners of the United States and the Standard Oil Company of New Jersey, and wandered out alone among the hills. For six months at a stretch they clambered and slipped and wrestled with Green Hell, breaking off bits of mountains and entering the facts in a notebook. They peered about for seepages —which are never directly above the oil field, but are diagonal backwashes from a layer some miles away—and grew daily leaner. They called themselves with characteristic modesty, geologists. I met one of them, a grave, pinched man, a little white about the temples, but when he tried to tell me of his job the loneliness had dried the words out of him. I expressed wonder that he could enjoy so grim a vigil in a country where trees grow like bristles on the faces of sheer cliffs. Drily he smiled:

"It's a good life on the whole," he said. "Better than a pot belly, anyway."

To these unassuming heroes of industry the Standard Oil Company owes its dividends. In every corner of the world hills have skipped like young rams at their bidding, the result of unintelligible jottings in faded notebooks. Wherever they can they take a pipe and a camp bed—they are most particular about this—and vanish into the great untamed. In due course they return, bearded and tongue-tied; and the vast machinery of drills and derricks, and valves and steam-engines newcast in Pittsburgh is hurried from the coast.

Tiger-Man and I paid visits to three of their camps,

and came away wiser for the encounters. At the first *Camiri* we made a blunder that we never repeated. We arrived at four in the afternoon, having missed our lunch because the delay on the Parapití had swallowed our supplies. We were too shy to ask for a meal during work hours, and they never dreamed that we were hungry, so we took some photographs, and afterwards shot a brace of parrots; and we vowed then and then, by the blood and feathers of the slain, to turn up at other locations within half an hour of feeding time. Religiously we kept our word.

The memory of Macherití, the second camp, bides with me yet. For close on forty miles we had ridden through blazing sunshine and broken canyon country. Up two hundred feet of soft, red sand that was as difficult to negotiate as snow; down again into the valleys where the fickle rivers had dried in the heat; through barren cactus patches we plodded our lonely way, until our saddles and our tempers had become equally hot and unhitched. As was our custom when weariness assailed us we spoke not at all, but left the other fellow to welter in his thirst. This was Tiger-Man's idea, and he was a prince of comrades; for in such an atmosphere of give and take a quarrel became quite impossible.

Suddenly we climbed a high, slippery bank, and Macherití, radiant in its promise of a night's rest, lay before us. A crimson, bulbous sun shone low above the Franciscan monastery, throwing it into black relief. Wide, tree-lined streets, savage boulevards, showed clearly the priestly influence towards tidiness, and an army of misbegotten dogs snapped at the heels of our mules. As we passed into the sunset, a loud hail issued from a hut.

"Say here," bellowed a voice, "you English?"

A lank figure in white came out from the shadows.

"Standard Oil?" asked Tiger-Man, shaking the hard hand.

"I should say so," boomed the cheery American. "Late of Oklahoma!"

"We wanted a few pictures of your place," I said.

A pair of shrewd, gray eyes switched from Tiger-Man to me.

"Sure thing. Come and spend the night. The boys love strangers."

With a wave of his arm, he indicated a mud and wattle hut.

"Beer!" he shouted. "You look dusty."

That drink was Olympian, but something far rarer was to follow. Just as darkness fell we rode into the location two miles from the village. It was cut out of the wilderness, a haven on a rank hillside, served by a constant stream, ice-cold, straight from the Cordilleras. To reach this small collection of neat houses we had to descend from the path and wade through the water between two tremendous boulders, smooth as pebbles, magnificent as the Pillars of Hercules. To say that we were welcomed would be trite. Half a dozen friendly and charming men collected us, showed us to a hot shower, and gave us towels. With a parting shot they left us to wallow in an ecstasy of soap.

"Supper in twenty minutes, boys. You've struck lucky. It's our day for ices!"

Ices in the forests of Bolivia! It seemed incredible, until we remembered the monotonous thud of that steam-engine from Pittsburgh. Our cup was full. Joyously we bathed.

Later, as we sat round a milk-white table-cloth and made pigs of ourselves over the ices, we led these hard-hewn men to talk of their profession. It was "shop," delivered with the gusto of exiles to sympathetic laymen, for they had seen no outsider for months, and their hearts shone in the telling. The man from Oklahoma opened the ball with a sly poke at his neighbor.

"We are rather short-handed just now," he drawled, staring at the electric light. "Jim will tell you why."

"Jim" came as near to a blush as a seasoned engineer may permit himself.

"Oh, that," he said, off-handed as a young father displaying his baby.

Pressed for details, he confessed that somehow or other an extra charge of dynamite had found its way into the blasting operations. One morning, round about lunch-time, a large slice of mountain had showered into the native quarters. "No damage at all," he assured us, "but the cowards ran." Could we understand such yellow behavior? Filled to the brim with the luxury of good cheer we told him emphatically that he was the worst-used man in Bolivia. He gave us a cigar.

As the evening drew on we became more and more attracted to these jolly Americans. They were so unlike the pompous, stiff-collared breed that haunts the caravanserais of Europe. Tough, rude health spoke from their tanned cheeks. Their eyes were the eyes of men keyed up to the acme of bodily vigor. They bore themselves with an air; and the almighty dollar never once passed their lips in relation to themselves.

"Guess we're poor men," said one, "we've to root for a living."

"Twelve hours a day," said another. "Week in, week out, Sundays included. You can't stop that damned drill for a Sabbatarian whim."

"Seems to suit you," I said, scanning their faces.

"No complaints," growled the man from Oklahoma. "We live like kings from bum all. Still, a few months' rest is good at the end of two years. Yes, sir."

So the talk rattled on, fine and free, as it does in wild places. Before long we were feeling pleasantly intimate, and story followed story with easy rhythm.

"Ever hear about our pay-car?" said one.

The others laughed grimly, showing their teeth, and suddenly the warmth went out of the room. It was exactly as if something ghastly had joined us.

"Tell 'em, Jim," they said.

"Waal," the drawl was sardonic, mirthless, hard as edged tools. "A goddamed bunch of bandits tried to ambush our pay-roll on the way from the border. They knew when it was due, so they squatted in the trees above the road and waited. But they had forgotten one thing—our autos travel in pairs, about half a mile apart, and for the life of them those sons of bitches could not guess which held the bills. I reckon they must have figured the first was a blind, for they let it through."

The dynamite man drew savagely at his pipe, and his eyes blazed behind the smoke. "In the second car, gentlemen, was six free-born Americans, pals of mine, that I had known for years. Then a volley came from the hill, and all was over bar the service for the dead; even the cushions were sliced up. The dollars were in number one, of course, but that's life."

"Good God," said Tiger-Man. "What happened?"

An awkward tension had fallen over the party. Our hosts looked at one another slantwise, as though doubting the wisdom of words. Then a harsh chuckle shattered the silence.

"The avengers shall be nameless," said the man from Oklahoma, "but they followed precedent."

Neither Tiger-Man nor I were young enough to speak just then. A single sentence would have wrecked the story for ever.

With quiet tact the man from Oklahoma gave us another ice.

For many a thirsty league before we came to Camatindi the great steel derrick of the oil-well showed black against the clouds. Though eight hours of riding under a sun had turned the ices to bitterness within us, that dark finger of progress softened our distress. It stood on a pale green eminence, far above the tree-line, so that it looked like a barbaric ornament on the breast of a half-clad lady. As we drew near we saw that it was approached by a winding path cut in a rock to the shape of the curved hillside. Waterfalls, sliding quite easily over the summit, made a tremendous fuss of their descent, which they accomplished in a series of flashing leaps so white that the clouds seemed as soiled as last week's linen.

We slept at the foot in the hut of an Indian cowherd.

Early next day we began the ascent. A pleasant freshness lingered in the trees, and as we wound in and out along the broad mule path, the sound of splashing water disturbed the great silence. Thirty or forty times a cascade dropped on to the track and fell bubbling into the rocky depths hundreds of feet below. A green, majestic emptiness, heightened by the cool shadows, set off our own insignificance, and made us realize the gigantic labor that had gone to the building of the road. Slowly we mounted.

At four thousand feet we emerged from the tree-line, and, like swimmers breaking surface after a dive, we gasped at our freedom from Green Hell. For six strenuous months we had plowed our way through the hills and thickets of the forests; our lungs had grown accustomed to the strange, dead atmosphere of decay; and our eyes had almost forgotten the existence of space. Now we stood and wondered, and our feelings might have

WHERE TALL STORIES ARE UNNECESSARY

been compared to those of prisoners long buried in the Bastille on climbing Notre Dame after their release.

In an angle of the path with the noise of water in our ears we looked out across the rolling leagues of the Gran Chaco. It was a brilliant day, and we could see for a hundred miles beyond the wooded folds of mountains that twined about our feet. Mile upon mile of silent, motionless green tapestry, it stretched away to the horizon that was slightly blurred by heat. To the southward the silver snake of the Rio Pilcomayo uncurled itself in the sunlight, only to be lost in the marshes beyond before it pitched over the edge of our vision. Suddenly, a stone rattled at my side, and Tiger-Man ran his mule against mine.

"There are five such horizons," he said, "between us and the Rio Paraguay."

Thus simply, as was his wont, the bearded philosopher-hunter showed me the dangers we had been spared. We had traversed the whole of that vast plain, in which streams were few and water holes fewer; we had starved and thirsted and gone without our sleep, and had gloried in the greatness of companionship; and yet it was only at this moment when we saw with the eyes of vultures, that awe, overwhelming and unshakeable, took possession of us. We felt like flies on the surface of the sea.

We sat without moving for twenty minutes in this unaccustomed temper of humility, and then Tiger-Man pointed to the foothills. A little puff of cloud, soft and round and opaque shot out of a concealed valley and started to climb towards us. Another followed, and yet another, until the entire plain was mottled by these curious white billows.

"Wind-dogs," said Tiger-Man. "We must hurry."

Sure enough, within a quarter of an hour, the main army of mist had caught up with the wind-dog vedettes, and the sun went quietly to sleep. In an instant we were isolated, pushing through a moving veil. It was cold and wet as a sea-fog, swirling and tossed, chilling us to the bone. It shut out the perspective of Green Hell, and made us wonder what precipice we should fall down next. The mules, born and bred in the plains, took fright, and whinnied their distress into the unresponsive gloom of the ascent. Soon we were groping in grim earnest, feeling our way along the rock wall, and guided only by the roar of the cascades. A few inches ahead I could see Tiger-Man, a bronze figure in the saddle, trying to induce his animal to walk in a straight line. Then it took to its heels, my mount bolted in sympathy, and for a mile we swept round corners at terrifying speed, until the gradient proved too steep and our beasts breathed themselves to a halt.

Half an hour later, guided by the snorting of a steam-engine, we bumped into the steel triangle of the oil derrick, and demanded lunch.

That afternoon revealed to us a Standard Oil Company in time of stress. As we toiled up the bare mountain from the living huts to the mine, a green and yellow torrent rushed past us down the hill. We followed it to its source, to where it splashed over the steps of the engine shed, and then, high above the racket of machinery, came a burst of nasal oaths. Tempestuous and florid, obviously from the heart, they poured through the cracks in the high, wooden walls, and halted us in our stride, for, deeply as we desired to explore the mysteries of petroleum, we did not wish to prejudice our chances by intrusion at such a moment. Suddenly, while we gazed at each other in disappointment, a glistening, oily head was poked round a corner, and a weary smile welcomed us.

"Guess you're intelligent beings," said a voice which was harsh from thirst. "Just bum around, keep clear of the wheels, and don't ask questions till your wits have done their damnedest. We're busy."

At first, everything seemed pointless in that smelly, din-filled shack. In consequence details piled themselves up in our brains and refused to fall into any ordered scheme. A filthy teapot, broken at the spout, lay on a shelf in the corner. A more than filthy man in overalls swayed on a step-ladder and grasped a handle that was clamped to a thick steel rope, one end of which disappeared into the ground, while the other curled over a pulley at the apex of the triangle, dizzily distant in the sky. With each beat of the engine the rope, taut as a bar, was lifted six inches into the air, and as it bumped down into place the man gave it a deft half turn. Over and over again this happened, and each time it dropped he listened for the sound of the fall with an anxious expression on his face. From time to time a lively, serious-looking native leaped from the floor into a pit that was lined with slimy balks of timber. It was all rather puzzling.

Then, without warning, the American held up his hand, and the engine groaned to a halt. Almost at once another one started, and the rope began to wind itself round a gigantic drum. Our friend came down from his ladder.

"Everything's gone wrong this afternoon," he said cheerfully, "we're in a seam of black shale, and the bit keeps sliding out of the true. The oil has been spurting up the shaft—possibly you met the surplus as you came up the hill. It will happen again before dark, sure as I'm a naturalized American."

By this time our minds had become attuned to the easy problems, and we were ready for technicalities.

"I'm called a tool-pusher," he explained, his lips glued to the spout of the teapot. "Yeah, water gets greasy if it ain't covered. I'm responsible for running a chain of steel pipes plumb vertical into the ground till they connect up with the petroleum, and God help me if I don't keep straight. How do I do it? That's simple. I just stand on that ladder and hold that rotten little handle and make a guess as to what my drill is doing half a mile away, somewhere round where you started to climb this morning."

The light of the true craftsman came into his eyes,

and he grinned. "Say, you need imagination in my job."

"How do you know what you're hitting?" asked Tiger-Man.

The American glanced at his wrist watch and walked over to a lever.

"I'll show you in a minute," he said.

Suddenly, out of the depths of the pit, a long, narrow yellow-green cylinder, dripping with oil, shot towards the summit of the triangle, in another second it would have crashed into the peak, but directly the gleam of it emerged, the lever was pulled down and the engine ceased. With intense curiosity we craned our necks and marveled at the majesty of the drill that hung, swaying slightly, half way up the tower.

"Now," said the tool-pusher, "watch me."

He lowered it into the pit and made a sign to the agile Indian. In an incredibly short time the little fellow had unhooked it from the rope and had replaced it with a similar instrument that shone like silver. A turn on the engine and it swung easily at the level of our heads.

"This," remarked the American, "is a valve."

He detached a fish-tailed appendage at the bottom of the cylinder and pressed it home.

"When it reaches the floor, nearly four thousand feet below, this head is driven into the barrel, and the mud squirts into the hollow interior. As you can see, it's twenty-five feet long and pretty wide. Directly I release the pressure the head falls back and the mess is trapped inside. Neat, eh?"

It was—very neat—and we watched the rope uncoil off the drum as it journeyed once more down the shaft. This time we looked at our watches when it started to come up, and it took eight solid minutes to ascend. That little fact more than any other convinced us of the imagination requisite to tool-pushers.

Towards evening, as we stood chatting to our new friend, there came a noise that sent him racing to the shaft. It was a curious sound, midway between a bubble and a hiss, almost as though some one was sucking at an enormous and unclean pipe while waves broke on the shingle. Quickly the disturbance grew, and before we could reach the pit the floor was covered with a seething tide of raw petroleum. We drew back in alarm, for it had the appearance of intense heat, frothing its energy in angry petulance, but when we stooped to dip our fingers it was harsh and cold with a peculiar gritty feeling all of its own. Higher it mounted and still higher, until it was several yards up the triangle in a feathery column of green and yellow foam. We watched entranced, hoping it would prove a real gusher, but the American did something technical and the flood fell away.

On the walk back to the living huts he pointed to a number of ten-foot tanks that made an ugly blot on the mountain.

"Funny birds, Indians," he said. "They know petroleum quite well, both by feel and smell, yet one of 'em tried to swim across that refinery. Naturally, he sank like a rock, and we had to send to the Pilcomayo for a boathook."

That, except for one incident, ended our acquaintance with the men of the Standard Oil; for we left for Yacuiba in the morning. I shall always remember them with gratitude, they took us at our face value and gave us what they had. A stout-hearted band of courteous gentlemen, I hope sincerely to meet them again.

The last incident happened in Yacuiba itself, and will ever stand out in my memory as an example of the highest form of generosity. Urrio was somewhere on the railway and we were unable to get into touch with him. Tiger-Man and I were completely stranded for we were two hundred miles from Urrio's next stopping place and we had not a penny between us. In this predicament we should neither of us been surprised if we had been regarded as needy beach-combers and shouldered aside. Yet the hotel-keeper, a Spaniard of immense girth with a head like an ostrich's egg, an ex-tenor of Grand Opera, allowed his bill to stand over until we reached Tarija. Moreover, a young American, an engineer of the Standard Oil Company, approached me on his own and offered financial assistance.

If this book should ever find its way into their hands I should like them to know that their belief in us was sincerely appreciated.

We did not see Urrio and Bee-Mason again until we were safe in the mountains at Sucre for, although Tiger-

Man and I walked and rode the two hundred miles to Tarija in five days, they had departed three hours before us.

Thus, to all intents and purposes, ended our trip.

CHAPTER XXV

Quite lately a Bolivian of high repute reproached me with the title of my book. "Green Hell!"

A land where thirst is the order of the day, and insects whine through the forests in search of blood; where food is scarce, hardship a commonplace, and vampires prey upon the baggage animals. That, he said, was the impression that I should give. Here is my answer.

Eastern Bolivia is without doubt an amazingly rich country. For many a long year those astute men of business, the Jesuits, held sway in the province of Chiquitos. Even to the moderately learned this plain fact speaks for itself, for although they were brilliant missionaries with the welfare of the natives at heart, they rarely took over a place that could not be made to pay, nor did they here. Cattle and cotton and fruit were grown in great quantities, and the hastiest dip into the archives of Santa Cruz will show that they ruled over a numerous and self-respecting flock.

Now this chronicle has never set out to be more than a record of a little band of men who went adventuring. From the very start we determined to go where no other man had gone since the days of Nuflo de Chavez. We were pioneers, cutting our way through a goodly portion of uncharted trees. Naturally, therefore, we encountered obstacles that were not in the ordinary run of life. We ran short of water because we had neither the time nor the energy at the end of a day's riding to dig twenty feet into the soil; though my divining rod told me it was there. We ran short of food because game never ventures far from water. There was nothing unusual in this. In Argentina, the richest country in South America, scarcely a stream flows across the pampas. It is a land of windmill-pumps which bring the water to the surface that the cattle may live. Rivers are the exception to the rule.

The insects, too, were worse for us than they will be for those who follow after. When a railway has opened up Chiquitos a large proportion will disappear, for their range of flight is limited to a few hundred yards, and they hate leaving the forest. Even the vampires yield easily to treatment. They live in hollow trees and, given the time and the patience, can be burned out while they sleep.

Of sickness there is little in this land of promise, and of sunstroke there is none. Those who visit the great eastern plain may expect to get sores on their legs just as Urrio and I did, but they will pass in six weeks and never appear again. Nor are they unknown in Africa and Australia. Finally, there is not one of our little party who would not return should the opportunity present itself, and, as I have tried to point out, we are much as other men are.

Our trip is over—that wonderful year in the wilds. Urrio, Bee-Mason and I still meet at intervals, and the friendship that sprang up so naturally in the jungles has not abated. Indeed, it is strengthened, because we have now had time to realize what we did. Together we journeyed in a measure through the sixteenth century. We learned something of the trials and dangers through which old Nuflo went, and our respect for certain wild characters of history has deepened. When we read of the Ancient Britons we can imagine the darkness of their woods, the dirt and instability of their houses; for we have seen them. The story of the Spanish Conquistadores is an open book to us, we recognize their terrors, we have stepped the road ourselves. In short, our interests have widened and our sympathies have become quick.

From time to time we hear from Tiger-Man, short letters in English, not so immaculate as his speech. He is at present in New York, trying to persuade a film company to back him in his hunting picture. May he succeed!

One more snap-shot and my tale is done. The scene is Urrio's club with a puzzled waiter hovering in the background. A table is laid for four, but one place is sadly vacant. Suddenly the glasses are filled, and three men of widely diverse interests, bound only by a common memory and a common taste for sky-lines, raise the wine to their lips. Their eyes are fixed on the empty chair that holds so much of their affections.

"Tiger-Man," we say.

And we long for a re-union.

INDEX

Alligators of the Paraguay River, 38, 40
Amazon River, 23, 232
Americans in Matto Grosso, 32
Anaconda, adventure with, 61-64
Arce, Father, 211
Argentina, 11, 334
Argentina and the Indians, 233
Argentinos, characteristics of, 12, 13
Asuncion, 7, 20, 28, 29, 31, 72, 151
Atahualpa, 230
Audiencia de Charcas, 88
Augustine monks, 231
Avenida de Mayo, 14
Aviation in Bolivia, 221 *et seq.*
Aymará Indians, 7
Ayolas, Juan de, 28

Bahia Negra, 30
Bee-Mason, J. C., 3 *et seq.*
Beni, Province of the, 89
Bird-life on the Rio Paraguay, 57
Birds on the Paraguay, 81
Bolivar, Simôn, 11
Bolivia, 3, 6-8, 9-16, 19 *et seq.*
Bolivia, Eastern, 127, 143, 333
Bolivian Air Force, 219
Bolivian bootleggers, 83
Bolivian caravan, 253
Bolivian farm home, 245 *et seq.*
Bolivian ox-carts, 237
Bolivian postman, 250
Bonaparte, Joseph, 11
Brazil, 19, 23
Buenos Aires, 8, 9-16, 30, 35, 72, 91, 298
Buenos Aires, Vice-Royalty of, 11

Cabot, Sebastian, 28
Camatindi, 323

Camp Grande, 33
Cathedral of San José, 213
Catholic Church and the conquest of Peru, 229
Cayman, South American, 27
Cayubara, river hog, 79
"Chaco," the, 15, 29, 89, 232, 233
Charqui industry, 36
Chavez, Nuflo de, 7, 14, 27, 28, 89, 96, 104, 210, 333
Chile, 11
Chiquitano burial rites, 175, 176
Chiquitano Indians, 88, 147, 149, 223
Chiquitos, province of, 7, 28, 89, 90, 143-145, 232, 333
Chiriguano Indians, 231, 234, 316, 317
Churrasco, 136
Cochabamba, 222, 252, 253, 297
Colombia, 11
Conquest of the Incas, 228 *et seq.*
Conquistadores, the, 10, 227, 228
Corumbá, Brazil, 20, 34, 42-45, 46, 50, 51, 72, 220, 247
Cuyabá, Brazil, 19, 33, 72, 195
Cuzco, 229

Danton, Lieut., 91, 116-123
Dialect of the Argentinos, 13
Dominican fathers, 231
d'Oissy, Pelletier, 222
D'Orbigny, 232

Eastern Bolivia, 127, 143, 333
Ecuador, 23
Egret colonies, 81

Farm home in Bolivia, 245 *et seq.*
Fish, the *piranha*, 93
  the *pintado*, 95

337

INDEX

Fishing at Lake Gaiba, 93
Fly pests, 238 *et seq.*
Fortins, 237, 238, 240
Franciscan monks, 231

Gaiba, 89-103, 114-123, 129, 311
Gaiba belle, a, 84
Garrapata, the Bolivian tick, 96
Galpon, 291
Guaraní Indians, 28, 203
Gran Chaco, 310, 325
"Green Hell," description of, 23-25

Harris, Mr., 115-123

Ibenns fly, the, 238
Incas, the, 227-234
Indian episode, 253 *et seq.*
Indian morality, 203
Indians, Aymará, 7
    Chiquitano, 88, 147, 149, 223
    Chiriguanos, 231, 234, 316, 317
    extinction of, 233
    Guaraní, 28, 203
    Quechua, 7, 88
    Tobas, 232, 234, 251, 265 *et seq.*
Irala, 28

"Jacarés," 26
Jaguar hunting, 67-76
Japanese in Matto Grosso, 32
Jesuits in Bolivia, 144, 212, 231, 232, 237
Jordan, Capt., 220

King vulture, the, 79

Lagunillas, 299, 310
Lake Gaiba, 7, 82, 93
Lake Mandioré, 82
Lake Uberaba, 82
La Paz, 89, 159, 220, 221, 310
Le Maître, Major, 222
Lima, 11, 88, 145
Lima, Vice-Royalty of, 11
Lucan River, 287

Macheriti, 317, 319
Madre de Dios River, 89

Maracaibo, 233
Maté drinking, 136
Matto Grosso, Province of, 31-36, 48, 256
Maximilian II, 210
Melgarejo, Bolivian politician, 50
Mojos province, 232
Moreto, Balthasar, 151
Mosquito pests, 48

Napoleon, 11
Negroes of Matto Grosso, 32

Oil wells of Bolivia, 318-323, 327-330
Orinoco River, 11, 23
Ox-carts, Bolivian, 237

Pacifiqui, 164
Palacio de Congreso, Buenos Aires, 14
Paraguay, 11, 19, 23, 30, 211
Paraguay River, 6, 7, 9, 23, 28, 46, 72, 105, 232, 237, 310, 325
Paraná River, 9, 19, 29
Parapití River, 313-316
Parrot hunting, 118
Pelotas, 286 *et seq.*
Pernambuco, 23, 181
Peru, 6, 9, 10, 11, 227-234
Peru, Incas of, 227-234
Pilcomayo River, 11, 29, 232, 234, 325
Pintado, the, 95
Piranha, the carnivorous fish, 37, 40, 41, 93-95
Pizzaro, 6, 231
Plate River, 8, 9, 10, 12
Postman of Bolivia, 250
Potosí, 50
Prestes, General, 91
Province of Chiquitos, 232, 333
Province of Mojos, 232
Puerto Esperanza, 37
Puerto Suarez, 83, 129, 220, 234, 238, 250, 272

Quebracho industry, 30
Quechua Indians, 7, 88

René-Moreno, Señor, 147, 202
Ricoleta cemetery, Buenos Aires, 14

INDEX   339

Rio de Janeiro, 6, 8, 221
Rio de la Plata, 8, 9, 10, 12, 28
Rio Grande, 285, 303, 305
Rio Paraguay, 6, 7, 9, 23, 28, 37, 46, 72, 105, 232, 237
Rio Paraná, 9, 19, 29
Rio Pilcomayo, 11, 29, 232, 234, 325
Rivers.
   Amazon, 23, 232
   La Plata, 8, 9, 10, 12, 28
   Lucan, 287
   Madre de Dios, 89
   Orinoco, 11, 23
   Paraguay, 6, 7, 9, 23, 28, 46, 72, 105, 232, 237, 310, 325
   Paraná, 9, 19, 29
   Parapití, 313-316
   Pilcomayo, 11, 29, 232, 234, 325
   Rio Grande, 285, 303, 305
   Salladillo, 287
   Uruguay, 9
Rosario, Argentina, 16, 17, 19, 23
Rousseau, Jean Jacques, 11

Salladillo River, 287
San José de Chiquitos, 207, 209-235, 292
San Juan, 180, 183, 201-206
San Lorenzo, 127-137
San Sebastián, 138, 139
Santalla, Major, 221
Santa Cruz de la Sierra, 7, 99, 145, 210, 220, 222, 231, 234, 237, 238, 251, 257, 274, 275, 288-292, 297-300
Santo Corazón, 142, 147-157, 158, 201, 232
São Paulo, 72
Siemel, Alejandro, 73-83, 129 *et seq.*
Snake charming, 97

South Americans, characteristics of, 18
Sports of Argentina, 12
Sports of Uruguay, 12
Standard Oil Company, 318
Sting-ray, the, 95
Storms, tropical, 235
Sucre, Bolivia, 88, 314, 331
Sucre, Marshal, 89
Syrians of Matto Grosso, 32

Tarantula, adventure with, 46, 247
Tarija, 231, 233, 311, 317, 331, 332
Tiburcio, native servant, 166, 172
Tiger hunting, 164-173
Tilbury, 4, 50
Tsusux, the, 82
Toba Indians, 232, 234, 251, 265 *et seq.*
Trans-Brazilian railway, 37
Tropical difficulties, 240 *et seq.*
Tropical storm, 235
Tucuman, 287

Upper Peru, 88
Urriolagoitia, Mamerto, 3 *et seq.*
Uruguay, 19
Uruguay River, 9

Vaca, Cabeza de, 28
Vaca, José, 66-71, 95, 96
Vampire bats, 201, 206, 260
Venezuela, 11
Vulture bats, 260

Women of Matto Grosso, 33-35
Worsley, Commander, 5

Xarayes marsh, 28

Yacuiba, 299, 331

www.ingramcontent.com/pod-product-compliance
Lightning Source LLC
Chambersburg PA
CBHW021753230426
43669CB00006B/66